The LNICST series publishes ICST's conferences, symposia and workshops.
LNICST reports state-of-the-art results in areas related to the scope of the Institute.
The type of material published includes

- Proceedings (published in time for the respective event)
- Other edited monographs (such as project reports or invited volumes)

LNICST topics span the following areas:

- General Computer Science
- E-Economy
- E-Medicine
- Knowledge Management
- Multimedia
- Operations, Management and Policy
- Social Informatics
- Systems

Vaneet Aggarwal · Tobias Harks · Sanjiv Kapoor
Editors

Game Theory for Networks

13th EAI International Conference, GameNets 2025
Cambridge, UK, March 17–18, 2025
Proceedings

 Springer

Editors
Vaneet Aggarwal
Purdue University
West Lafayette, IN, USA

Tobias Harks
Universität Passau
Passau, Germany

Sanjiv Kapoor
Illinois Institute of Technology
Chicago, IL, USA

ISSN 1867-8211 ISSN 1867-822X (electronic)
Lecture Notes of the Institute for Computer Sciences, Social Informatics
and Telecommunications Engineering
ISBN 978-3-032-12914-7 ISBN 978-3-032-12915-4 (eBook)
https://doi.org/10.1007/978-3-032-12915-4

Preface

This volume contains the papers and extended abstracts presented at the 13th EAI International Conference on Game Theory for Networks (GAMENETS), held from March 17–18, 2025, at Magdalene College in Cambridge, UK.

The purpose of GAMENETS is to bring together researchers from Computer Science, Economics, Mathematics and Networking to present and discuss original research at the intersection of Networks and Game Theory. The works accepted for publication in this volume cover topics of Algorithmic Game Theory, Networking including mechanism design, two-sided markets, network security, wireless networks, computational aspects of games, scheduling games, and computational social choice.

The papers accepted range from investigating network markets to scheduling network resources. The first set of papers cover Cournot competitive markets over wireless networks, propose novel hypergraph information structures for Cournot competition, and investigate social influence and behavior in Fisher markets. The papers utilize models and techniques from game theory that include evolutionary games and tâtonnement-type algorithms. The next set of papers incorporate behavior in multi-agent systems, including deception to alter the behavior of other players in N-player oligopoly markets and the use of emotions that impacts their strategic changes. One of the results considers the notion of irrational behavior that results in herd-following behavior by following the majority, resulting in rational players actually gaining due to this behavior. Scheduling games is another important topic considered in a set of papers. One of the papers considers mechanism design for a provisioning game utilizing sequential invitations to commit to the mechanism. Network resource scheduling in the context of rank-ordering is considered in environments with either identical or unrelated machines. Motivated by beam forming in 5G networks, allocation of resources via interval scheduling is the subject of study of another research reported here. The final set of papers consider applications, the use of Shapely value in cooperative games to control wild fires, as well as adversarial games in blockchain mining.

The Program Committee, consisting of 23 top researchers from the field, reviewed 28 submissions and decided to accept 11 papers. Each paper had three reviews, with additional reviews solicited as needed. We are very grateful to the Program Committee for their insightful reviews and discussions. The review process was conducted entirely electronically via Easy Chair -we gratefully acknowledge this support. To accommodate the publishing traditions of different fields, authors of accepted papers could ask that only a one-page abstract of the paper appeared in the proceedings. Among the 11 accepted papers, the authors of 1 paper selected this option.

Furthermore, due to the general support by EAI, we were able to provide a best paper award. The PC decided to give the award to the paper Interval Scheduling Games by Vipin Ravindran Vijayalakshmi, Marc Schroder and Tami Tamir.

The program included three invited talks by leading researchers in the field: Sanjiv Goyal (Cambridge University, UK), Matthew Elliot (Cambridge University, UK), and Randall Berry (Northwestern University, USA).

We would like to thank all the authors for their interest in submitting their work to GameNets 2025, as well as the PC members and the external reviewers for their great work in evaluating the submissions. We also want to thank EAI and Springer for their generous financial support. We are grateful to Radka Vasileiadis and Timea Madarova at EAI for their help with the conference website and organization.

Vaneet Aggarwal
Tobias Harks
Sanjiv Kapoor

Organization

Steering Committee

Victor C.M. Leung	University of British Columbia, Canada
Arumugam Nallanathan	Queen Mary University of London, UK

Organizing Committee

General Chair

Sanjiv Kapoor	Illinois Tech, USA

TPC Chair and Co-Chairs

Sanjiv Kapoor	Illinois Tech, USA
Vaneet Aggarwal	Purdue University, USA
Tobias Harks	University of Passau, Germany

Technical Program Committee

Randall Berry	Northwestern University, USA
Vittorio Bilo	University of Salento, Italy
Martin Gairing	University of Liverpool, UK
Arnob Ghosh	New Jersey Institute of Technology, USA
Shweta Jain	Indian Institute of Technology, India
Pascal Lenzner	Hasso Plattner Institute Potsdam, Germany
Xiangyang Li	University of Science and Technology, China
Richard Ma	National University of Singapore, Singapore
Jason Marden	University of California, Santa Barbara, USA
Washim Mondal	Indian Institute of Technology Kanpur, India
Parinaz Naghizadeh	University of California San Diego, USA
Duong Nguyen	Arizona State University, USA
Dario Paccagnan	Imperial College London, UK
Kevin Schewior	University of Southern Denmark, Denmark

Marc Schroder	Maastricht University, Netherlands
Tami Tamir	Reichman University, Israel
Eirini Eleni Tsiropoulou	University of New Mexico, USA
Guido Schaefer	CWI Amsterdam, Netherlands
S. Sivaranjani	Purdue University, USA

Contents

Applications of Game Theory

Games and Markets

Markets for Intermittent Service Using Intermittent Spectrum

Martial Felix[(✉)] [ID] and Randall Berry [ID]

Northwestern University, Evanston, IL 60201, USA
{martial.felix, rberry}@northwestern.edu

Abstract. In this paper, we develop a Cournot competition model to analyze a competitive wireless communications market where service providers (SPs) utilize both proprietary bandwidth—exclusively owned and consistently available—and intermittent bandwidth, which becomes available sporadically. Previous studies have considered such a setting where SPs offer a non-intermittent service, meaning that users must be served at all times. Here, we instead consider SPs that offer an intermittent service, where users can tolerate delays in service but at a cost. Our model captures how the availability of intermittent bandwidth affects the service latency experienced by users, the strategies adopted by SPs, and their resulting revenues. Through theoretical analysis, we find that intermittent bandwidth can significantly impact market dynamics, lowering barriers to entry and enabling new entrants to compete effectively against established incumbents. This increased competition can lead to favorable outcomes for consumers, such as lower prices and improved service quality. We support our findings with simulations that illustrate how intermittent bandwidth can be used and its effects on the market. Our study highlights the strategic importance of intermittent bandwidth in shaping competitive markets and offers insights into how it can be leveraged to enhance efficiency and innovation in the telecommunications industry.

Keywords: Spectrum sharing · Service latency · Cournot competition · Auctions

1 Introduction

The rapid growth of data-intensive applications and services has led to an unprecedented demand for wireless spectrum. Service providers (SPs) are continuously seeking ways to meet this escalating need. Certain spectrum resources reserved for critical operations—such as military communications, emergency services, and hospitals—are not utilized all of the time. These restricted bandwidths often remain idle during periods of non-use, presenting an opportunity to alleviate bandwidth scarcity in civilian applications.

The work was supported in part by the US National Science Foundation grants CNS-2148183, SES-2332054, and AST-2132700-024.

V. Aggarwal et al. (Eds.): GameNets 2025, LNICST 657, pp. 3–17, 2026.
https://doi.org/10.1007/978-3-032-12915-4_1

Leveraging intermittent access to these underutilized bandwidth resources can provide significant benefits. By allowing service providers to use restricted bandwidth when it is not occupied by primary users, we can enhance network capacity and improve service quality for end-users. The Citizens Broadband Radio Service (CBRS) deployed in the 3.5 GHz band in the U.S. offers such a service [7]. However, the intermittent nature of such bandwidth poses challenges in terms of service reliability, latency, and overall user experience [4].

In this paper, we develop a game theoretic model to analyze a competitive market where SPs utilize both proprietary bandwidth and intermittent access to restricted bandwidth. We investigate how the incorporation of intermittent bandwidth affects service latency, pricing strategies, and the revenues of service providers. Our model captures the dynamics of a market where bandwidth resources are not consistently available, reflecting real-world scenarios where restricted bandwidth can be temporarily allocated to other users.

Our work extends existing models of Cournot competition with congestion [1,2,8] where SPs deliver uninterrupted services, ensuring that users are continuously served. In this study, we explore SPs that offer intermittent services using intermittent bandwidth, accepting that users may experience delays in service, albeit with associated costs. Through theoretical analysis and simulations, we demonstrate that intermittent bandwidth can significantly impact market dynamics. Notably, we find that new entrants can leverage intermittent bandwidth to effectively compete against incumbents with proprietary bandwidth. This has important implications for consumer surplus and social welfare, as increased competition can lead to lower prices and improved services.

2   Related Works

This article contributes to a body of research focused on competition in industries where firms utilize congestible resources, and customer utility is influenced by the delivered price (also known as the total price), which includes both the service price and a congestion cost. This type of research has been conducted in various fields, including but not limited to, transportation [6,15], service industries [3,9], and closer to our work, telecommunications including both wired [1,2,8] and wireless services [10,13].

Our model differs significantly from the work presented in these papers in several key aspects. One of the primary distinctions between our model and the models presented in these other papers lies in the basis of competition. In the existing research, the competition among participants is primarily driven by price (Bertrand Models). This means that the various entities involved compete by adjusting their prices in response to market conditions or strategic considerations. In contrast, our model emphasizes competition based on quantity (Cournot Model), wherein participants compete by varying the amounts of resources or products they offer.

Furthermore, another significant difference is related to the availability of underlying resources. In the previously discussed papers, the resources in question are consistently available, implying that there are no interruptions or fluctuations in their availability. However, our model diverges from this approach by incorporating intermittently available resources. This means that the resources our model considers are subject to interruptions and variability in their availability.

Some papers have individually addressed and relaxed one of these assumptions. For example, Perakis and Sun [14] and Mu and Berry [12] studied Cournot models with congestion but without intermittency. Our model is inspired by the work of Berry et al. [5], who developed a model of Cournot competition with congestion that was also used by Mu and Berry [11] but we generalized it to take into account users that accept to not be served when the bandwidth is not available.

3   Model and Assumptions

We examine a competitive market consisting of n Service Providers (SPs), each vying for the same pool of clients. Each SP i decides to offer services to w_i clients. When a client is served by SP i, they experience a latency l_i. This latency represents the utility lost in average for the time a client must wait to transfer one arbitrary unit of data. If SP i has only X_i units of dedicated spectrum, then the latency is considered to be proportional to its number of clients w_i and inversely proportional to X_i. Mathematically, this is expressed as

$$l_i = \frac{w_i}{X_i}. \tag{1}$$

If the SP is using intermittent bandwidth, the latency calculation changes and depends on how SP i serves its traffic when the intermittent band is not available. One approach, as in [5], is for SP i to offload all of its traffic from the intermittent band onto its licensed band. This results in an average latency given by:

$$l_i = \alpha \frac{w_i}{X_i + W_i} + (1 - \alpha) \frac{w_i}{X_i}. \tag{2}$$

Here, W_i represents the intermittent bandwidth and $\alpha \in [0, 1]$ is the probability of W_i being available at any given time. Note with this model, all clients are always served, but they do experience a larger latency when the intermittent band is not available. As X_i approaches 0, note that the latency in (2) blows up. This suggests that if a SP has a small amount (or no) licensed spectrum, the latency its clients experience may become prohibitively large. Here, we consider an alternative approach for using an intermittent band. Namely the SP could instead make the client wait for the intermittent band to become available. Of course, this is only feasible if the client is tolerant to the resulting delay. We consider a discrete-time model, where the number of time-slots a client must wait before the intermittent band becomes available is modeled as a Bernoulli trial, as shown in Fig. 1a. The client incurs a cost of C per unit time from waiting, so that the total cost incurred is C multiplied by the number of time-slots spent waiting. Figure 1a shows the expected waiting time given that a node has a packet available - this matches a two-state Markov chain model for availability shown in Fig. 1b - where the states are available and not available and the transition from available to not, happens with probability $1 - \alpha$ and from not available to available, happens with probability α. For this model, we note that the steady-state probability of being available will be α which is consistent with (2).

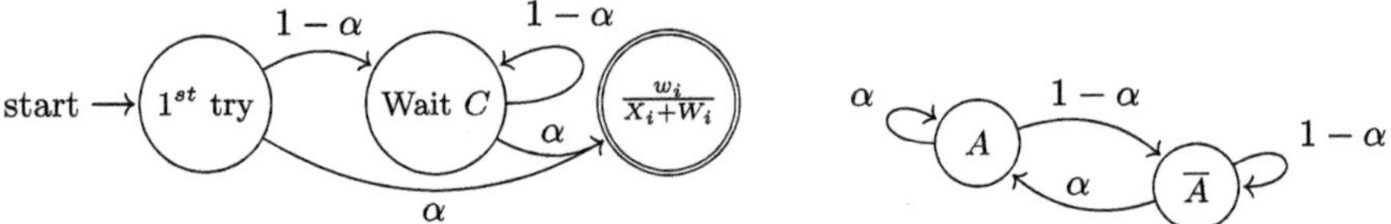

(a) Model for the waiting cost due to intermittent spectrum.

(b) Two state Markov chain model for availability. $A = W_i$ available

Fig. 1. Illustrations of the waiting cost model.

The number of time units the channel is unavailable, G follows a geometric distribution with an expected value: $E[G] = \sum_{k=0}^{\infty} k(1-\alpha)^k \alpha = \frac{1-\alpha}{\alpha}$. We can then express the expected waiting time before connection as:[1]

$$f(\alpha, C) = C\frac{1-\alpha}{\alpha}. \tag{3}$$

Given this, the total expected latency when waiting can be expressed as:

$$\begin{aligned} l_i &= \alpha\frac{w_i}{X_i + W_i} + (1 - \alpha)\left(f(\alpha, C) + \frac{w_i}{X_i + W_i}\right) \\ &= \frac{w_i}{X_i + W_i} + (1 - \alpha)f(\alpha, C). \end{aligned} \tag{4}$$

More generally, we allow a SP to decide between waiting and offloading, which gives

$$l_i = \alpha\frac{w_i}{X_i + W_i} + (1 - \alpha)\min\left\{\frac{w_i}{X_i}, f(\alpha, C) + \frac{w_i}{X_i + W_i}\right\}. \tag{5}$$

Note that when X_i goes to zero, the minimum in (5) will always be given by waiting.

Given w_i for each SP i, we assume that the market *delivered price* is given by a downward slopping inverse demand curve, i.e., $p_d = k - \sum_i w_i$, where k is the total demand. The price that clients are willing to pay is defined as the

---

[1] Note that f is increasing hyperbolically when α is decreasing, $f(1, C) = 0$, $f(0, C) = +\infty$ and $f(\frac{1}{2}, C) = C$.

difference between the delivered price and the latency ($p_i = p_d - l_i$). The revenue for SP i is then, this price multiplied by the number of clients ($R_i = p_i w_i$). Since this is a Cournot model, each SP i attempts to maximize its revenue by choosing w_i. We seek to characterize a market equilibrium, where no SP can unilaterally improve its revenue. This model effectively captures the dynamics of SP competition, client service latency, and the impact of intermittent bandwidth on overall service quality and profitability. For a given equilibrium, we are also interested in the consumer surplus generated by the market. The consumer surplus is the difference between the total amount consumers are willing to pay for the service and the actual cost they incur. It directly captures the coverage of the total demand by the SPs. Having defined the model, we can now explore various scenarios.

4 Results and Simulations

In this section, we present our main theoretical results and support them with simulations to illustrate the impact of intermittent bandwidth on market dynamics.

4.1 Competition Among Service Providers Using Only Intermittent Bandwidth

We first consider a scenario where all SPs have access only to intermittent bandwidth, so that $X_i = 0$ for all i. Since $X_i = 0$, waiting is the only option when W_i is not available. In this case, from (4), note that waiting simply adds a constant terms $((1 - \alpha)f(\alpha, C))$ to the latency, which is equivalent to reducing the demand by that amount in a market without intermittent spectrum.

Lemma 1. *In a market with n SPs using only intermittent bandwidth, in equilibrium, if $(1 - \alpha)f(\alpha, C) < k$, SP i will choose to serve:*

$$w_i = \frac{k - (1 - \alpha)f(\alpha, C)}{\left(1 + \frac{2}{W_i}\right)\left(1 + \sum\limits_{j=1}^{n} \frac{1}{1 + \frac{2}{W_j}}\right)}. \tag{6}$$

If $(1 - \alpha)f(\alpha, C) \geq k$, the only equilibrium is $w_i = 0$.
The resulting revenue for SP i is:

$$R_i = -\left(1 + \frac{1}{W_i}\right)w_i^2 + \left(k - (1 - \alpha)f(\alpha, C) - \sum\limits_{j=1, j\neq i}^{n} w_j\right)w_i. \tag{7}$$

The proof is in Sect. 6.

Note that the condition $(1 - \alpha)f(\alpha, C) \leq k$ means that the expected cost of waiting is less than the maximum amount a client is willing to pay. If this is not true, a SP cannot profit from serving any users. The left-hand side of this condition is increasing in C and decreasing in α.

To illustrate this result, we simulate a market with three SPs, one SP with a larger amount of intermittent bandwidth and two SPs with smaller amounts of bandwidth. Figure 2 shows the number of clients served by each SP, as well as their revenues, as a function of α, the probability that the intermittent bandwidth is available. It also shows the total consumer surplus. The numbers of clients and the revenues of SP 2 and 3 are the same since $W_2 = W_3$.

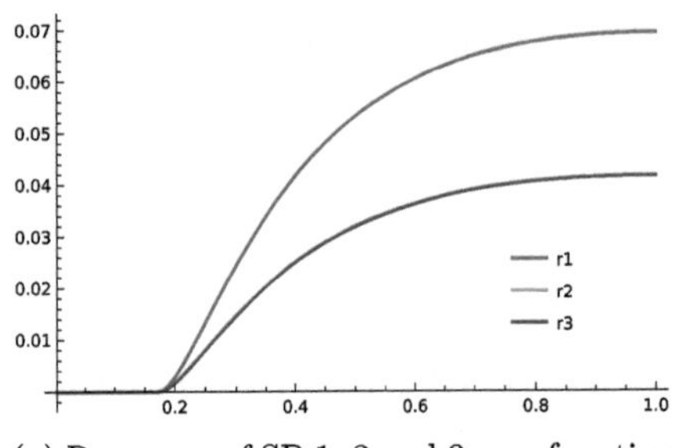 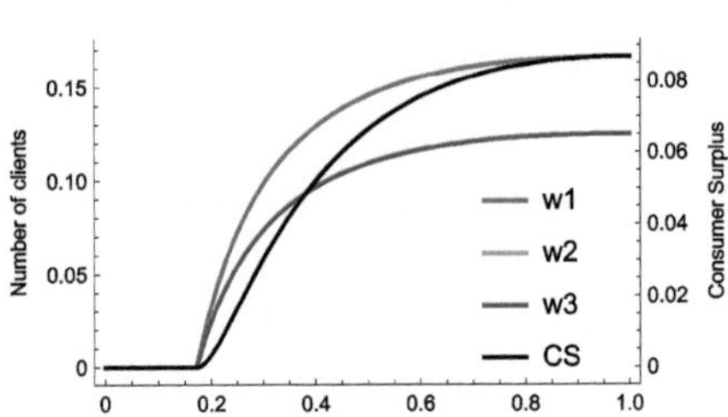

(a) Revenues of SP 1, 2 and 3 as a function of α.

(b) Number of clients of SP 1, 2 and 3 and total consumer surplus as a function of α.

Fig. 2. Results for a setting with intermittent bandwidth only with $W_1 = 1$, $W_2 = W_3 = 0.5$, $C = 0.25$, and $k = 1$.

We can see in Fig. 2 that initially the clients served stays at zero as there is not enough availability - then, as α grows, it rapidly rises and eventually flattens out - this suggests that the greatest gains are for moderate levels of availability. The revenue and consumer surplus follow a similar pattern.

This scenario allows us to understand better how intermittent bandwidth allows the creation of a market when used by itself. However, it also raises questions about whether relying solely on intermittent bandwidth is enough for new service providers to compete with incumbents that already own non-intermittent spectrum.

4.2   Competition Between Two Service Providers with Different Bandwidth Access

Next, we consider a market with two SPs where SP 1 has both proprietary and intermittent bandwidth, while SP 2 has only intermittent bandwidth. Both intermittent bands have the same probability α of being available.

Lemma 2. *In this scenario, SP 1 and SP 2 will choose to serve w_1 and w_2 clients, respectively, with revenues:*

$$R_1 = \max\left\{{}^1R_1, {}^2R_1\right\}. \tag{8}$$

$$R_2 = -\left(1 + \frac{1}{W_2}\right) w_2^2 + \left(k - (1-\alpha)f(\alpha, C) - w_1\right) w_2. \tag{9}$$

Here:

$$^1R_1 = -\left(1 + \frac{\alpha}{W_1 + X_1} + \frac{1-\alpha}{X_1}\right) w_1^2 + (k - w_2)w_1. \tag{10}$$

$$^2R_1 = -\left(1 + \frac{1}{W_1 + X_1}\right) w_1^2 + \left(k - (1-\alpha)f(\alpha, C) - w_2\right) w_1. \tag{11}$$

If $(1-\alpha)f(\alpha, C) < k$, the optimal number of clients for SP 1 and SP 2 is given by:

$$w_1 = \begin{cases} \dfrac{2k(1+\frac{1}{W_2}) + (1-\alpha)f(\alpha,C) - k}{4(1 + \frac{\alpha}{W_1+X_1} + \frac{1-\alpha}{X_1})(1+\frac{1}{W_2}) - 1}, & \text{if } ^1R_1 > {}^2R_1 \\ (k - (1-\alpha)f(\alpha, C))\dfrac{2(1+\frac{1}{W_2})-1}{4(1+\frac{1}{W_1+X_1})(1+\frac{1}{W_2})-1}, & \text{otherwise.} \end{cases} \tag{12}$$

$$w_2 = \begin{cases} \dfrac{2(k-(1-\alpha)f(\alpha,C))(1+\frac{\alpha}{W_1+X_1}+\frac{1-\alpha}{X_1}) - k}{4(1+\frac{\alpha}{W_1+X_1}+\frac{1-\alpha}{X_1})(1+\frac{1}{W_2})-1}, & \text{if } ^1R_1 > {}^2R_1 \\ (k - (1-\alpha)f(\alpha, C))\dfrac{2(1+\frac{1}{W_1+X_1})-1}{4(1+\frac{1}{W_2})(1+\frac{1}{W_1+X_1})-1}, & \text{otherwise.} \end{cases} \tag{13}$$

If $(1-\alpha)f(\alpha, C) \leq k$, then $w_2 = 0$ and:

$$w_1 = \frac{k}{2\left(1 + \frac{\alpha}{W_1+X_1} + \frac{1-\alpha}{X_1}\right)}. \tag{14}$$

The proof is in Sect. 6.

In this setting, SP 1 must decide between offloading or waiting when the intermittent spectrum is not available. Here, $^1R_1$ and $^2R_1$ represents the revenue SP 1 obtains by offloading or waiting, respectively. The quantities that both SPs choose, in turn depend on which of these options is selected. We simulate this scenario to observe how SP 1 and SP 2 adjust their client bases as α varies. Figure 3 shows the revenues and the consumer surplus.

In this figure, we can identify three different phases. When α is small, only SP 1 is in the market and the bigger α grows, the more revenue SP 1 can get. At one point, α is big enough for SP 2 to enter the market (around $\alpha = 0.2$ in Fig. 3). Finally, at one point (around $\alpha = 0.6$), α is big enough for SP 1 to always make its clients wait for the intermittent bandwidth availability. At this moment, SP 2 becomes less attractive than SP 1, thus the discontinuity in SP 2's revenue and in the consumer surplus. Note that SP 1's revenue is relatively flat while SP 2 revenue increases quickly when it enters the market, it is also interesting that at the discontinuity -even though SP 2 appears to be less competitive - consumers benefit.

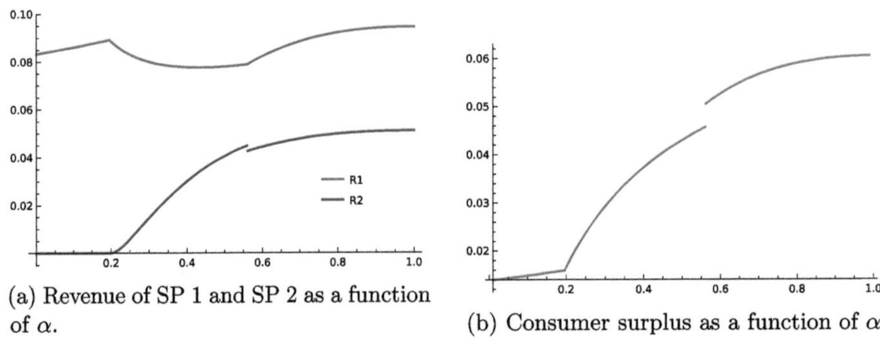

(a) Revenue of SP 1 and SP 2 as a function of α.

(b) Consumer surplus as a function of α.

Fig. 3. Results for a setting with proprietary bandwidth $X_1 = 0.5$ for SP 1, an intermittent bandwidth $W_1 = 0.5$, $W_2 = 0.5$ for SP 1 and SP 2, respectively. $C = 0.25$, and $k = 1$.

This scenario shows that granting intermittent bandwidth to a new provider can foster effective competition. But can a new SP secure that bandwidth through a traditional second-price auction[2] and still compete successfully?

4.3 Auction for Intermittent Bandwidth

We now consider a two-stage game where SPs bid in a second-price auction for a single intermittent band of spectrum with bandwidth W. As in the previous section, we consider a setting with two SPs, where SP 1 has proprietary bandwidth X_1 and SP 2 has no proprietary band. In a second-price auction, each SP will submit a bid for the intermittent band. The band is awarded to the SP with the highest bid and that SP pays the bid of the other SP (i.e., the second highest bid). It is well know that a second price auction is incentive compatible so that it is a weakly dominant strategy for each SP to bid its true value obtained from winning the intermittent band. In this case that value is the difference in its revenue when it wins the band and its revenue when it losses the band. The following lemma will enable us to calculate these bids.

Lemma 3. *In a second-price auction between SP 1 (with proprietary bandwidth X_1) and SP 2 (without proprietary bandwidth):*
If SP 1 wins the auction, then SP 2 serves no client and SP 1 serves:

$$
{}_1w_1 = \begin{cases} \dfrac{k}{2(1+\frac{\alpha}{W+X_1}+\frac{1-\alpha}{X_1})}, & \text{if } f(\alpha,C) > \dfrac{k}{1-\alpha}\left(1 - \sqrt{\dfrac{1+\frac{1}{W+X_1}}{1+\frac{\alpha}{W+X_1}+\frac{1-\alpha}{X_1}}}\right) \\ \dfrac{k-(1-\alpha)f(\alpha,C)}{2(1+\frac{1}{W+X_1})}, & \text{otherwise.} \end{cases} \tag{15}
$$

---

[2] Here we focus on a second-price auction as it is well known to be incentive compatible and result in the socially optimal allocation.

In the case where SP 2 wins the auction, SP 1 and SP 2 serves $_2w_1$ and $_2w_2$ respectively:

$$_2w_1 = \frac{2k(1 + \frac{1}{W}) + (1 - \alpha)f(\alpha, C) - k}{4(1 + \frac{1}{X_1})(1 + \frac{1}{W}) - 1}. \tag{16}$$

$$_2w_2 = \frac{2(k - (1 - \alpha)f(\alpha, C))(1 + \frac{1}{X_1}) - k}{4(1 + \frac{1}{X_1})(1 + \frac{1}{W}) - 1}. \tag{17}$$

The proof is in Sect. 6.

Using these expressions, we next show simulation results for the outcome of such an auction in Figs. 4, 5 and 6. A similar auction model was studied in [5] where SPs could only offload traffic. In [5], both SPs needed proprietary bandwidth to participate in the auction. It was shown that the SP with the larger amount of proprietary bandwidth always won the auction. Interestingly, our simulations (see Fig. 4) reveal that when waiting is allowed, the smaller SP (SP 2) can now win the auction in certain cases, even without any proprietary band. This corresponds to the intermediate values of α in Fig. 4, where SP 2 serves a non-zero amount of customers. As we can see in Fig. 5, the bids have three different phases. When α is small, SP 2 can not use the intermittent band even if it wins, while SP 1 can use the band with offloading, leading to a small increase in its revenue. In this case, SP 2 bids zero and SP 1 bids its marginal increase in revenue from winning. Once α becomes large enough (larger than 0.2), both SP 2 can use the band with waiting, while SP 1 still prefers offloading. Initially, SP 1 outbids SP 2, preventing it from entering the market. However when α is large enough, the gains for SP 2 exceed those for SP 1 and SP 2 is able to win the auction and enter the market. Finally, when α is large enough, SP 1 also seeks to use the band with waiting and in this case, it eventually outbids SP 2. Figure 6 shows how the bids vary with C for a fixed α. In this case, there is a middle range of C value for which SP 2 wins the auction. This result suggests that intermittent spectrum can lower entry barriers, potentially benefiting consumers through lower prices and improved services.

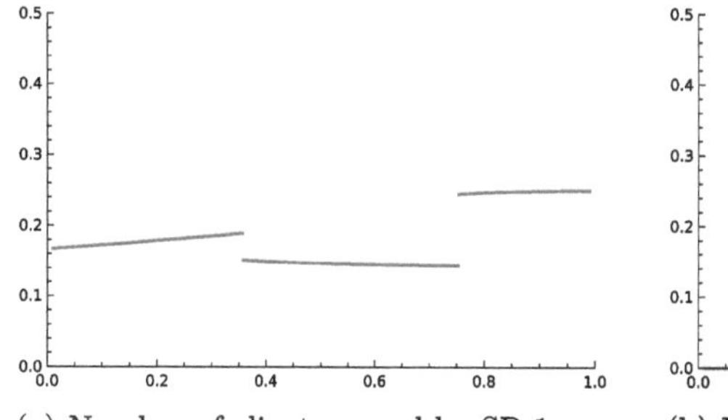
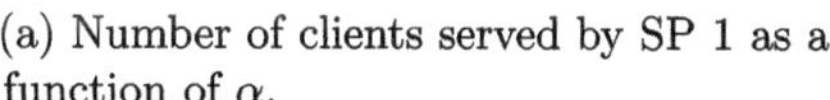

(a) Number of clients served by SP 1 as a function of α.

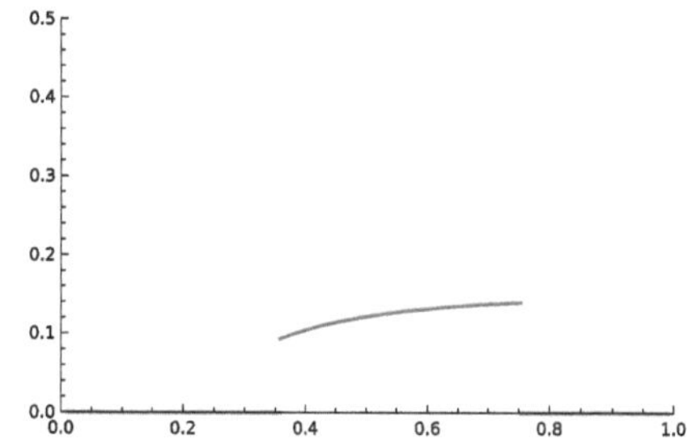

(b) Number of clients served by SP 2 as a function of α.

Fig. 4. Number of clients with $X_1 = 0.5$, $W = 0.5$, $C = 0.25$, and $k = 1$.

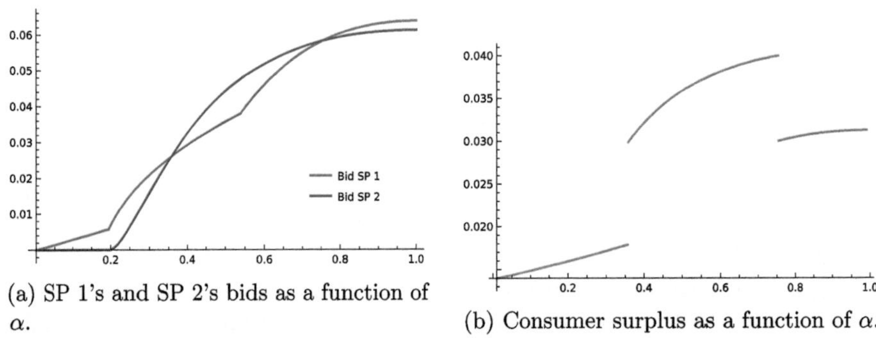

(a) SP 1's and SP 2's bids as a function of α.

(b) Consumer surplus as a function of α.

Fig. 5. Bids and consumer surplus with $X_1 = 0.5$, $W = 0.5$, $C = 0.25$, and $k = 1$.

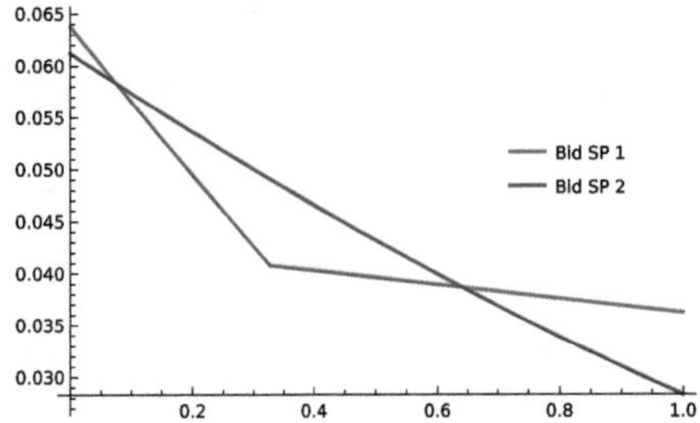

Fig. 6. SP 1's and SP 2's bids as a function of C with $X_1 = 0.5$, $W = 0.5$, $\alpha = 0.6$, and $k = 1$.

5   Conclusion

In this paper, we have developed a model to analyze the competitive dynamics among SPs who utilize both proprietary and intermittent bandwidth. Our findings reveal that the availability of intermittent bandwidth significantly impacts service latency, pricing strategies, SP revenues, and overall market competition.

Intermittent bandwidth can disrupt markets dominated by incumbents with proprietary bandwidth. In scenarios where SPs rely solely on intermittent bandwidth, increasing the availability probability α allows SPs to serve more clients. When an incumbent SP with proprietary bandwidth competes with a new entrant using intermittent bandwidth, higher α lowers entry barriers. The entrant can capture significant market share as α increases, challenging the incumbent's dominance. Our simulations illustrate that beyond a certain threshold, the entrant can successfully compete. The auction scenario further highlights the strategic importance of intermittent bandwidth. Our findings show that under certain conditions, an SP without proprietary bandwidth can outbid an incumbent in acquiring intermittent bandwidth, thus entering the market and serving clients. This outcome underscores the potential of intermittent bandwidth to promote competition and innovation in the market.

These results have important implications for policy and regulation. Facilitating access to intermittent bandwidth, perhaps through spectrum sharing policies or dynamic spectrum access, can encourage competition and benefit consumers through lower prices and improved services. Moreover, understanding the role of intermittent resources can help regulators design better frameworks to manage shared resources and promote efficient utilization.

However, it is important to acknowledge the limitations of our model, which rely on several simplifying assumptions. For instance, we assume rational behavior and perfect knowledge among SPs, linear latency and we restrict our analysis to pure Cournot competition, excluding the possibility of mixed pricing strategies or hybrid approaches that SPs could adopt. The intermittent bandwidth availability is modeled as a simple Bernoulli process with probability α, which may oversimplify the stochastic and often complex nature of real-world spectrum dynamics. Furthermore, we assume uniform sensitivity among clients to waiting times (parameterized by C), which may not account for varying user tolerances and preferences.

Future research could extend our model to address these limitations and help bridge the gap between theoretical models and the complex realities of modern telecommunications markets.

6   Proofs

Proof (Proof of Lemma 1). Each Service Provider i in the set $\{1, 2, \ldots, n\}$ competes to serve a common pool of clients. We focus specifically on Service Provider i, its latency is given by:

$$l_i = \alpha \frac{w_i}{W_i} + (1 - \alpha)(f(\alpha, C) + \frac{w_i}{W_i}) = (1 - \alpha)f(\alpha, C) + \frac{w_i}{W_i}. \qquad (18)$$

The price that clients are willing to pay for the service provided by SP i is calculated by subtracting the latency and the total number of clients served by all SPs from the total demand k. The price expression is:

$$p_i = p_d - l_i = k - \sum_j^n w_j - \frac{w_i}{W_i} - (1 - \alpha)f(\alpha, C)$$

$$= k - (1 - \alpha)f(\alpha, C) - \sum_{j=1, j \neq i}^n w_j - w_i(1 + \frac{1}{W_i}). \qquad (19)$$

The revenue of SP i can be derived by multiplying the price p_i by the number of clients w_i served by SP i:

$$R_i = p_i w_i = \left(k - (1-\alpha)f(\alpha, C) - \sum_{j=1, j\neq i}^{n} w_j - w_i(1 + \frac{1}{W_i}) \right) w_i$$

$$= -(1 + \frac{1}{W_i})w_i^2 + \left(k - (1-\alpha)f(\alpha, C) - \sum_{j=1, j\neq i}^{n} w_j \right) w_i. \tag{20}$$

This is a concave quadratic revenue function of w_i, indicating that there is a unique optimal number of clients w_i that maximizes SP i's revenue. From the first order optimality conditions, we have that the optimal number of clients to maximize the revenue in (20) is given by:

$$w_i = \frac{k - (1-\alpha)f(\alpha, C) - \sum_{j=1, j\neq i}^{n} w_j}{2(1 + \frac{1}{W_i})}. \tag{21}$$

By solving this system of equations for all n SPs, we determine the equilibrium number of clients each SP serves. The equilibrium solution is given by (6). This is only valid when $k - (1-\alpha)f(\alpha, C) > 0$, otherwise the optimal number of clients must be zero for each SP i.

Proof (Proof of Lemma 2). SP 1 has access to both proprietary bandwidth X_1 and intermittent bandwidth W_1. SP 2 only has access to intermittent bandwidth W_2. According to our model, the latencies are:

$$l_1 = \alpha \frac{w_1}{W_1 + X_1} + (1-\alpha) \min \left\{ \frac{w_1}{X_1}, f(\alpha, C) + \frac{w_1}{W_1 + X_1} \right\},$$
$$l_2 = \frac{w_2}{W_2} + (1-\alpha)f(\alpha, C). \tag{22}$$

The revenue for each service provider can be expressed as follows. For SP 1:

$$R_1 = p_1 w_1 = (p_d - l_1)w_1$$
$$= (k - w_1 - w_2 - \alpha \frac{w_1}{W_1 + X_1} - (1-\alpha) \min \{ \frac{w_1}{X_1}, f(\alpha, C) + \frac{w_1}{W_1 + X_1} \})w_1$$
$$= \max \{ {}^1R_1, {}^2R_1 \}. \tag{23}$$

With:

$${}^1R_1 = -(1 + \frac{\alpha}{W_1 + X_1} + \frac{1-\alpha}{X_1})w_1^2 + (k - w_2)w_1. \tag{24}$$

$${}^2R_1 = -(1 + \frac{1}{W_1 + X_1})w_1^2 + (k - (1-\alpha)f(\alpha, C) - w_2)w_1. \tag{25}$$

For SP 2:

$$
\begin{aligned}
R_2 = p_2 w_2 &= (p_d - l_2) w_2 \\
&= (k - w_1 - w_2 - \frac{w_2}{W_2} - (1-\alpha)f(\alpha, C))w_2 \\
&= -(1 + \frac{1}{W_2})w_2^2 + (k - (1-\alpha)f(\alpha, C) - w_1)w_2.
\end{aligned}
\tag{26}
$$

These revenue functions are concave with respect to w_1 and w_2, indicating that there are optimal numbers of clients w_1 and w_2 that maximize the revenues for SP 1 and SP 2, respectively.

By solving the optimization problems, we determine the equilibrium values for the number of clients each service provider serves. If the first revenue possible for SP 1 ($^1R_1$) is higher than the second ($^1R_1$), the optimal number of clients for SP 1 and SP 2 can be expressed as:

$$
w_1 = \frac{2k(1 + \frac{1}{W_2}) + (1-\alpha)f(\alpha, C) - k}{4(1 + \frac{\alpha}{W_1 + X_1} + \frac{1-\alpha}{X_1})(1 + \frac{1}{W_2}) - 1}.
\tag{27}
$$

$$
w_2 = \frac{2(k - (1-\alpha)f(\alpha, C))(1 + \frac{\alpha}{W_1 + X_1} + \frac{1-\alpha}{X_1}) - k}{4(1 + \frac{\alpha}{W_1 + X_1} + \frac{1-\alpha}{X_1})(1 + \frac{1}{W_2}) - 1}.
\tag{28}
$$

If the proprietary bandwidth X_1 is too small to be effectively utilized on its own, SP 1 might choose not to use it when W_1 is unavailable. In such a case, the optimal number of clients for SP 1 and SP 2 can be found using:

$$
w_1 = (k - (1-\alpha)f(\alpha, C)) \frac{2(1 + \frac{1}{W_2}) - 1}{4(1 + \frac{1}{W_1 + X_1})(1 + \frac{1}{W_2}) - 1}.
\tag{29}
$$

$$
w_2 = (k - (1-\alpha)f(\alpha, C)) \frac{2(1 + \frac{1}{W_1 + X1}) - 1}{4(1 + \frac{1}{W_2})(1 + \frac{1}{W_1 + X_1}) - 1}.
\tag{30}
$$

We are back to the first scenario, with SP 1 having $W_1 + X_1$ as intermittent bandwidth and SP 2 having W_2.

Those two possibilities are only valid when $k - (1-\alpha)f(\alpha, C) > 0$, otherwise the optimal number of clients, for SP 2 must be 0 and SP 1 has a monopoly and use W_1 when it's available without making its clients wait. From $^1R_1$, with $w_2 = 0$, we get (14).

Proof (Proof of Lemma 3).
If SP 1 wins the auction, SP 2 will be excluded from competing in the market and SP 1 latency will be:

$$
_1l_1 = \alpha \frac{_1w_1}{W + X_1} + (1-\alpha) \min \left\{ \frac{_1w_1}{X_1}, f(\alpha, C) + \frac{_1w_1}{W + X_1} \right\}.
\tag{31}
$$

And its revenue is given by:

$$_1R_1 = {}_1p_{11}w_1$$

$$= {}_1w_1 \left(k - {}_1w_1 - \alpha \frac{{}_1w_1}{W + X_1} - (1-\alpha) \min \left\{ \frac{{}_1w_1}{X_1}, f(\alpha, C) + \frac{{}_1w_1}{W + X_1} \right\} \right)$$

$$= \max \{ {}_1^1R_1, {}_1^2R_1 \}.$$

$$(32)$$

With:

$$_1^1R_1 = - \left(1 + \frac{\alpha}{W + X_1} + \frac{1-\alpha}{X_1} \right) {}_1w_1{}^2 + k {}_1w_1. \tag{33}$$

$$_1^2R_1 = - \left(1 + \frac{1}{W + X_1} \right) {}_1w_1{}^2 + \left(k - (1-\alpha)f(\alpha, C) \right) {}_1w_1. \tag{34}$$

Those two revenues are concave in ${}_1w_1$, so SP 1 chooses:

$$_1w_1 = \begin{cases} \frac{k}{2\left(1 + \frac{\alpha}{W+X_1} + \frac{1-\alpha}{X_1}\right)}, & \text{if } f(\alpha, C) > \frac{k}{1-\alpha}\left(1 - \sqrt{\frac{1 + \frac{1}{W+X_1}}{1 + \frac{\alpha}{W+X_1} + \frac{1-\alpha}{X_1}}}\right) \\ \frac{k - (1-\alpha)f(\alpha,C)}{2\left(1 + \frac{1}{W+X_1}\right)}, & \text{otherwise.} \end{cases} \tag{35}$$

Indeed, we can show that ${}_1^1R_1$ can be higher than ${}_1^2R_1$ if and only if:

$$\frac{k}{1-\alpha}\left(1 - \sqrt{\frac{1 + \frac{1}{W+X_1}}{1 + \frac{\alpha}{W+X_1} + \frac{1-\alpha}{X_1}}}\right) < f(\alpha, C) < \frac{k}{1-\alpha}\left(1 + \sqrt{\frac{1 + \frac{1}{W+X_1}}{1 + \frac{\alpha}{W+X_1} + \frac{1-\alpha}{X_1}}}\right).$$

$$(36)$$

Since a SP cannot have a negative number of clients, we know that, $f(\alpha, C)$ shouldn't be higher than $\frac{k}{1-\alpha}$. Otherwise, SP 1 wins the auction and we are back in the same situation as the previous scenario, so we get back to (14). Conversely, if SP 2 wins the auction, it will have access to the intermittent bandwidth W, while SP 1 retains only its proprietary bandwidth X_1. In this case, SP 2 might be able to actually enter the market and compete with SP 1. Under this scenario the latencies are: ${}_2l_1 = \frac{{}_2w_1}{X_1}$ and $l_2 = \frac{{}_2w_2}{W} + (1-\alpha)f(\alpha, C)$ for SP 1 and SP 2, respectively.

The respective revenues for SP 1 and SP 2 are:

$$_2R_1 = {}_2w_1 \left(k - {}_2w_1 - {}_2w_2 - \frac{{}_2w_1}{X_1} \right) = - \left(1 + \frac{1}{X_1} \right) {}_2w_1{}^2 + (k - {}_2w_2){}_2w_1. \tag{37}$$

And,

$$_2R_2 = {}_2w_2 \left(k - {}_2w_1 - {}_2w_2 - \frac{{}_2w_2}{W} - (1-\alpha)f(\alpha, C) \right)$$

$$= - \left(1 + \frac{1}{W} \right) {}_2w_2{}^2 + (k - (1-\alpha)f(\alpha, C) - {}_2w_1){}_2w_2. \tag{38}$$

Which are both concave in $_2w_1$ and $_2w_2$ respectively. So, the SPs choose:

$$_2w_1 = \frac{2k(1 + \frac{1}{W}) + (1 - \alpha)f(\alpha, C) - k}{4(1 + \frac{1}{X_1})(1 + \frac{1}{W}) - 1}. \tag{39}$$

$$_2w_2 = \frac{2(k - (1 - \alpha)f(\alpha, C))(1 + \frac{1}{X_1}) - k}{4(1 + \frac{1}{X_1})(1 + \frac{1}{W}) - 1}. \tag{40}$$

Once again, this is only true if $(1 - \alpha)f(\alpha, C) < k$, otherwise, we also get back to (14).

References

1. Acemoglu, D., Ozdaglar, A.: Competition and efficiency in congested markets. Math. Oper. Res. **32**(1), 1–31 (2007)
2. Acemoglu, D., Ozdaglar, A.: Competition in parallel-serial networks. IEEE J. Sel. Areas Commun. **25**(6), 1180–1192 (2007)
3. Armony, M., Haviv, M.: Price and delay competition between two service providers. Eur. J. Oper. Res. **147**(1), 32–50 (2003)
4. Berry, R., Hazlett, T.W., Honig, M., Laneman, J.N.: Evaluating the CBRS experiment. In: Proceedings of TPRC 2023: The Research Conference on Communications, Informaiton and Internet Policy (2023)
5. Berry, R., Honig, M., Nguyen, T., Subramanian, V., Vohra, R.: The value of sharing intermittent spectrum. Manage. Sci. **66**(11), 5242–5264 (2020)
6. Engel, E., Fischer, R., Galetovic, A.: Toll competition among congested roads. Working Paper 239, National Bureau of Economic Research (1999)
7. Federal communications commission: amendment of the commission's rules with regard to commercial operations in the 3550-3650 MHZ band (2015)
8. Hayrapetyan, A., Tardos, E., Wexler, T.: A network pricing game for selfish traffic. Distrib. Comput. **19**, 255–266 (2007)
9. Levhari, D., Luski, I.: Duopoly pricing and waiting lines. Eur. Econ. Rev. **11**, 17–35 (1978)
10. Maillé, P., Tuffin, B., Vigne, J.-M.: Competition between wireless service providers sharing a radio resource. In: Bestak, R., Kencl, L., Li, L.E., Widmer, J., Yin, H. (eds.) NETWORKING 2012. LNCS, vol. 7290, pp. 355–365. Springer, Heidelberg (2012). https://doi.org/10.1007/978-3-642-30054-7_28
11. Mu, K., Berry, R.: Market impacts of pooling intermittent spectrum. In: 2024 IEEE International Symposium on Dynamic Spectrum Access Networks (DySPAN), pp. 189–196 (2024)
12. Mu, K., Xie, Z., Kadota, I., Berry, R.: Impact of geographical separation on spectrum sharing markets. In: 22nd Internation Symposium on Modeling and Optimization in Mobile, Ad Hoc and Wireless Networks (WiOpt) (2024)
13. Nguyen, T., Zhou, H., Berry, R.A., Honig, M.L., Vohra, R.: The cost of free spectrum. Oper. Res. **64**(6), 1217–1229 (2016)
14. Perakis, G., Sun, W.: Efficiency analysis of cournot competition in service industries with congestion. Manage. Sci. **60**(11), 2684–2700 (2014)
15. Xiao, F., Yang, H., Han, D.: Competition and efficiency of private toll roads. Transport. Res. Part B: Methodol. **41**(3), 292–308 (2007)

A Hypergraph Evolutionary Game Theoretic Cournot Model for Networked Markets

Ioannis Papastaikoudis[1]([⊠]), Jonathan Newton[2], Jeremy Watson[3], and Ioannis Lestas[4]

[1] Judge Business School (CERF), University of Cambridge, Trumpington Street, Cambridge CB2 1AG, Cambridgeshire, U.K.
`ip352@cam.ac.uk`
[2] Institute of Economic Research, University of Kyoto, Yoshida-honmachi, Sakyo-ku, 606-8501 Tokyo, Kansai, Japan
`newton@kier.kyoto-u.ac.jp`
[3] Faculty of Engineering, University of Canterbury, Private Bag 4800, 8140 Christchurch, Canterbury, New Zealand
`jeremy.watson@canterbury.ac.nz`
[4] Department of Engineering, University of Cambridge, Trumpington Street, Cambridge CB2 1PZ, Cambridgeshire, U.K.
`icl20@cam.ac.uk`

Abstract. We propose a novel hypergraph information structure for a Cournot network competition model and formulate it as a distributed optimization problem which we solve with continuous-time evolutionary game theoretic techniques that result in a dynamical system. The proposed hypergraph structure is more efficient and compact in terms of information transmission than a bipartite graph and exhibits faster convergence of the respective distributed evolutionary dynamical system. The equilibrium point of the distributed evolutionary dynamical system is unique and has the economic interpretation of the market clearing point. Thus, fast attainment is associated with economic benefits like price stability and efficient resource allocation.

Keywords: Cournot Network Model · Evolutionary Game Theory · Hypergraphs

JEL Classification C61 · C62 · C73 · D4 · D85

1 Introduction

The Cournot competition model is a well established economic model due to the seminal work of Cournot himself in 1838. In modern day economics with the extensive use of networks [20] it was inevitable for the Cournot competition model to be expanded in the network setting. The network Cournot competition (NCC) is able to facilitate the case of multiple markets and firms that have

© ICST Institute for Computer Sciences, Social Informatics and Telecommunications Engineering 2026
Published by Springer Nature Switzerland AG 2026. All Rights Reserved
V. Aggarwal et al. (Eds.): GameNets 2025, LNICST 657, pp. 18–41, 2026.
https://doi.org/10.1007/978-3-032-12915-4_2

supply and demand interconnections in an inter-regional economic environment. Works on Cournot netwok models can be found in [1,4,10,19] and others with the main common aspect of these works to be the usage of a bipartite graph for the description of the model communication structure. Usually the above models do not use a unique communication matrix in their proposed solution algorithm to describe the interactions of the agents involved. Instead they use searching algorithms among the different agents by trying to utilize their pairwise interactions working directly on the network space something that may have quite a big computational cost in the case of a large number of agents. For this reason we propose the use of a matrix that could represent the network communication structure, e.g., an adjacency matrix or a Laplacian matrix directly in the solution algorithm. This approach provides a computationally convenient automation of the solution process of the network Cournot model.

In a Cournot competition model it is often used game theoretic notions to describe its behavior and more specifically that of Nash equilibrium as a solution concept which is achieved via optimization methods. Game theory was introduced in the seminal work of [33] and is the formal study of conflict and cooperation among multiple agents. In this work we will not make use of standard game theory but we will use instead evolutionary game theory. In evolutionary game theory (EGT) are introduced the concepts of a population of players and the interpretation of payoff as fitness. The traditional mathematical framework of evolutionary game theory is that of a dynamical system [11,17,29,42] where the deterministic dynamics of the population are described with the use of differential equations in well-mixed and infinitely large populations. The learning and strategy adjustment of the agents are heavily based on the concept of the evolutionary stable strategy (ESS) which was introduced in [41] and is a similar concept to strict Nash equilibrium [31]. The most widely used dynamic strategy adjustment mechanism is the replicator dynamic equation [43] where if a strategy is a strict Nash equilibrium then it is an asymptotically stable fixed point of the replicator equation [17]. Real populations are not infinitely large but rather finite and they are neither well mixed. These obstacles were overcome with the introduction of networks in the study of EGT as in [14,15,34] where this combined study has led to evolutionary graph theory [23,35]. In this work we will focus on replicator dynamics since we are mostly interested on the graph theoretical structure of the model. Other types of evolutionary dynamics such as Smith dynamics, projected dynamics, logit dynamics could easily be accommodated in our hypergraph setting in a similar fashion as in [3]. We chose to use evolutionary game theory since we are interested on the evolution of the population strategies distribution regarding the respective operating firms of their market, a process that affects directly the price of the good by also taking into account the operating cost of the firms to the other markets in a simultaneous way.

For the proposed Cournot competition model due to its network structure and since we are looking for the optimal population distribution of the different markets given their links with the respective firms we believe it is more efficient to make use of distributed optimization techniques in order to find the optimum for the firms' profit functions. Distributed optimization can be traced back to the seminal work of [44] with a review on the topic provided in [47] and a common way of solving such problems is the use of first order methods as in [21] and [32] that result to a dynamical system. We focus on continuous time dynamical systems where this continuous time approach has multiple real world applications as we discuss later on. The equilibrium point of the dynamical system coincides with the optimum solution of the firms' distributed profit maximization problem and is actually the Nash equilibrium in the proposed oligopolistic setting that has the economic interpretation of firms getting an equal share in terms of profit from all the available markets depending on their local network interconnections. Due to [3] it is established a connection among distributed optimization and evolutionary/population game theory via the concept of distributed evolutionary dynamics where the strategies of a population (the choice of firms) are being described with the use of a graph. The coupled trajectories that reach the optimum solution of a static distributed optimization problem can be viewed as a dynamic evolutionary process. From our proposed structure of the profit functions, i.e., strictly concave inverse demand functions for the markets and stricty convex cost functions for the respective firms we will be able to use a special subclass of evolutionary games, the stable games that were introduced in [16] and have the property that their dynamics converge to a unique, stable Nash equilibrium point that coincides with the optimum solution of the distributed optimization problem.

The equilibrium point of our proposed algorithm is a Nash equilibrium and despite of having the property of providing an equal share for all operating firms across all markets it also has the economic interpretation that all buyers and sellers are satisfied with the quantity acquired/sold. In other words it is the market-clearing point, i.e., the point where supply meets demand for all markets and firms simultaneously. The evolutionary nature of the population strategies, i.e., their choices regarding the operating firms in their market can also be viewed as tâtonnement processes that bring supply into consistency with demand and they are decentralized based on the given network communication structure. Relevant literature regarding decentralized tâtonnement processes is provided in [7,12,25,27,28,37]. Our algorithm is also a price determination mechanism and an efficient resource allocation mechanism by ensuring that the quantity of goods or services supplied matches the quantity demanded and facilitates the actual exchange of goods, services, or financial instruments between buyers and sellers. An aspect of great importance of the equilibrium point is the requirement for efficiency and speed. Fast market clearing reduces the risk of price fluctuations and improves market efficiency, e.g., high-frequency trading (HFT) firms use algorithms to execute trades almost in continuous time, ensuring instant market clearing which has various other benefits like transaction costs. Automated trading systems have lower transaction costs by reducing the need for manual intervention and thus making trading more accessible and increase market participation. Other examples of continuous time trading are the foreign exchange

(Forex) market where continuous trading provides high liquidity and real-time price adjustments while the case is the same for stock markets and electricity markets. In our setting we focus on the commodity market where we assume the trade of one homogeneous good that is produced by different firms and is sold among different markets like the electricity market [30]. Our results could also be expanded to the financial market [38] or the e-commerce [24] respectively.

In this work we propose a novel information structure that is based on hypergraphs. Hypergraphs were introduced in [9] and they are a generalization of graphs since they allow more than two nodes to be linked in the same edge (hyperedge). We choose hypergraphs in order for both the markets (population groups of buyers) and the firms to have more complex and not just pairwise interactions. The nodes of the hypergraph are partitioned into blocks where each block corresponds to a specific market and each node within a block corresponds to the population of the market that chooses to buy from a specific firm. Regarding the hyperedges we have that each hyperedge corresponds to a firm and its respective trade channels. The proposed hypergraph information structure is able to describe the same situation as a bipartite graph but is much less complex since it does not use nodes for the representation of firms, these are being described by the hyperedges and as a result, we have less number of nodes and hyperedges describing the supply and demand relationships. Also a hypergraph can lead to better convergence rate than its respective graph analogue since it describes the same information in a more "centralized" way compared to the pairwise interactions of the bipartite graph. Our claims regarding complexity and convergence rate have been demonstrated in [36] for the comparison of a hypergraph and its respective clique expansion graph. The clique expansion of a bipartite graph, i.e., its substitution of the supply and demand relationships with complete subgraphs can be viewed as superior to bipartite graphs in terms of convergence rate for consensus algorithms (Nash equilibrium has a consensus interpretation in our setting) due to the higher connectivity [13] of clique expansion graphs something that hints the superiority of hypergraphs over bipartite graphs which we will demonstrate numerically in this work. Overall, the proposed hypergraph information structure is much more efficient than its respective bipartite graph analogue. Hypergraphs have been used as information structures in distributed optimization settings in works like [46] and [39] while they have also been used in the evolutionary game theoretic setting in works like [8] and [26]. It is important to note that in terms of comparative statics the choice of the different graphical structures does not affect the asymptotic strategies, i.e., the equilibrium point nor the objective value since the different graph communications depict the same underlying information structure.

At this point we would like to mention that the inverse demand/price of the good for each market depends solely on the different populations of this market while the cost function of a firm depends on the populations of the different markets where the firm has a presence. This situation actually hints two types of interactions. The first type corresponds to the interactions of each market's sub-populations where we will describe the markets with the use of blocks and their respective sub-populations as nodes within these blocks. It is important to note that each sub-population represents a strategy, i.e., the choice to buy from a specific firm. The second type corresponds to the interactions of the firms with the sub-populations of various markets which we will describe with the use of a hypergraph where the hyperedges represent the firms and their supply channels with the sub-populations of the different markets. We assume that the union of these two types of interactions creates a connected graphical structure in the sense that every node, i.e., every markets sub-population is directly or indirectly linked with any other node via the hyperedges of the firms. In many stable game interpretations of Cournot models the cost functions were assumed constant but our proposed information structure allows us to include them in the model without deviating from the theory of stable games. For the proposed dynamical system we will provide a Lyapunov based stability analysis proof.

The paper is organized as follows: Section 2 presents the mathematical tools that will be used throughout the paper such as non linear control theory [22], convex analysis [6], matrix theory [18], evolutionary game theory [40] and graph/hypergraph theory [45]. In Sect. 3 we present the information structure of the Cournot competition model. In Sect. 4 we present the respective distributed optimization problem along with the distributed evolutionary dynamics that solve the optimization problem and we provide the stability analysis of the algorithm. Finally, in Sect. 5 we present the matrix representation of the evolutionary dynamical system which we will utilize for the main results of this paper. A numerical example is provided alongside with the evolution of the theory.

2   Preliminaries

2.1   Non Linear Control Theory

In this work we consider a system Σ, with the following state space expression

$$\dot{x}(t) = f(x(t)) \tag{1}$$

where $x(t) \in \mathbb{R}^n$ is the state of the system and the function $f : \mathbb{R}^n \to \mathbb{R}^n$ is considered to be Lipschitz continuous. A function $V : \mathbb{R}^n \to \mathbb{R}$ that satisfies $\|x\| \to \infty \Rightarrow V(x) \to \infty$ is called radially unbounded. The Lie derivative of function V is denoted by $\dot{V} : \mathbb{R}^n \to \mathbb{R}$ and is defined as:

$$\dot{V}(x) = \nabla V(x)^T \cdot \dot{x} = \nabla V(x)^T \cdot f(x).$$

Theorem 1. *Let x^* be an equilibrium point of (1). If $V : \mathbb{R}^n \to \mathbb{R}$ is radially unbounded and $\dot{V}(x) < 0, \forall\, x \neq x^*$ then x^* is globally asymptotically stable and V is a valid Lyapunov function of (1).*

Definition 1. *A domain $\mathcal{D} \subseteq \mathbb{R}^n$ is called invariant for the system $\dot{x} = f(x)$ if*

$$\forall\, x(t_0) \in D \Rightarrow x(t) \in D, \ \forall\, t \in \mathbb{R}.$$

Definition 2. *A domain $\mathcal{D} \subseteq \mathbb{R}^n$ is called positively invariant for the system $\dot{x} = f(x)$, if*

$$\forall\ x(t_0) \in D \Rightarrow x(t) \in D,\ \forall\ t \geq t_0.$$

Theorem 2 (LaSalle's Invariance Principle). *Let $\Omega \subset D$ be a compact positively invariant set with respect to $\dot{x} = f(x)$. Let $V : D \to \mathbb{R}$ be a continuously differentiable function such that $\dot{V}(x) \leq 0$ in Ω. Let $\mathcal{X}$ be the set of all points in Ω where $\dot{V}(x) = 0$. Let M be the largest invariant set in $\mathcal{X}$. Then every solution starting in Ω approaches M as $t \to \infty$.*

2.2   Convex Analysis

Definition 3. *A differentiable function $f : \mathbb{R}^n \to \mathbb{R}$ is said to be convex if the following inequality holds for all $x, y \in \mathbb{R}^n$*

$$f(x) - f(y) \leq \nabla f(x)^T (x - y). \tag{2}$$

The function is said to be strictly convex if the inequality (2) strictly holds whenever $x \neq y$. We say that a function f is concave if $-f$ is convex and similarly we say that f is strictly concave if $-f$ is strictly convex.

Lemma 1. *Consider a convex function $f : \mathbb{R}^n \to \mathbb{R}$. Then, its gradient $\nabla f : \mathbb{R}^n \to \mathbb{R}^n$ is monotonical increasing, i.e., the following inequality holds for any $x, y \in \mathbb{R}^n$*

$$(\nabla f(x) - \nabla f(y))^T (x - y) \geq 0. \tag{3}$$

If f is strictly convex, the inequality strictly holds as long as $x \neq y$. In that case, ∇f is called strictly monotonical increasing. In the cases of concave and strictly concave functions the inequality (3) is in the opposite direction.

2.3   Matrix Theory

A symmetric matrix $M \in \mathbb{R}^{n \times n}$ is called positive (negative) semidefinite $M \succeq 0$ $(M \preceq 0)$ if $x^T M x \geq 0$ $(x^T M x \leq 0)$ for every nonzero $x \in \mathbb{R}^n$ where x^T is the transpose of x. If we have strict inequality we say that matrix M is positive (negative) definite $M \succ 0$ $(M \prec 0)$. A square matrix $P \in \mathbb{R}^{n \times n}$ is called an orthogonal projection matrix if $P^2 = P$ and $P = P^T$. For a matrix $M \in \mathbb{R}^{n \times n}$ we denote the spectrum of matrix M by $\mathcal{S}(M)$.

2.4   Evolutionary Game Theory

Consider a population of mass $m > 0$ comprised of a continuum of agents in a strategic interaction. We assume, without loss of generality, that the mass of the population is equal to one, i.e., $m = 1$. The set of available strategies for the agents is given by $\mathcal{S} = \{1, ..., n\}$. The populations states, which describe the distribution of strategy choices by players, constitute a simplex defined by

$\mathbb{X} = \{x \in \mathbb{R}^n_+ : \sum_{i \in \mathcal{S}} x_i = 1\}$ where $x_i \geq 0$ represents the fraction of the population that corresponds to the agents choosing the strategy $i \in \mathcal{S}$. The tangent space of $\mathbb{X}$ is denoted by $\mathbb{TX} = \{z \in \mathbb{R}^n_+ : \sum_{i=1}^{n} z_i = 0\}$. We denote the payoff vector which is assigned to population state x by $p \in \mathbb{R}^n$ where the components p_i of vector p correspond to the players choosing strategy i. We will focus on static payoffs of the form

$$p(t) = F(x(t)). \tag{4}$$

Definition 4. *Given a payoff function $F : \mathbb{X} \to \mathbb{R}^n$, the population state $x^{NE} \in \mathbb{X}$ is a Nash equilibrium of F if it holds that*

$$x_i^{NE} > 0 \Rightarrow i \in \max_{j \in \{1,..,n\}} F_j(x^{NE}).$$

Definition 5. *Let $F : \mathbb{R}^N_+ \to \mathbb{R}^n$ be a population game (PG). If there exists a continuously differentiable potential function $V : \mathbb{R}^n_+$ that satisfies $\nabla V(x) = F(x) \; \forall \; x \in \mathbb{R}^n_+$, then F is a full potential game.*

Definition 6. *The population game $F : \mathbb{X} \to \mathbb{R}^n$ is a stable game if: $(y - x)^T(F(y) - F(x)) \leq 0$, for all $x, y \in \mathbb{X}$.*

An alternative characterization of stable games due to [40] is the following.

Theorem 3. *Let the population game $F : \mathbb{X} \to \mathbb{R}^n$ be continuously differentiable. F is a stable game if and only if $z^T DF(x)z \leq 0$, for all $z \in \mathbb{TX}$ and $x \in \mathbb{X}$ where $DF(x)$ is the Jacobian matrix of $F(x)$.*

Lemma 2. *In a stable game there is a unique Nash equilibrium.*

Definition 7. *A function $\tau : \mathbb{R}^n \times \mathbb{X} \to \mathbb{R}^{n \times n}_+$ is a revision protocol which has as input a population state x and the respective payoff vector $F(x)$, and as output a nonnegative matrix T whose elements $\tau_{ij}(F(x), x)$ represent the conditional switch rate from strategies i to j, where $i, j \in \mathcal{S}$.*

A population game combined with a revision protocol results to evolutionary dynamics (ED). Evolutionary dynamics describe how the population state evolves over time in response to given payoffs. We focus on evolutionary dynamic models that admit state space representation of the following form:

$$\dot{x}(t) = \mathcal{F}(p(t), x(t)), \; x(0) \in \mathbb{X}$$

where $p(t), x(t)$ and $\dot{x}(t)$ take values in $\mathbb{R}^n, \mathbb{X}$ and $\mathbb{TX}$ respectively. We assume that the vector field $\mathcal{F} : \mathbb{R}^n \times \mathbb{X} \to \mathbb{TX}$ is well defined.

2.5   Graphs and Hypergraphs

Graphs. A graph $\mathcal{G} = (\mathcal{V}, \mathcal{E})$ is an ordered pair, where $\mathcal{V} = \{v_1, ..., v_n\}$ is the node set while $\mathcal{E} = \{e_1, ..., e_m\}$ is the edge set. The degree of a node v_i denoted by $|v_i|$ is the total number of edges that are adjacent to this node. The total number of nodes in the graph is called the order of the graph and is denoted by $|\mathcal{V}|$. We define by D_V the diagonal $|\mathcal{V}| \times |\mathcal{V}|$ matrix whose entries are the degrees of each node

$$D_V = \text{diag}\{|v_1|, ..., |v_n|\}.$$

The adjacency matrix of graph $\mathcal{G}$, denoted by A, is a $|\mathcal{V}| \times |\mathcal{V}|$ matrix whose (i, j)-th entry is given by

$$A_{ij} = \begin{cases} 1, & (i,j) \in \mathcal{E} \\ 0, & \text{otherwise.} \end{cases}$$

The Laplacian matrix of graph $\mathcal{G}$, denoted by L, is a $|\mathcal{V}| \times |\mathcal{V}|$ matrix given by the following formula,

$$L = D_V - A. \tag{5}$$

For the rest of the paper we will use instead of the Laplacian matrix the normalized Laplacian matrix given by the formula

$$L = I - D_V^{-1} A. \tag{6}$$

A complete graph is a graph that has an edge between every two vertices. A subgraph $\mathcal{G}'$ of graph $\mathcal{G}$ is a graph all of whose points and edges are contained in $\mathcal{G}$.

Hypergraphs. A hypergraph is a pair $\mathcal{H} = (\mathcal{V}, \mathcal{E})$ where $\mathcal{V}$ is the finite set of nodes and $\mathcal{E}$ is the set of hyperedges. For the set of hyperedges we have that a hyperedge can join any number of nodes and not just two as it is in the case of a graph. We call the cardinality of the node set as the order of $\mathcal{H}$ and we denote it with $|\mathcal{V}|$. We call the cardinality of the edge set as the size of $\mathcal{H}$ and we denote it with $|\mathcal{E}|$. Assuming that the node set is $\mathcal{V} = \{v_1, ..., v_n\}$ the degree of ith node is denoted by $|v_i|$ and is equal with the number of hyperedges adjacent to this node. If $\mathcal{E} = \{\mathcal{E}_1, ..., \mathcal{E}_m\}$ is the set of hyperedges by $|\mathcal{E}_j|$ we represent the size of j-th hyperedge which is the total number of nodes adjacent to this hyperedge. We have that $|\mathcal{E}_j| \geq 2 \ \forall \ j$ and in the case that $|\mathcal{E}_j| = 2$ we say that $\mathcal{E}_j$ is a "standard" edge. We denote by D_V the diagonal $|\mathcal{V}| \times |\mathcal{V}|$ matrix whose entries are the degrees of each node, by D_E the diagonal $|\mathcal{E}| \times |\mathcal{E}|$ matrix whose entries are the sizes of each hyperedge and by E the $|\mathcal{V}| \times |\mathcal{E}|$ incidence matrix whose (i, j)-th entry is determined as:

$$e_{ij} = \begin{cases} 1, & v_i \in \mathcal{E}_j \\ 0, & \text{otherwise.} \end{cases}$$

The Laplacian of hypergraph (Bolla's Laplacian) [5] is the $|\mathcal{V}| \times |\mathcal{V}|$ matrix defined as:

$$L^H = D_V - E D_E^{-1} E^T. \tag{7}$$

The hypergraph Laplacian matrix is a positive semidefinite matrix, i.e., $L^H \succeq 0$. The clique of a hyperedge $\mathcal{E}_j$ is a complete graph of the hyperedge's adjacent nodes with $|\mathcal{E}_j|(|\mathcal{E}_j| - 1)/2$ pairwise interactions. We call a graph as the clique expansion of a hypergraph if we substitute all the hyperedges with their respective cliques.

Graphical Evolutionary Game Theory. For the case that a population is not well mixed we may use a graphical structure in order to describe it, i.e., $\mathcal{G} = (\mathcal{V}, \mathcal{E})$ where the node set $\mathcal{V} = \{v_1, ..., v_n\}$ corresponds to the strategies x_i, $\forall\ 1 \leq i \leq n$ available to the respective subpopulations while the edge/hyperedge set corresponds to the interactions among these strategies. For a well mixed population the graphical structure is always complete, i.e., all the nodes/strategies interact with each other. The mean dynamics for a non well mixed population for an undirected and unweighted graphical structure is given by the following relationship:

$$\dot{x}_i = \sum_{j \in \mathcal{N}_i} x_j \tau_{ji} - x_i \sum_{j \in \mathcal{N}_i} \tau_{ij}, \forall\ i \in \mathcal{V}. \tag{8}$$

where by τ_{ij} we denote the revision protocol from strategy i to strategy j and by $\mathcal{N}_i$ we denote the local interactions of node i, where this can be interpreted as a neighborhood for the case of a graph or as a hyperedge for the case of the hypergraph. We will make the following assumption for the graphical structure $\mathcal{G}$ and Nash equilibrium for the evolutionary graph theoretic setting.

- The graphical structure $\mathcal{G}$ that describes the population structure is connected.
- The Nash equilibrium x^* belongs to the interior of the simplex $\mathbb{X}$, i.e., $x^* \in \text{int}(\mathbb{X})$, where $\text{int}(\mathbb{X}) = \{x \in \mathbb{R}^n_{++} : \sum_{i \in \mathcal{V}} x_i = 1\}$.

3 Hypergraph Information Structure

3.1 Markets Information Structure

We assume that we have a global market that is partitioned in K local markets and N firms that operate within these local markets by selling a single homogeneous good. This partition of the local markets can be based on geographical, cultural or various other reasons. The global population $\mathbb{X}$ is partioned according to the local markets, i.e., $\mathbb{X} = \bigcup_{i=1}^{K} \mathbb{X}^i$ where $\mathbb{X}^i$ corresponds to the population of ith market. Within each market, the set of available strategies $\mathcal{S}^i$ coincides with the number of firms operating to the specific market. As a result, the sub-populations of each market are partitioned based on the firm/strategy that they choose from $\mathcal{S}^i$. The total set of strategies for all markets is given by $\mathcal{S} = \bigcup_{i=1}^{K} \mathcal{S}^i$ and it is natural some of the available strategies among the markets to be common since the same firm will operate to these markets. The agents of a subpopulation within the ith market can only switch strategies from the strategy subset $\mathcal{S}^i$ that corresponds to their population, i.e, an agent within a market can switch only to the firms that operate within the ith market. A suitable graphical representation of this situation would be a complete graph where for the ith market we have $\mathcal{G}_i = (\mathcal{V}_i, \mathcal{C}_i)$ where the node set $\mathcal{V}_i$ describes the available strategies of $\mathcal{S}^i$ and the edge set $\mathcal{C}_i$ describes the interconnections among these strategies. As a result, from the global economy scope we have K complete subgraphs where all of them are disjoint with each other, i.e., the graph $\mathcal{G}$ of the global economy can be described as $\mathcal{G} = (\mathcal{V}, \mathcal{C}) = \bigcup_{i=1}^{K} \mathcal{G}_i$ and $\mathcal{G}_i \bigcap \mathcal{G}_j = \emptyset$, $\forall\, i \neq j$. Since the subgraphs are fully connected we know that they can be viewed as the clique expansion of hyperedges [2] and as a result, we can substitute the graph $\mathcal{G} = (\mathcal{V}, \mathcal{C})$ with a hypergraph $\mathcal{H} = (\mathcal{V}, \mathcal{E})$ where each hyperedge $\mathcal{E}_i \ \forall\ 1 \leq i \leq K$ similarly with its clique analogue corresponds to the ith market and is disjoint with all other hyperedges. We will describe each market as a block with its available strategies as nodes within the block linked via a hyperedge. Below we present an example of a graph as the union of complete subgraphs and its respective hypergraph.

Example 1. In Fig. 1a we have a graph which is the union of complete subgraphs and it can be viewed as the clique expansion graph of the hypergraph in Fig. 1b.

(a) The graph   (b) The hypergraph

Fig. 1. Hypergraph and its respective clique expansion graph.

3.2   Firms Information Structure

From what we have seen so far the local markets seem unrelated and independent of each other and they could be studied independently. What we want is to study the behavior of all these seemingly unrelated markets from a unified scope in the sense of a Cournot model. What actually links these markets is the operation of common firms among them. For the description of the firms operation among the different markets we will make use of another hypergraph $\mathcal{H}' = \{\mathcal{V}, \mathcal{E}'\}$ where the node set $\mathcal{V} = \{\mathcal{V}_1, ..., \mathcal{V}_K\}$ corresponds to the K markets and the nodes within each $\mathcal{V}_i$ correspond to the different population groups that buy from different firms respectively. The hyperedge set $\mathcal{E}' = \{\mathcal{E}'_1, ..., \mathcal{E}'_N\}$ is partitioned with respect to the firms where each $\mathcal{E}'_j, 1 \leq j \leq N$ corresponds to the jth firm. We will denote by x_i^j the node that represents the population group of market i that buys from jth firm. We assume that each firm might or might not be able to supply a particular market but it has to supply at least two markets and as a result, each firm has s_j different selling options where $2 \leq s_j \leq K$. Similarly, each market buys from at least two firms and has b_i different buying options where $2 \leq b_i \leq N$. Overall we have K markets and N firms that have supply and demand relationships with each other according to hypergraph $\mathcal{H}$. For the complete information description of our model we make use of the hypergraph $\mathcal{H}'$ that describes the subpopulation interconnections within the markets and the hypergraph $\mathcal{H}$ that describes the operation of the firms in the markets. The resulting hypergraph is of the form $\mathcal{N} = \{\mathcal{V}, \mathcal{A}\}$ where $\mathcal{A} = \mathcal{E} \cup \mathcal{E}'$. The resulting hypergraph $\mathcal{N}$ is connected in the sense that exists a path from a node to any other node within $\mathcal{N}$. It is important to note that in our evolutionary dynamics approach of the network Cournot model we will mainly use the markets hypergraph $\mathcal{H}$. Below we present an example to better illustrate our information structure.

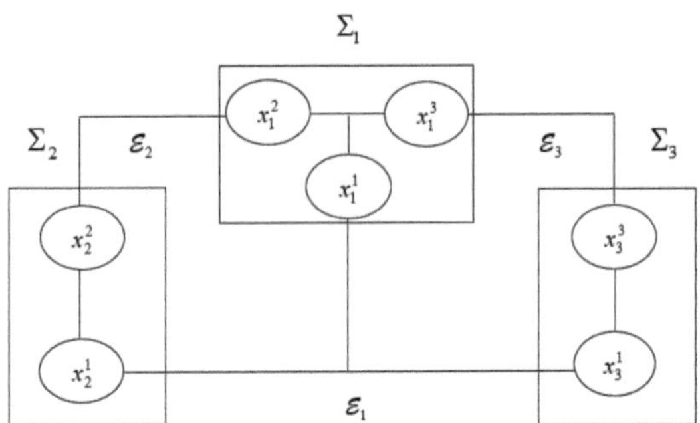

Fig. 2. Hypergraph Cournot Model.

Example 2. In Figure 2 we have a global market that is represented by a hypergraph $\mathcal{N} = \{\mathcal{V}, \mathcal{A}\}$ where the node set $\mathcal{V}$ is partitioned in three local markets $\Sigma_1, \Sigma_2, \Sigma_3$, i.e., $\mathcal{V} = \{\mathcal{V}_1, \mathcal{V}_2, \mathcal{V}_3\}$ and three operating firms, i.e., $\mathcal{E} = \{\mathcal{E}_1, \mathcal{E}_2, \mathcal{E}_3\}$. More specifically we have that the strategy set of each of the markets subpopulations is given by $\mathbb{S}_1 = \mathcal{V}_1 = \{x_1^1, x_1^2, x_1^3\}$, $\mathbb{S}_2 = \mathcal{V}_2 = \{x_2^1, x_2^2\}$ and $\mathbb{S}_3 = \mathcal{V}_3 = \{x_3^1, x_3^3\}$ respectively since the first market buys from all three firms, the second market buys from the first and the second firm while the third market buys from the first and the third firm. We notice in Figure 2 that within each of the three markets all subpopulations/nodes interact with each other via non enumerated hyperedges. The node set $\mathcal{V}$ and the set $\mathcal{E}$ of the non enumerated hyperedges constitute the markets hypergraph $\mathcal{H} = \{\mathcal{V}, \mathcal{E}\}$ as it was discussed in the theory and denotes the strategy switching ability for the subpopulation of each market. For the markets hypergraph $\mathcal{H} = \{\mathcal{V}, \mathcal{E}\}$ we have that

$$D_V = I_{7\times 7}, D_E = \begin{pmatrix} 3 & 0 & 0 \\ 0 & 2 & 0 \\ 0 & 0 & 2 \end{pmatrix}, E = \begin{pmatrix} 1 & 0 & 0 \\ 1 & 0 & 0 \\ 1 & 0 & 0 \\ 0 & 1 & 0 \\ 0 & 1 & 0 \\ 0 & 0 & 1 \\ 0 & 0 & 1 \end{pmatrix} \text{ with the hypergraph Laplacian of}$$

$\mathcal{H}$ given by

$$L^H = \begin{pmatrix} \frac{2}{3} & \frac{-1}{3} & \frac{-1}{3} & 0 & 0 & 0 & 0 \\ \frac{-1}{3} & \frac{2}{3} & \frac{-1}{3} & 0 & 0 & 0 & 0 \\ \frac{-1}{3} & \frac{-1}{3} & \frac{2}{3} & 0 & 0 & 0 & 0 \\ 0 & 0 & 0 & \frac{1}{2} & \frac{-1}{2} & 0 & 0 \\ 0 & 0 & 0 & \frac{-1}{2} & \frac{1}{2} & 0 & 0 \\ 0 & 0 & 0 & 0 & 0 & \frac{1}{2} & \frac{-1}{2} \\ 0 & 0 & 0 & 0 & 0 & \frac{-1}{2} & \frac{1}{2} \end{pmatrix}.$$

In order to demonstrate the hypergraph superiority in terms of information transmission over its bipartite graph analogue we present in figure 3 its respective bipartite graph which needs 10 nodes and 7 edges in order to describe the same supply and demand relationship as the hypergraph that only needs 7 nodes and 3 hyperedges and describes the same information transmission setting in a much more compact way.

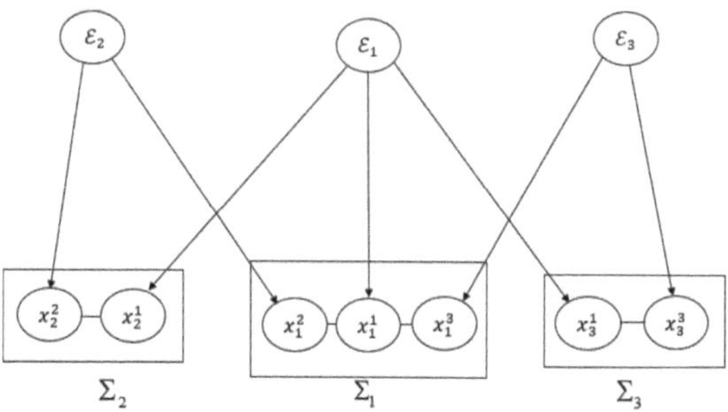

Fig. 3. Bipartite Graph Cournot Model.

In order for us to have an equivalent Laplacian matrix with the same dimensions as with the hypergraph Laplacian matrix in order to facilitate our convergence rate comparisons later on we will use the clique expansion graph generated by the bipartite graph which is expected to converge faster than the bipartite graph due to its higher connectivity [13]. The clique expansion graph is presented in figure 4 where we notice that it has 7 nodes and 5 supply and demand edges which are still more than its hypergraph analogue but less than its bipartite graph analogue.

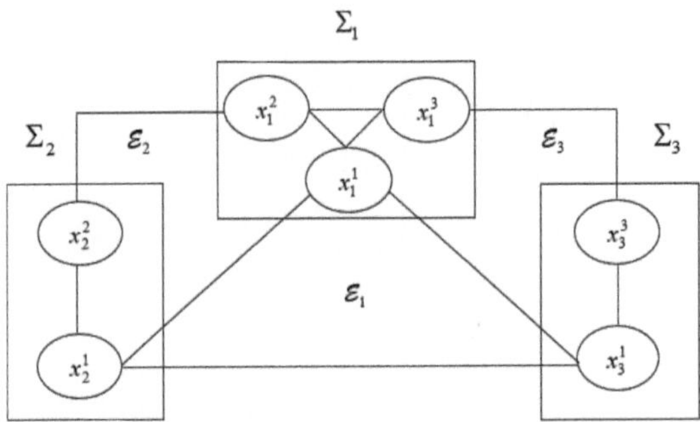

Fig. 4. Clique Expansion Graph Cournot Model.

Given that the degree matrix D_V and the adjacency matrix of the clique expansion graph are

$$D_V = \begin{pmatrix} 2 & 0 & 0 & 0 & 0 & 0 & 0 \\ 0 & 2 & 0 & 0 & 0 & 0 & 0 \\ 0 & 0 & 2 & 0 & 0 & 0 & 0 \\ 0 & 0 & 0 & 1 & 0 & 0 & 0 \\ 0 & 0 & 0 & 0 & 1 & 0 & 0 \\ 0 & 0 & 0 & 0 & 0 & 1 & 0 \\ 0 & 0 & 0 & 0 & 0 & 0 & 1 \end{pmatrix}, A = \begin{pmatrix} 0 & 1 & 1 & 0 & 0 & 0 & 0 \\ 1 & 0 & 1 & 0 & 0 & 0 & 0 \\ 1 & 1 & 0 & 0 & 0 & 0 & 0 \\ 0 & 0 & 0 & 0 & 1 & 0 & 0 \\ 0 & 0 & 0 & 1 & 0 & 0 & 0 \\ 0 & 0 & 0 & 0 & 0 & 0 & 1 \\ 0 & 0 & 0 & 0 & 0 & 1 & 0 \end{pmatrix}$$

respectively. Then the clique expansion graph Laplacian matrix is given by

$$L^C = \begin{pmatrix} 1 & \frac{-1}{2} & \frac{-1}{2} & 0 & 0 & 0 & 0 \\ \frac{-1}{2} & 1 & \frac{-1}{2} & 0 & 0 & 0 & 0 \\ \frac{-1}{2} & \frac{-1}{2} & 1 & 0 & 0 & 0 & 0 \\ 0 & 0 & 0 & 1 & -1 & 0 & 0 \\ 0 & 0 & 0 & -1 & 1 & 0 & 0 \\ 0 & 0 & 0 & 0 & 0 & 1 & -1 \\ 0 & 0 & 0 & 0 & 0 & -1 & 1 \end{pmatrix}$$

4   Distributed Evolutionary Dynamics Formulation

4.1   Distributed Optimization Formulation

The aggregate demand for the homogeneous good within ith market is given by a function $a_i : \mathbb{R}_+^{s_j} \to \mathbb{R}_+$. The variable corresponding to the aggregate demand function of ith market is of the form $x_i = (x_i^1, ..., x_i^{b_i})$. Let $p_i : \mathbb{R}_+^{b_i} \to \mathbb{R}_+$ denote the inverse demand (price) of market i, which we assume to be a decreasing strictly concave function of aggregate demand which has the following analytical expression:

$$p_i(a_i(x_i)) = \ln(x_i + l_i), l_i \geq 1, \forall\, 1 \leq i \leq N. \tag{9}$$

The cost function of the homogenous good for the jth firm is given by a function $c^j : \mathbb{R}_+^{s_j} \to \mathbb{R}_+$. The variable corresponding to the demand function of jth firm is of the form $x^j = (x_1^j, ..., x_{s_j}^j)$ and the cost function is a strictly convex function that has the following analytical expression:

$$c^j(x^j) = ||x^j||_2^2. \tag{10}$$

Given the inverse demand and cost functions, the payoff function of firm j is given by the formula

$$f_j(\mathbf{x}_j) = \sum_{i \in \mathcal{E}_j} [x_j^i p_i(a_i(x_i)) - c_j(x^j)] \,\forall\, 1 \leq j \leq K$$

where $\mathbf{x}_j$ is the unified variable of firm j that is affected by the respective price functions and the cost function associated with jth firm. Function $f = (f_1, ..., f_K)$ is a full potential game with full potential function $F = (F_1, ..., F_K)$ where

$$F_j(\mathbf{x}_j) = \sum_{i=1}^{s_j} \int_0^{a_i(x_i)} (x_j^i) p(z) dz - \int_0^{x^j} c^j(z) dz. \tag{11}$$

The potential function is also a strictly concave potential function and hence the potential game is also a stable game and admits a unique Nash equilibrium. For all markets and firms we assume that we have a population with unit mass, i.e, $\sum_{i,j} x_i^j = 1, \forall\, i, j$. We can describe the Cournot competition problem with the following optimization formulation

$$\max_{\mathbf{x}_j} \sum_{j=1}^{K} F_j(\mathbf{x}_j)$$

$$\text{s.t.} \sum_{i=1}^{N} \sum_{j=1}^{K} x_i^j = 1$$

$$x_i^j > 0, \forall\, i, j. \tag{12}$$

We notice that there are couplings among the profit functions of the different firms and for this reason the problem can be viewed as a distributed optimization problem. For the solution of the problem a full potential game is formulated as

$$G = \left[\left(\frac{\partial F_1}{\partial \mathbf{x}_1}\right), ..., \left(\frac{\partial F_K}{\partial \mathbf{x}_K}\right)\right], \left(\frac{\partial F_j}{\partial \mathbf{x}_j}\right) = f_j \,\forall\, 1 \leq j \leq K \tag{13}$$

and we will make use of a distributed algorithm in order to better capture the aforementioned couplings among the variables.

Example 3. Continuing the previous example the network Cournot competition problem for the given network setting can be expressed as the following distributed optimization problem

$$\max_{\mathbf{x}_j} \sum_{j=1}^{3} F_j(\mathbf{x}_j)$$

$$\text{s.t.} \sum_{i=1}^{3} \sum_{j=1}^{3} x_i^j = 1$$

$$x_i^j > 0, \ \forall \ i, j$$

where we have the variables of the market prices to be:

$$x_1 = (x_1^1, x_1^2, x_1^3), x_2 = (x_2^1, x_2^2), x_3 = (x_3^1, x_3^3),$$

while the variables for the firms' costs are:

$$x^1 = (x_1^1, x_2^1, x_3^1), x^2 = (x_1^2, x_2^2), x^3 = (x_1^3, x_3^3).$$

Given both sets of variables the objective functions are:

$$F_1 = x_1^1 p_1(x_1) + x_2^1 p_2(x_2) + x_3^1 p_3(x_3) - c_1(x^1)$$

$$F_2 = x_1^2 p_1(x_1) + x_2^2 p_2(x_2) - c_2(x^2)$$

$$F_3 = x_1^3 p_1(x_1) + x_3^3 p_3(x_3) - c_3(x^3).$$

4.2 Hypergraph Distributed Evolutionary Dynamics

For the solution of the distributed optimization problem (12) we will make use of the following distributed replicator dynamics (DRDs) presented below:

$$\dot{x}_i^j = x_i^j \left(f_i \sum_{j \in \mathcal{E}_i, j \neq i} x_i^j - \sum_{j \in \mathcal{E}_i, j \neq i} x_i^j f_j \right), \ \forall \ i \in \mathcal{V}. \tag{14}$$

Below we will provide a stability analysis of the DRDs as they are presented in (14). Firstly, we define the simplex

$$D = \left\{ \sum_{i=1}^{N} \sum_{j=1}^{K} x_i^j = 1 | x_i^j \geq 0 \ \forall \ i, j \right\} \tag{15}$$

and we have the following theorem.

Theorem 4. *The simplex D is an invariant set under the DRDs in (14).*

Proof. The simplex D has to satisfy two conditions: $\sum_{i,j} x_i^j = 1$ (mass conservation) and $x_i^j \geq 0$, for all i, j (nonnegativeness). The first condition is equivalent with showing that $\sum_{i,j} \dot{x}_i^j = 0$ under the distributed mean dynamics in (8). These dynamics can be written by using the elements e_{ij} of the symmetric matrix $E(D_E)^{-1}E^T$ in the following way where E and D_E are the incidence and size degree matrices of hypergraph $\mathcal{H}$ respectively.

$$\dot{x}_i^j = \sum_{j \in \mathcal{E}_i, j \neq i} e_{ij}\tau_{ji}x_i^j - x_i^j \sum_{j \in \mathcal{E}_i, j \neq i} e_{ij}\tau_{ij}, \forall\, i,j.$$

Hence,

$$\sum_{i \in \mathcal{V}} \dot{x}_i^j = \sum_{i \in \mathcal{V}} \sum_{j \in \mathcal{E}_i, j \neq i} e_{ij}\tau_{ji}x_i^j - \sum_{i \in \mathcal{V}} x_i^j \sum_{j \in \mathcal{E}_i, j \neq i} e_{ij}\tau_{ij}$$

Since $\mathcal{H}$ is undirected (i.e., $e_{ij} = e_{ji}$), we have

$$\sum_{i \in \mathcal{V}} \dot{x}_i^j = \sum_{i \in \mathcal{V}} \sum_{j \in \mathcal{E}_i, j \neq i} e_{ji}\tau_{ji}x_i^j - \sum_{i \in \mathcal{V}} \sum_{j \in \mathcal{E}_i, j \neq i} e_{ji}\tau_{ji}x_i^j = 0,$$

where $\tau_{ij} = x_j[f_i - f_j]_+$ with $[x]_+ = x$ if $x > 0$ and $[x]_+ = 0$ if $x \leq 0$. Finally, we prove the non-negativeness condition for DRDs. Nonnegativeness of each x_i^j is satisfied given the fact that $\dot{x}_i^j = 0$ if $x_i^j = 0$ under DRDs in (14). Thus, if $x_i^j(0) \geq 0$, then $x_i^j(t) \geq 0 \,\forall\, t \geq 0$.

Below, we provide our results on convergence of the distributed replicator dynamics to a Nash equilibrium (NE).

Theorem 5. *Let f be the full potential game (13) with strictly concave potential function $F(x)$, and let $x^* \in NE(f)$. Since the graphical structure that we study is connected and assuming the Nash equilibrium x^* belongs to the interior of simplex D in (15), then x^* is asymptotically stable under the DRDs in (14).*

Proof. Since $x^* \in \mathrm{NE}(f)$ and $x^* \in \mathrm{int}(D)$ we conclude that $f_i(x^*) = f_j(x^*)$, for all $i, j \in \mathcal{E}$, which is the hyperedge set of hypergraph $\mathcal{H}$. Moreover, it is easily verifiable that $x^* = \mathrm{argmax}_{x \in D}F(x)$ by applying the KKT conditions. Additionally, since $F(x)$ is strictly concave from (11), we can take $E_F(x) = F(x^*) - F(x)$ as a candidate Lyapunov function. The derivative of $E_F(x)$ along the trajectories of DRDs is given by

$$\dot{E}_F(x) = -(\nabla F(x))^T \dot{x} = -f^T \dot{x} = -f^T L^{(x)} f$$

where $L^{(x)} = [l_{ij}^{(x)}]$ is a matrix whose entries $l_{ij}^{(x)}$ are given for DRDs by:

$$l_{ij}^{(x)} = \begin{cases} -a_{ij}x_i x_j, & \text{if } i \neq j \\ \displaystyle\sum_{k \in \mathcal{E}_i, k \neq i} a_{ik}x_i x_k & \text{if } i = j \end{cases}$$

We notice that $L^{(x)}$ is the Laplacian of the undirected hypergraph given by the tuple $\mathcal{H}^{(x)} = (\mathcal{V}, \mathcal{E}, \mathcal{A}^{(x)})$, where $\mathcal{A}^{(x)} = [a_{ij}^{(x)}]$ is the matrix whose entries are defined as follows:

$$a_{ij}^{(x)} = \begin{cases} a_{ij} x_i x_j, & \text{if } j \in \mathcal{E}_i \\ 0, & \text{otherwise.} \end{cases}$$

Thus $L^{(x)} \succeq 0$ and $\dot{E}_F(x) \leq 0$. Therefore, x^* is stable under the DRDs. Considering that $x^* \in \text{int}(D)$ is stable, the compact set $\Omega = \text{int}(D)$ around x^* can be defined such that if $x(0) \in \Omega$, then $x(t) \in \Omega$ for all $t \geq 0$. Thus, if $x(0) \in \Omega$, the null space of $L^{(x)}$ is equal to span1 since $\mathcal{H}^{(x)}$ is connected due to the fact that $\mathcal{H}^{(x)}$ and $\mathcal{H}$ have the same topology in Ω. Hypergraph $\mathcal{H}$ is connected due to the links provided by $\mathcal{H}'$ to its hyperedges. In this case, $\dot{E}_F(x) = 0$ iff $f_i = f_j \; \forall \; i, j \in \mathcal{E}$, i.e., $\dot{E}_F(x) = 0$ only in x^* which results from LaSalle's invariance principle since the largest invariant set in Ω is the set $\{x^*\}$ and as a result, x^* is asymptotically stable.

5 Matrix Representation of Distributed Evolutionary Dynamics

The distributed evolutionary dynamics in (14) have the following matrix representation in the network setting,

$$\dot{x} = \Sigma \cdot f$$

where $\dot{x}$ and f represent the vectors of dynamics and profit functions respectively while Σ represents the system matrix which is of the following form,

$$\Sigma = \begin{pmatrix} X_1 & \cdots & 0 \\ \vdots & \ddots & \vdots \\ 0 & \cdots & X_N \end{pmatrix}$$

where

$$X_i = \begin{pmatrix} x_i^1 \sum x_i^{-1} & -x_i^1 x_i^2 & \cdots & -x_i^1 x_i^{p_i} \\ \vdots & \vdots & \ddots & \vdots \\ -x_i^{p_i} x_i^1 & \cdots & -x_i^{p_i - 1} x_i^{p_i} & x_i^{p_i} \sum x_i^{-p_i} \end{pmatrix} \quad \forall \; i = 1, ..., N$$

with $x_i^{-j} = (x_i^1, ..., x_i^{j-1}, x_i^{j+1}, ..., x_i^{p_i}) \; \forall \; j = 1, ..., p_i$. It is important to note that the representation of the system matrix is achieved by utilizing the structure of the Laplacian matrix which allows to acquire the system matrix representation with much less computational cost. In order to include the network information of the respective graphical structure that will be used (either the clique expansion graph or the hypergraph) for the description of the markets we propose the following alternative distributed evolutionary dynamical system representation

$$\dot{x} = (\Sigma \odot L') \cdot f$$

where by $\odot$ we denote the Hadamard (pairwise) matrix product and by L' we denote the modified Laplacian matrix of the respective graphical structure which is going to have the same sparsity with the Laplacian matrix and all the elements of each block that correspond to the respective market will have the same element that will describe the interactions of each node with all the other nodes of the market. For the case of the clique expansion graph we will have that the modified Laplacian matrix to be of the form

$$L^{C'} = \begin{pmatrix} L_1^{C'} & \cdots & 0 \\ \vdots & \ddots & \vdots \\ 0 & \cdots & L_N^{C'} \end{pmatrix}$$

where

$$L_i^{C'} = \begin{pmatrix} \frac{1}{D_i-1} & \frac{-1}{D_i-1} & \cdots & \frac{-1}{D_i-1} \\ \frac{-1}{D_i-1} & \frac{1}{D_i-1} & \cdots & \frac{-1}{D_i-1} \\ \vdots & \vdots & \ddots & \vdots \\ \frac{-1}{D_i-1} & \frac{-1}{D_i-1} & \cdots & \frac{1}{D_i-1} \end{pmatrix} \quad \forall\ D_i \geq 2,$$

with D_i denoting the node degree of ith clique, i.e., the total number of nodes in ith clique. For the case of the hypergraph we have

$$L^{H'} = \begin{pmatrix} L_1^{H'} & \cdots & 0 \\ \vdots & \ddots & \vdots \\ 0 & \cdots & L_N^{H'} \end{pmatrix}$$

where

$$L_i^{H'} = \begin{pmatrix} \frac{D_i-1}{D_i} & -\frac{D_i-1}{D_i} & \cdots & -\frac{D_i-1}{D_i} \\ -\frac{D_i-1}{D_i} & \frac{D_i-1}{D_i} & \cdots & -\frac{D_i-1}{D_i} \\ \vdots & \vdots & \ddots & \vdots \\ -\frac{D_i-1}{D_i} & -\frac{D_i-1}{D_i} & \cdots & \frac{D_i-1}{D_i} \end{pmatrix} \quad \forall\ D_i > 2.$$

Remark 1. The modified Laplacian matrix secures that the summation of the row elements of matrix $\Sigma \odot L'$ will sum to zero due to the structure of the diagonal elements of the system matrix Σ.

Example 4. Continuing the previous examples we have that the DRDs take the following form in our example

$$\dot{x}_1^1 = x_1^1[f_1(x_1^2 + x_1^3) - (x_1^2 f_2 + x_1^3 f_3)]$$
$$\dot{x}_1^2 = x_1^2[f_2(x_1^1 + x_1^3) - (x_1^1 f_1 + x_1^3 f_3)]$$
$$\dot{x}_1^3 = x_1^3[f_3(x_1^1 + x_1^2) - (x_1^1 f_1 + x_1^2 f_2)]$$

$$\dot{x}_2^1 = x_2^1[f_1 x_2^2 - x_2^2 f_2]$$

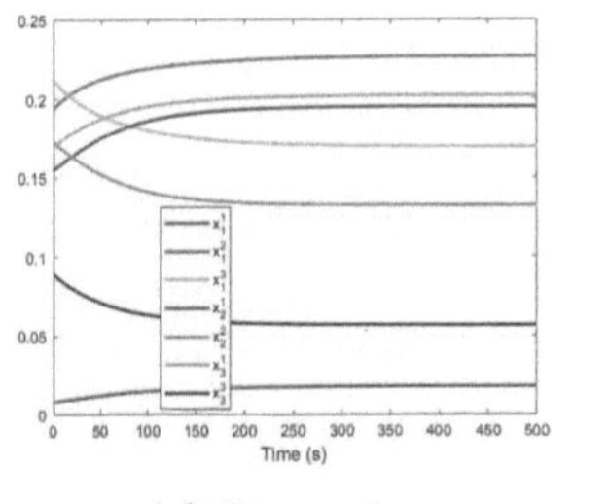

(a) Strategies

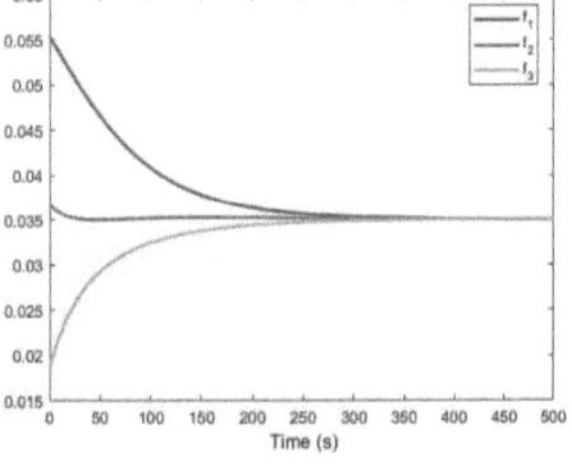

(b) Profit Functions

Fig. 5. Convergence plots of strategies and profit functions.

$$\dot{x}_2^2 = x_2^2[f_2 x_2^1 - x_2^1 f_1]$$

$$\dot{x}_3^1 = x_3^1[f_1 x_3^3 - x_3^3 f_3]$$

$$\dot{x}_3^3 = x_3^3[f_3 x_3^1 - x_3^1 f_1].$$

Assuming that the logarithmic price functions for the three markets have parameters $l_1 = \frac{6}{5}, l_2 = \frac{3}{2}$ and $l_3 = \frac{5}{4}$ in (9) respectively, the cost functions of the firms in (10) and random initial conditions for variables x_i^j we can see in Figure 5a the convergent values of all the subpopulation strategies under DRDs while in Figure 5b we observe the convergence to the common profit value of the firms. The above dynamical system can be written also in the following matrix form.

$$
\begin{pmatrix} \dot{x}_1^1 \\ \dot{x}_1^2 \\ \dot{x}_1^3 \\ \dot{x}_2^1 \\ \dot{x}_2^2 \\ \dot{x}_3^1 \\ \dot{x}_3^3 \end{pmatrix} =
\begin{pmatrix}
x_1^1(x_1^2 + x_1^3) & -x_1^1 x_1^2 & -x_1^1 x_1^3 & 0 & 0 & 0 & 0 \\
-x_1^2 x_1^1 & x_1^2(x_1^1 + x_1^3) & -x_1^2 x_1^3 & 0 & 0 & 0 & 0 \\
-x_1^3 x_1^1 & -x_1^3 x_1^2 & x_1^3(x_1^1 + x_1^2) & 0 & 0 & 0 & 0 \\
0 & 0 & 0 & x_2^1 x_2^2 & -x_2^1 x_2^2 & 0 & 0 \\
0 & 0 & 0 & -x_2^1 x_2^2 & x_2^1 x_2^2 & 0 & 0 \\
0 & 0 & 0 & 0 & 0 & x_3^1 x_3^3 & -x_3^1 x_3^3 \\
0 & 0 & 0 & 0 & 0 & -x_3^1 x_3^3 & x_3^1 x_3^3
\end{pmatrix}
\cdot
\begin{pmatrix} f_1 \\ f_2 \\ f_3 \\ f_1 \\ f_2 \\ f_1 \\ f_3 \end{pmatrix}
$$

where

$$
\Sigma =
\begin{pmatrix}
x_1^1(x_1^2 + x_1^3) & -x_1^1 x_1^2 & -x_1^1 x_1^3 & 0 & 0 & 0 & 0 \\
-x_1^2 x_1^1 & x_1^2(x_1^1 + x_1^3) & -x_1^2 x_1^3 & 0 & 0 & 0 & 0 \\
-x_1^3 x_1^1 & -x_1^3 x_1^2 & x_1^3(x_1^1 + x_1^2) & 0 & 0 & 0 & 0 \\
0 & 0 & 0 & x_2^1 x_2^2 & -x_2^1 x_2^2 & 0 & 0 \\
0 & 0 & 0 & -x_2^1 x_2^2 & x_2^1 x_2^2 & 0 & 0 \\
0 & 0 & 0 & 0 & 0 & x_3^1 x_3^3 & -x_3^1 x_3^3 \\
0 & 0 & 0 & 0 & 0 & -x_3^1 x_3^3 & x_3^1 x_3^3
\end{pmatrix}.
$$

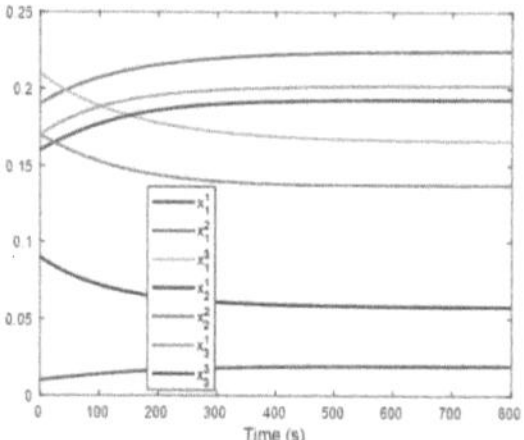

(a) Strategies with Clique Graph

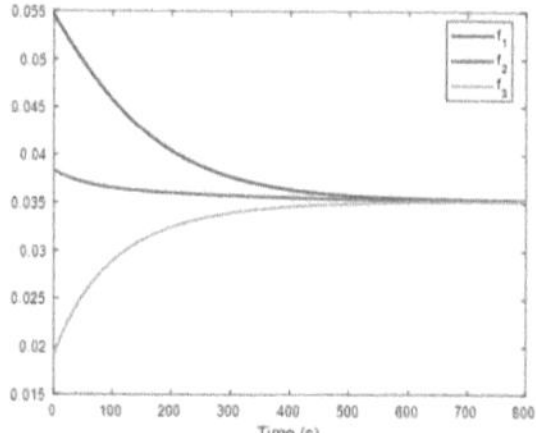

(b) Profit Functions with Clique Graph

Fig. 6. Convergence plots of strategies and profit functions with Clique Expansion Graph Communication.

In our example for the case of the clique expansion graph we have the modified clique expansion graph Laplacian matrix is

$$
L^{C'} = \begin{pmatrix}
\frac{1}{2} & \frac{-1}{2} & \frac{-1}{2} & 0 & 0 & 0 & 0 \\
\frac{-1}{2} & \frac{1}{2} & \frac{-1}{2} & 0 & 0 & 0 & 0 \\
\frac{-1}{2} & \frac{-1}{2} & \frac{1}{2} & 0 & 0 & 0 & 0 \\
0 & 0 & 0 & 1 & -1 & 0 & 0 \\
0 & 0 & 0 & -1 & 1 & 0 & 0 \\
0 & 0 & 0 & 0 & 0 & 1 & -1 \\
0 & 0 & 0 & 0 & 0 & -1 & 1
\end{pmatrix}
$$

As a result, the system matrix $\Sigma \odot L^{C'}$ will be of the following form,

$$
\Sigma \odot L^{C'} = \begin{pmatrix}
\frac{x_1^1(x_1^2+x_1^3)}{2} & \frac{-x_1^1 x_1^2}{2} & \frac{-x_1^1 x_1^3}{2} & 0 & 0 & 0 & 0 \\
\frac{-x_1^2 x_1^1}{2} & \frac{x_1^2(x_1^1+x_1^3)}{2} & \frac{-x_1^2 x_1^3}{2} & 0 & 0 & 0 & 0 \\
\frac{-x_1^3 x_1^1}{2} & \frac{-x_1^3 x_1^2}{2} & \frac{x_1^3(x_1^1+x_1^2)}{2} & 0 & 0 & 0 & 0 \\
0 & 0 & 0 & \frac{x_2^1 x_2^2}{2} & \frac{-x_2^1 x_2^2}{2} & 0 & 0 \\
0 & 0 & 0 & \frac{-x_2^1 x_2^2}{2} & \frac{x_2^1 x_2^2}{2} & 0 & 0 \\
0 & 0 & 0 & 0 & 0 & \frac{x_3^1 x_3^3}{2} & \frac{-x_3^1 x_3^3}{2} \\
0 & 0 & 0 & 0 & 0 & \frac{-x_3^1 x_3^3}{2} & \frac{x_3^1 x_3^3}{2}
\end{pmatrix}
$$

The convergence of the strategies and profit functions with the use of clique expansion graph communication is presented in Figures 6a and 6b respectively.

For the case of the hypergraph we have that the modified hypergraph Laplacian matrix is

$$
L^{H'} = \begin{pmatrix}
\frac{2}{3} & \frac{-2}{3} & \frac{-2}{3} & 0 & 0 & 0 & 0 \\
\frac{-2}{3} & \frac{2}{3} & \frac{-2}{3} & 0 & 0 & 0 & 0 \\
\frac{-2}{3} & \frac{-2}{3} & \frac{2}{3} & 0 & 0 & 0 & 0 \\
0 & 0 & 0 & \frac{1}{2} & \frac{-1}{2} & 0 & 0 \\
0 & 0 & 0 & \frac{-1}{2} & \frac{1}{2} & 0 & 0 \\
0 & 0 & 0 & 0 & 0 & \frac{1}{2} & \frac{-1}{2} \\
0 & 0 & 0 & 0 & 0 & \frac{-1}{2} & \frac{1}{2}
\end{pmatrix}.
$$

As a result, the system matrix $\Sigma \odot L^{H'}$ will be of the following form,

$$\Sigma \odot L^{H'} = \begin{pmatrix} \frac{2x_1^1(x_1^2+x_1^3)}{3} & \frac{-2x_1^1x_1^2}{3} & \frac{-2x_1^1x_1^3}{3} & 0 & 0 & 0 & 0 \\ \frac{-2x_1^2x_1^1}{3} & \frac{2x_1^2(x_1^1+x_1^3)}{3} & \frac{-2x_1^2x_1^3}{3} & 0 & 0 & 0 & 0 \\ \frac{-2x_1^3x_1^1}{3} & \frac{-2x_1^3x_1^2}{3} & \frac{2x_1^3(x_1^1+x_1^2)}{3} & 0 & 0 & 0 & 0 \\ 0 & 0 & 0 & \frac{x_2^1x_2^2}{2} & \frac{-x_2^1x_2^2}{2} & 0 & 0 \\ 0 & 0 & 0 & \frac{-x_2^1x_2^2}{2} & \frac{x_2^1x_2^2}{2} & 0 & 0 \\ 0 & 0 & 0 & 0 & 0 & \frac{x_3^1x_3^3}{2} & \frac{-x_3^1x_3^3}{2} \\ 0 & 0 & 0 & 0 & 0 & \frac{-x_3^1x_3^3}{2} & \frac{x_3^1x_3^3}{2} \end{pmatrix}$$

The convergence of the strategies and profit functions with the use of the hypergraph communication is presented in Figures 7a and 7b respectively.

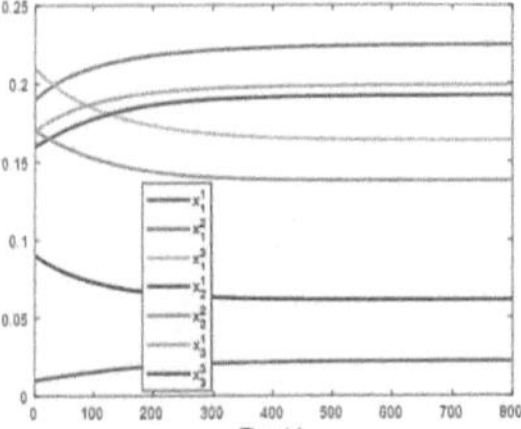

(a) Strategies with Hypergraph

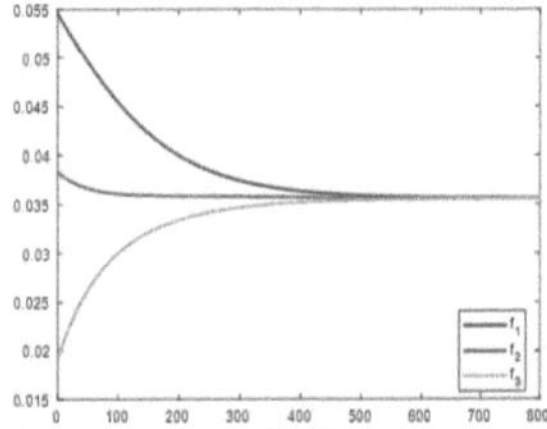

(b) Profit Functions with Hypergraph

Fig. 7. Convergence plots of strategies and profit functions with Hypergraph Communication.

We observe that the fastest convergence of the profit functions is achieved in the general case without the use of a matrix that would encapsulate the information of the network structure but as we discussed in the introduction this is the case with the higher computational cost. For the cases of the hypergraph and the clique expansion graph, the superiority of the hypergraph over its clique expansion graph is clearly demonstrated in Figs. 7 and 6 respectively. We would also like to point out that in terms of comparative statics the equilibrium points of strategies and their respective asymptotic values of the profit functions are the same.

6   Conclusion

We have proposed a novel information structure for a Cournot network model in the continuous-time evolutionary game theoretic setting with the use of a hypergraph. We have also formulated the problem with the use of distributed optimization methodology and we solved it with distributed evolutionary dynamics where we used directly the respective network communication matrix for less computational cost. The proposed hypergraph communication structure is more efficient and compact in terms of information transmission and faster in terms of convergence rate than a bipartite graph, something that was demonstrated numerically. Finally, by using non linear control theoretic techniques we showed that the equilibrium point of the evolutionary dynamical system solves the network Cournot optimization problem, i.e., it is a market clearing point, it is unique and asymptotically stable.

References

1. Abolhassani, M., Bateni, M.H., Hajiaghayi, M.T., Mahini, H., Sawant, A.: Network COURNOT competition. In: Liu, T.-Y., Qi, Q., Ye, Y. (eds.) WINE 2014. LNCS, vol. 8877, pp. 15–29. Springer, Cham (2014). https://doi.org/10.1007/978-3-319-13129-0_2
2. Agarwal, S., Branson, K., Belongie, S.: Higher order learning with graphs. In: Proceedings of the 23rd International Conference on Machine Learning, pp. 17–24 (2006)
3. Barreiro-Gomez, J., Obando, G., Quijano, N.: Distributed population dynamics: optimization and control applications. IEEE Trans. Syst. Man Cybern. Syst. **47**(2), 304–314 (2016)
4. Bimpikis, K., Ehsani, S., Ilkılıç, R.: Cournot competition in networked markets. Manage. Sci. **65**(6), 2467–2481 (2019)
5. Bolla, M.: Spectra, Euclidean representations and clusterings of hypergraphs. Discret. Math. **117**(1–3), 19–39 (1993)
6. Boyd, S.P., Vandenberghe, L.: Convex Optimization. Cambridge University Press (2004)
7. Cheng, J.Q., Wellman, M.P.: The WALRAS algorithm: a convergent distributed implementation of general equilibrium outcomes. Comput. Econ. **12**, 1–24 (1998)
8. Civilini, A., Anbarci, N., Latora, V.: Evolutionary game model of group choice dilemmas on hypergraphs. Phys. Rev. Lett. **127**(26), 268301 (2021)
9. Claude, B.: Graphs and Hypergraphs. University of Paris, second, revised (1973)
10. Flåm, S.D., Horvath, C.: Network games; adaptations to NASH-COURNOT equilibrium. Ann. Oper. Res. **64**, 179–195 (1996)
11. Gintis, H.: Game Theory Evolving: A Problem-Centered Introduction to Modeling Strategic Behavior. Princeton university press (2000)
12. Gintis, H.: The emergence of a price system from decentralized bilateral exchange. Contrib. Theor. Econ. **6**(1) (2006)
13. He, Z.: Optimization of convergence rate via algebraic connectivity. arXiv preprint arXiv:1912.06536 (2019)
14. Helbing, D., Yu, W.: Migration as a mechanism to promote cooperation. Adv. Complex Syst. **11**(04), 641–652 (2008)
15. Hofbauer, J.: The spatially dominant equilibrium of a game. Ann. Oper. Res. **89**, 233–251 (1999)
16. Hofbauer, J., Sandholm, W.H.: Stable games and their dynamics. J. Econ. Theory **144**(4), 1665–1693 (2009)
17. Hofbauer, J., Sigmund, K.: The theory of evolution and dynamical systems: mathematical aspects of selection (1988)
18. Horn, R.A., Johnson, C.R.: Matrix Analysis. Cambridge university press (2012)

19. Ilkilic, R.: Cournot competition on a network of markets and firms (2009)
20. Jackson, M.O., et al.: Social and Economic Networks, vol. 3. Princeton university press Princeton (2008)
21. Kelly, F.P., Maulloo, A.K., Tan, D.K.H.: Rate control for communication networks: shadow prices, proportional fairness and stability. J. Oper. Res. Soc. **49**, 237–252 (1998)
22. Khalil Hassan, K., Grizzle Jessy, W.: Nonlinear Systems, vol. 3 (2002)
23. Lieberman, E., Hauert, C., Nowak, M.A.: Evolutionary dynamics on graphs. Nature **433**(7023), 312–316 (2005)
24. Lin, W., Pang, J.Z., Bitar, E., Wierman, A.: Networked cournot competition in platform markets: access control and efficiency loss. ACM SIGMETRICS Perform. Eval. Rev. **45**(2), 15–17 (2017)
25. List, J.A.: Testing neoclassical competitive theory in multilateral decentralized markets. J. Polit. Econ. **112**(5), 1131–1156 (2004)
26. Liu, T., Wang, Y.-H., Cheng, D.-Z.: Dynamics and stability of potential hyper-networked evolutionary games. Int. J. Autom. Comput. **14**(2), 229–238 (2017). https://doi.org/10.1007/s11633-017-1056-0
27. Malamud, S., Rostek, M.: Decentralized exchange. Am. Econ. Rev. **107**(11), 3320–3362 (2017)
28. Mandel, A., Gintis, H.: Decentralized pricing and strategic stability of walrasian general equilibrium. J. Math. Econ. **63**, 84–92 (2016)
29. McNamara, J.M., Gasson, C.E., Houston, A.I.: Incorporating rules for responding into evolutionary games. Nature **401**(6751), 368–371 (1999)
30. Metzler, C., Hobbs, B.F., Pang, J.S.: Nash-cournot equilibria in power markets on a linearized dc network with arbitrage: formulations and properties. Netw. Spat. Econ. **3**, 123–150 (2003)
31. Nash, J.F., Jr.: Equilibrium points in N-person games. Proc. Natl. Acad. Sci. **36**(1), 48–49 (1950)
32. Nedic, A.: Distributed gradient methods for convex machine learning problems in networks: distributed optimization. IEEE Signal Process. Mag. **37**(3), 92–101 (2020)
33. Neumann, J., Morgenstern, O., et al.: Theory of games and economic behavior (1947)
34. Nowak, M.A., May, R.M.: Evolutionary games and spatial chaos. Nature **359**(6398), 826–829 (1992)
35. Ohtsuki, H., Pacheco, J.M., Nowak, M.A.: Evolutionary graph theory: breaking the symmetry between interaction and replacement. J. Theor. Biol. **246**(4), 681–694 (2007)
36. Papastaikoudis, I., Watson, J., Lestas, I.: A decentralized control approach in hypergraph distributed optimization decomposition cases. Appl. Netw. Sci. **9**(1), 1–25 (2024)
37. Reiter, S., Simon, C.P.: Decentralized dynamic processes for finding equilibrium. J. Econ. Theory **56**(2), 400–425 (1992)
38. Rondina, G., Shim, M.: Financial prices and information acquisition in large cournot markets. J. Econ. Theory **158**, 769–786 (2015)
39. Samar, S., Boyd, S., Gorinevsky, D.: Distributed estimation via dual decomposition. In: 2007 European Control Conference (ECC), pp. 1511–1516. IEEE (2007)
40. Sandholm, W.H.: Population Games and Evolutionary Dynamics. MIT press (2010)
41. Smith, J.M., Price, G.R.: The logic of animal conflict. Nature **246**(5427), 15–18 (1973)

42. Smith, J.M.: Evolution and the theory of games. In: Did Darwin get it right? Essays on games, sex and evolution, pp. 202–215. Springer (1982). https://doi.org/10.1007/978-1-4684-7862-4_22
43. Taylor, P.D., Jonker, L.B.: Evolutionary stable strategies and game dynamics. Math. Biosci. **40**(1–2), 145–156 (1978)
44. Tsitsiklis, J.N.: Problems in decentralized decision making and computation. Ph.D. thesis, Massachusetts Institute of Technology (1984)
45. Voloshin, V.I.: Introduction to graph and hypergraph theory. (No Title) (2009)
46. Wang, L., Wu, H., Ding, Y., Chen, W., Poor, H.V.: Hypergraph-based wireless distributed storage optimization for cellular D2D underlays. IEEE J. Sel. Areas Commun. **34**(10), 2650–2666 (2016)
47. Yang, T., et al.: A survey of distributed optimization. Annu. Rev. Control. **47**, 278–305 (2019)

On Stability and Learning of Competitive Equilibrium in Generalized Fisher Market Models: A Variational Inequality Approach

Mandar Datar[(✉)]

CEA-Leti, Université Grenoble Alpes, 38000 Grenoble, France
`mandar.datar@cea.fr`

Abstract. In this work, we study a generalized Fisher market model that incorporates social influence. In this extended model, buyers' utilities depend not only on their own resource allocation but also on the allocations received by their competitors. We propose a novel competitive equilibrium formulation for this generalized Fisher market using a variational inequality approach. This framework effectively captures competitive equilibrium in markets that extend beyond the traditional assumption of homogeneous utility functions. We analyze key structural properties of the proposed variational inequality problem, including monotonicity, stability, and uniqueness. Additionally, we present two decentralized learning algorithms for buyers to achieve competitive equilibrium: a two-timescale stochastic approximation-based tâtonnement method and a trading-post mechanism-based learning method. Finally, we validate the proposed algorithms through numerical simulations.

Keywords: Generalized Fisher Market · Competitive Equilibrium · Generalized Nash Equilibrium · Variational Inequality Problem · Decentralized Learning

1 Introduction

Markets have historically functioned as fundamental mechanisms for allocating resources since the dawn of human civilization. From meticulously recorded commodity prices in ancient Babylon to modern-day global exchanges, markets facilitate the exchange of goods through intricate pricing systems. The fundamental principles governing these exchanges, encapsulated in the notion of equilibrium, have been the focal point of economic inquiry for centuries. In the late 19th century, the French economist Léon Walras established the foundations of modern market theory with the introduction of the concept of Walrasian equilibrium,

---

The author is currently affiliated with CEA-Leti, Grenoble, France, and was previously associated with Inria Sophia Antipolis and the University of Avignon, France, during the course of this work.

V. Aggarwal et al. (Eds.): GameNets 2025, LNICST 657, pp. 42–60, 2026.
https://doi.org/10.1007/978-3-032-12915-4_3

also known as a competitive equilibrium (CE) [48]. In informal terms, an equilibrium can be defined as a set of prices at which the supply and demand of all goods in the market are in balance.

Despite Walras' foundational contributions, the precise conditions guaranteeing the existence of such prices remained unresolved until Arrow's groundbreaking work [3]. By leveraging Kakutani's fixed point theorem, Arrow and Debreu not only settled the question of existence for a broad class of economic models but also established a fundamental basis for what is now known as general equilibrium theory [33]. However, despite the significance of their result, the non-constructive nature of the proof leaves the challenge of computing equilibrium prices largely unaddressed. Indeed, the pursuit of computing equilibrium prices has been a long-standing and significant area of research within the field of economics. Walras pioneered a decentralized price-adjustment process termed *tâtonnement* aimed at reflecting real market dynamics and conjecturing its convergence to equilibrium prices. Initially, optimism surrounding this concept was reinforced by Arrow et al. in [2,4], who illustrated convergence in continuous tâtonnement procedures under specific market conditions, notably the weak gross substitutes (WGS) property. However, the influential counterexample presented in Scarff's study [44] undermined the assumption of universal convergence, underscoring the complex challenges inherent in equilibrium computation.

The study of computational complexity in economic settings has provided profound insights into the challenges inherent in finding equilibrium solutions. It has been established that the task of computing even an approximate competitive equilibrium is PPAD-hard [11], thereby reinforcing the notion that equilibrium attainment in economic systems is inherently challenging. However, amidst these challenges, Fisher markets [9] have emerged as a notable exception. In contrast to the broader Arrow-Debreu framework, Fisher markets represent a specialized context where competitive equilibria can be efficiently computed under certain conditions. In Fisher markets, there are no firms; instead, buyers possess a single type of commodity, which serves either as an artificial currency or as a fixed endowment defining their budget constraints within the market.

Eisenberg and Gale, in their studies [21,22], and the subsequent generalization of their work by Jain et al. in [30], demonstrated that if the utilities of buyers in the market are continuous, concave and homogeneous of degree one[1](CCH), the market equilibrium can be determined by solving a convex optimization problem, commonly referred to as the Eisenberg-Gale (EG) program. While the EG program offers a centralized solution for finding equilibrium, it does not accurately represent real-world markets where agents interact with each other. Consequently, the algorithmic game theory community has been keen on developing algorithms that more realistically describe markets and their equilibrium concepts. Over the past two decades, considerable effort has been directed

---

[1] A function is called as a homogeneous function of any degree k' if; when each of its elements is multiplied by any number $t > 0$; then the value of the function is multiplied by t^k .

towards designing polynomial-time algorithms that enable buyers to compute competitive equilibria in Fisher markets in a decentralized manner. For example, [5,7,10,12–15,28,37,38]. Furthermore, recent studies, including [19,35], and [39], have highlighted practical applications of the Fisher market model, demonstrating its growing relevance in real-world contexts. However, most of these approaches rely on the EG program and are thus limited to CCH markets.

In recent years, there has been a growing interest in generalizing the Fisher market model through the introduction of several innovative variants and the development of the corresponding computational methods. Gao et al. in [26] introduced the concept of infinite-dimensional Fisher markets, expanding the traditional Fisher market model to encompass equilibrium for a continuum of items. In [27], Gao et al. and in [31], Jalota et al. studied an online variant of the Fisher market setting, in which users arrive sequentially with privately known utilities and budgets. Zhao et al. in [49] introduced the Fisher market with social influence, incorporating social dynamics into the traditional Fisher market model. This variant considers how buyers' preferences and decisions are shaped by the behavior and choices of other market participants. Prior to this, Datar et al. in [18] explored competition in wireless communication markets, implicitly linking their analysis to a Fisher market with social influence, though without formalizing it. Despite these advancements, a key limitation of these extended models is that they are all rooted in the EG program and are typically constrained to cases where buyers have CCH utility functions.

In this work, we aim to transcend these limitations by investigating methods to characterize market equilibrium in Fisher markets beyond homogeneous utility functions and by developing algorithms to achieve these equilibria. To achieve this objective, we revisit the foundational work of Arrow and Debreu [20], who pioneered the concept of generalized Nash equilibrium problem (GNEP)[2] or games to demonstrate the existence of competitive equilibrium in a general economy model. We begin by modeling the Fisher market as a GNEP, thereby demonstrating the existence of a commutative equilibrium. However, solving a GNEP is inherently complex. Thus, to make it computationally tractable, we reframe it as a variational inequality problem. This reformulation simplifies the problem by focusing on the Karush-Kuhn-Tucker (KKT) conditions at equilibrium, which can be expressed as variational inequalities. This approach allows us to develop polynomial-time algorithms capable of efficiently computing the equilibrium.

---

[2] In their seminal work, Arrow and Debreu introduced the concept now widely recognized as the generalized Nash equilibrium problem (GNEP), originally termed the social equilibrium problem. Over time, this concept has been identified by various names, such as pseudo-game, equilibrium programming, coupled constraint equilibrium problem, and abstract economy, depending on its application domain. In this paper, we adopt the term GNEP to denote this problem due to its broad applicability across different contexts.

2 Our Contributions

We model the market equilibrium problem in the generalized Fisher market as a generalized Nash equilibrium problem and develop a novel variational inequality (VI) problem based on the KKT conditions derived from the best responses of buyers at the Nash equilibrium (NE) of the (GNEP). Our analysis demonstrates that the solution to the proposed (VI) problem delineates the competitive equilibrium of the Fisher market. Furthermore, we investigate key properties of variational equilibrium to the VI problem, including its monotonicity, stability, and uniqueness.

We establish a connection between the variational inequality problem and the prior literature on Fisher markets where buyers exhibit CCH utility functions. Specifically, we demonstrate that the well-known Eisenberg-Gale program in non-social-influential Fisher markets and the buyers-auctioneer game in social-influential Fisher markets [49] are special cases of the variational inequality problem.

We present two decentralized algorithms for computing the competitive equilibrium in Fisher markets, employing two well-known approaches: the *tâtonnement* process and the buyer-centric trading post mechanism[3] [45]. Our first algorithm introduces a novel variation compared to the traditional *tâtonnement* approach by integrating the concept of two-time-scale stochastic approximation techniques. For the second algorithm, our analysis demonstrates that the trading post-mechanism-based learning scheme closely mirrors the discrete replicator. Leveraging stochastic approximation techniques, we establish that the proposed algorithm converges effectively in polynomial time. Finally, to validate the proposed algorithms, we conducted numerical simulations aimed at computing the competitive equilibrium in a Fisher market scenario where buyers exhibit non-homogeneous utility functions.

3 Preliminaries

3.1 Generalized Nash Equilibrium Problem (GNEP)

A generalized Nash equilibrium problem or game is characterized by a tuple $\mathcal{G} := (\mathcal{N}, (\mathcal{A}_n)_{n \in \mathcal{N}}, (\mathcal{X}_n)_{n \in \mathcal{N}}, (\phi_n)_{n \in \mathcal{N}})$. Here, $\mathcal{N}$ represents a set of players $\{1, \ldots, N\}$, where each player $n \in \mathcal{N}$ governs their action $\mathbf{a}_n \in \mathcal{A}_n \subseteq \mathbb{R}^{d_n}$. The joint action space of the players, denoted as $\mathcal{A} = \prod_{n \in \mathcal{N}} \mathcal{A}_n$, encompasses all possible combinations of individual actions. Each player n is associated with an objective function $\phi_n : \mathcal{A} \to \mathbb{R}$, which is concave and continuous in $\mathbf{a}_n$ and relies on both their own action $\mathbf{a}_n$ and the actions $\mathbf{a}_{-n}$ of all other players. This dependence is represented as $\phi_n(\mathbf{a}_n, \mathbf{a}_{-n})$. Given a particular $\mathbf{a}_{-n} \in \mathcal{A}_{-n} = \prod_{m \in \mathcal{N}, m \neq n} \mathcal{A}_m$, each player n endeavors to maximize their

---

[3] The same mechanism has been called by different names in different application domains, for example, the Kelly mechanism [32] in computer networks, and the proportional share scheme by [25].

objective function by selecting a feasible action such that $\mathbf{a}_n \in \mathcal{X}_n(\mathbf{a}_{-n}) \subseteq \mathcal{A}_n$. Here, the feasible action space or the strategy space of each player depends on the actions of others. Where $\mathcal{X}_n : \mathcal{A}_{-n} \rightrightarrows \mathcal{A}_n$ is a non empty, continuous, convex and compact map. The generalized Nash equilibrium problem (GNEP) involves N constrained optimization problems. In essence, for each player n, it tackles the optimization problem $Q_n(\mathbf{a}_{-n})$,

$$
\boxed{
\begin{aligned}
Q_n(\mathbf{a}_{-n}) \quad &\underset{\mathbf{a}_n}{\text{maximize}} \quad \phi_n\left(\mathbf{a}_n, \mathbf{a}_{-n}\right), \\
&\text{subject to} \quad \mathbf{a}_n \in \mathcal{X}_n(\mathbf{a}_{-n}).
\end{aligned}
}
$$

a generalized Nash equilibrium $\mathbf{a}^* = (\mathbf{a}_1^*, \ldots, \mathbf{a}_N^*)$ in a generalized game is a state where no player n desires to unilaterally deviate from their strategy in the equilibrium profile $\mathbf{a}^*$. Moreover, this equilibrium $\mathbf{a}^*$ must satisfy the constraints of each agent $n \in \mathcal{N}$, denoted as $\mathbf{a}_n^* \in \mathcal{X}_n(\mathbf{a}_{-n}^*)$.

Definition 1 (Genralized Nash equilibrium (GNE)). *A strategy profile $(\mathbf{a}^*)$ is a generalized Nash equilibrium (GNE) of the game $\mathcal{G}$ if $a_n^* \in SOL(Q_n(\mathbf{a}_{-n}^*))$ for all $n \in \mathcal{N}$, i.e., $\phi_n(\mathbf{a}_n^*, \mathbf{a}_{-n}^*) \geq \phi_n(\mathbf{a}_n, \mathbf{a}_{-n}^*)$ for all $\mathbf{a}_n \in \mathcal{X}_n(\mathbf{a}_{-n}^*)$ and all $n \in \mathcal{N}$.*

In the above definition $SOL(Q_n(.))$ represents the solution of the optimization problem $Q_n(.)$. If in a game $\mathcal{G}$, the objective function of each player $n \in \mathcal{N}$ $\phi_n()$ is concave and the feasible action set $\mathcal{X}_n(\mathbf{a}_{-n})$ is convex and compact, then the existence of GNE is guaranteed by the work of [3]

Definition 2 (Variational Inequality (VI) problem). *Consider a nonempty, closed, convex set $\mathcal{C} \subset \mathbb{R}^n$ and a mapping $F : \mathcal{C} \to \mathbb{R}^n$. The variational inequality (VI) problem is defined as follows:*

$$
\boxed{
\begin{aligned}
VI(\mathcal{C}, F) \quad &\textit{Find } \mathbf{a}^* \in \mathcal{C} \textit{ such that,} \\
&\langle F(\mathbf{a}^*), \mathbf{a} - \mathbf{a}^* \rangle \leq 0, \quad \forall \mathbf{a} \in \mathcal{C}.
\end{aligned}
}
$$

Here, $\langle \cdot, \cdot \rangle$ denotes the inner product in $\mathbb{R}^n$. This inequality essentially expresses a maximization condition for the functional $F(\mathbf{a})$ over the set $\mathcal{C}$, ensuring that $\mathbf{a}^*$ is a solution where the gradient $F(\mathbf{a}^*)$ is orthogonal to the tangent space of $\mathcal{C}$ at $\mathbf{a}^*$.

Now, let us introduce the concept of Variational Equilibrium (VE) in GNEP, which arises particularly in scenarios when GNEP involves coupled or shared constraints. Consider a convex compact set denoted as $\mathcal{C} \subset \mathbb{R}^d$, where $d = \sum_n d_n$, the sum of dimensions for each player n in-game $\mathcal{G}$ and $\mathcal{C}$ set represent the shared constraints of the game $\mathcal{G}$. Now, for each player n, we define $\mathcal{X}_n(\mathbf{a}_{-n})$ as the set of feasible strategies.

$$
\mathcal{X}_n(\mathbf{a}_{-n}) = \{\mathbf{a}_n \in \mathcal{A}_n \mid (\mathbf{a}_n, \mathbf{a}_{-n}) \in \mathcal{C}\} \tag{1}
$$

Definition 3 (Variational Equilibrium (VE)). *A strategy profile* $(\mathbf{a})$ *is called a Variational Equilibrium (VE) of a game* $\mathcal{G}$ *with shared constraints* $\mathcal{C}$ *if* $\mathbf{a} \in SOL(VI(\mathcal{C}, F))$, *where* $F(\mathbf{a}) = (\nabla_{\mathbf{a}1}\phi 1, \ldots, \nabla_{\mathbf{a}N}\phi N)$ *represents the pseudo-gradient of the utility profiles of the players, and* $\nabla_{\mathbf{a}_n}$ *denotes the partial derivative with respect to* $\mathbf{a}_n$.

Definition 4 (Monotone Game). *A game with profiles of strategies* $\mathbf{a}$ *and profiles of utility functions* ϕ *is called a Monotone, strictly monotone (Diagonally strict concave (DSC) [42]), or Strongly monotone game if for every distinct* $\mathbf{a}$ *and* $\mathbf{a}'$,

$$\text{Monotone:} \quad \langle F(\mathbf{a}) - F(\mathbf{a}'), \mathbf{a} - \mathbf{a}' \rangle \leq 0, \tag{2}$$

$$\text{Strictly Monotone:} \quad \langle F(\mathbf{a}) - F(\mathbf{a}'), \mathbf{a} - \mathbf{a}' \rangle < 0, \tag{3}$$

$$\text{Strongly Monotone:} \quad \langle F(\mathbf{a}) - F(\mathbf{a}'), \mathbf{a} - \mathbf{a}' \rangle < c \, \|\mathbf{a} - \mathbf{a}'\| \tag{4}$$

where c *is a positive with* F *the concatenation of the gradients of the players' utility functions*

$$F(\mathbf{a}) = \left[\nabla_1 \phi_1(\mathbf{a}), \nabla_2 \phi_2(\mathbf{a}), \ldots, \nabla_N \phi_N(\mathbf{a}) \right], \tag{5}$$

where $\nabla_n \phi_n(\mathbf{a})$ *denotes the gradient of objective function of player* n *with respect to his own strategy* $\mathbf{a}_n$.

3.2 Generalized Fisher Market

The generalized Fisher market, defined as

$$\mathcal{M} := \left\langle \mathcal{N}, \left(\mathbf{x}_n \in \mathbb{R}^K \right)_{n \in \mathcal{N}}, (U_n)_{n \in \mathcal{N}}, (B_n)_{n \in \mathcal{N}}, \mathbf{p} \in \mathbb{R}^K \right\rangle,$$

consists of a set of buyers denoted as $\mathcal{N} = \{1, 2, \ldots, N\}$ who have demands for a set of divisible goods or resources, represented as $\mathcal{K} = \{1, 2, \ldots, K\}$. Each buyer n expresses its resource allocation preferences through a vector $\mathbf{x}_n = (x_{n1}, x_{n2}, \ldots, x_{nK})$, where x_{nk} signifies the quantity of resource k required by buyer n. The collective preferences of the resources of all buyers are encapsulated in the vector formed by all these strategies and are represented as $\mathbf{x} := (\mathbf{x}_n)_{n=1}^{N}$. Each buyer n is associated with a utility function denoted as $U_n(\mathbf{x}_n, \mathbf{x}_{-n})$: $\mathbb{R}^{K \times N} \to \mathbb{R}_+$, indicating the quantified value or utility accrued by the buyer n upon acquiring $\mathbf{x}_n$ resources, while its adversaries have been assigned $\mathbf{x}_{-n} := (\mathbf{x}_m)_{m \neq n}^{N}$. In contrast to the traditional Fisher market, where buyers' utility depends solely on their acquired resources, we examine a broader scenario where buyers' utility depends not only on their resources but also on those of their opponents.

Assumption 1. *For each buyer* $n \in \mathcal{N}$, U_n *is continuous in* $\mathbf{x}$, *concave in* $\mathbf{x}_n$, *and satisfies no saturation*

Without loss of generality, we assume that each good k has a unit capacity, and each buyer n is endowed with a positive monetary budget B_n such that $\sum_n B_n = 1$. Let $\mathbf{p} = (p_1, \ldots, p_K)$ be a price vector representing the prices for all resources, where p_k denotes the price per unit for the resource k. Given the set of prices $\mathbf{p} \in \mathbb{R}_+^K$ for the resources, the feasible demand set of the buyer n is defined as the set of demands that satisfies its budget.

$$\mathcal{X}_n(\mathbf{p}) = \left\{ \mathbf{x}_n \mid \mathbf{x}_n \in \mathbb{R}^m, \sum_k x_{nk} p_k = B_n \right\} \tag{6}$$

We assume that buyers exhibit rational, self-interested behaviour, with each buyer seeking to maximize their individual utility. In this context, they consider the decisions made by their peer buyers when determining their own actions, where the decision problem for each buyer n is given as

$$Q_n(\mathbf{x}_{-n}; \mathbf{p}) \qquad \underset{\mathbf{x}_n}{\text{maximize}} \quad U_n(\mathbf{x}_n, \mathbf{x}_{-n}),$$
$$\text{subject to} \quad \mathbf{x}_n \in \mathcal{X}_n(\mathbf{p}). \tag{7}$$

Given resource prices, buyers strategic interaction gives rise to a non-cooperative game, denoted as $\mathcal{G}(\mathbf{p}) \triangleq \left\langle \mathcal{N}, (\mathbf{x}_n \in \mathbb{R}^K)_{n \in \mathcal{N}}, (\mathcal{X}_n(\mathbf{p}))_{n \in \mathcal{N}}, (U_n)_{n \in \mathcal{N}} \right\rangle$, comprising the set of players $\mathcal{N}$, their respective strategy spaces $(\mathcal{X}_n(\mathbf{p})) \, n \in \mathcal{N}$, and their utility functions $(U_n)_{n \in \mathcal{N}}$ and Let $\mathcal{X}(\mathbf{p}) = \mathcal{X}_1(\mathbf{p}) \times \mathcal{X}_2(\mathbf{p}) \times \ldots \mathcal{X}_N(\mathbf{p})$ defines the joint action space for the game. Here, we deliberately use the notation $\mathcal{G}(\mathbf{p})$ to emphasize the dependency of the game on the prices of goods, $\mathbf{p}$. The outcome of this game is determined by a Nash equilibrium.

Definition 5. *A strategy profile $(\mathbf{x}^*) \in \mathcal{X}(\mathbf{p})$ is called a Nash equilibrium (NE) of the game $\mathcal{G}(\mathbf{p})$ if*
$$U_n(\mathbf{x}_n^*, \mathbf{x}_{-n}^*) \geq U_n(\mathbf{x}_n, \mathbf{x}_{-n}^*)$$
for all $\mathbf{x}_n \in \mathcal{X}_n(\mathbf{p})$ and for all $n \in \mathcal{N}$.

In this work, we operate under the assumption that the game induced through the strategic interactions of buyers is Monotone.

Assumption 2. *We assume that the game $\mathcal{G}(\mathbf{p})$ exhibits strict monotonicity.*

Throughout the remainder of this paper, the term Fisher market refers to the generalized Fisher market unless explicitly stated otherwise. The traditional Fisher market, devoid of social influence, can be seen as a special instance within the framework of the generalized Fisher market, where utility functions remain unaffected by opponents' allocations.

Definition 6 (Demand Function). *If the game $\mathcal{G}(\mathbf{p})$ has a unique NE for each $\mathbf{p} \in \mathcal{P} \subset \mathbb{R}_+^K$, this gives rise to a function:*

$$\mathbf{x}_n^*(\mathbf{p}) : \mathcal{P} \to \mathbb{R}_+^K \tag{8}$$
$$\mathbf{p} \mapsto \mathbf{x}_n^*(\mathbf{p}), \tag{9}$$

which is called the demand function.

Definition 7 (Aggregate Excess Demand Function). *We now define the aggregate excess demand function:*

$$z_k(\mathbf{p}) : \mathcal{P} \to \mathbb{R} \quad \forall k \in \mathcal{K} \tag{10}$$

$$\mathbf{p} \mapsto z_k(\mathbf{p}) = \left(\sum_n x_{nk}^*(\mathbf{p}) - 1 \right). \tag{11}$$

By grouping these components into a vector, we introduce:

$$\mathbf{z}(\mathbf{p}) := (z_1(\mathbf{p}), \ldots, z_K(\mathbf{p})) \in \mathbb{R}^K. \tag{12}$$

Definition 8. *A competitive equilibrium for the market $\mathcal{M}$ is defined as a pair of prices and an allocation $(\mathbf{p}^*, \mathbf{x}^*)$, where the market clears its resources and buyers obtain their favorite resource bundles. Mathematically, $(\mathbf{p}^*, \mathbf{x}^*)$ is a CE if the following two conditions are satisfied.*

C1 *Given the resource price vector, every buyer n spends its budget such that it receives a resource bundle $\mathbf{x}_n^*$ that maximizes its utility.*

$$\mathbf{x}_n^* \in \arg\max \left\{ U_n(\mathbf{x}_n, \mathbf{x}_{-n}^*) \mid \mathbf{x}_n \in \mathcal{X}_n(\mathbf{p}^*) \right\}, \ \forall n \in \mathcal{N}. \tag{13}$$

C2 *Either the total demand for each resource meets its capacity and is positively priced; otherwise, that resource has a zero price, i.e., we have:*

$$p_k^* \left(\sum_n x_{nk}^* - 1 \right) = 0, \quad \forall k \in \mathcal{K}. \tag{14}$$

4 Competitive Equilibrium Problem

In this study, our objective is to develop a method to determine competitive equilibrium in a generalized Fisher market. Initially, we illustrate that this equilibrium can be attained through a pseudo-game or GNEP involving both the set of buyers and an auctioneer.

Definition 9 (Auctioneer-Buyer Pseudo-Game). *We consider a game $\widehat{\mathcal{G}}$ consisting of players: N buyers and an auctioneer. Actions: Each buyer chooses an allocation $\mathbf{x}_n \in \mathcal{A}_n = \mathbb{R}_+^K$, and the auctioneer chooses prices $\mathbf{p} \in \mathcal{A}_{N+1} = \mathbb{R}_+^K$. Action space: The feasible action space for each buyer n is $\mathcal{X}_n(\mathbf{p})$, as defined in (6), while for the auctioneer, it is $\mathcal{P} = \left\{ \mathbf{p} \mid \mathbf{p} \in \mathbb{R}_+^K, \sum_k p_k = 1 \right\}$. Utility: For the buyers, $\phi_n = U_n$. For the auctioneer, $\phi_{N+1} = \sum_{k \in \mathcal{K}} p_k \left(\sum_{n \in \mathcal{N}} x_{nk} - 1 \right)$.*

Theorem 1 ([49]). *For any Fisher market $\mathcal{M}$, where the buyers' utilities satisfy the assumption 1, the set of competitive equilibria corresponds precisely to the set of generalized Nash equilibria (GNE) of the associated auctioneer-buyer pseudogame $\widehat{\mathcal{G}}$.*

Thus far, we have studied a connection between the CE in a Fisher market and the GNE in an Auctioneer-Buyer pseudo-game, with its existence being ensured under mild conditions. However, a fundamental challenge remains: How can we effectively compute the GNE in this game? The task of determining a NE in a GNEP is generally recognized as challenging. However, within a subset of GNEPs where players share common coupled convex constraints, the problem can be reformulated as a variational inequality (VI) problem [23], with its solution called a variational equilibrium (VE). This type of equilibrium has been well studied and has efficient polynomial-time algorithms for solution. Unfortunately, in our specific scenario, the shared coupled constraint between players, expressed as $\sum_{k \in \mathcal{K}} \sum_{n \in \mathcal{N}} p_k x_{nk} = 1$, does not exhibit joint convexity. Consequently, the game cannot be directly resolved as a VI problem. However, we introduce a novel formulation of the VI problem, different from the standard framework, and demonstrate that its solution coincides precisely with the game $\widehat{\mathcal{G}}$, i.e., CE of the market $\mathcal{M}$. Before exploring the VI formulation, we first examine the KKT conditions at the GNE of the game $\widehat{\mathcal{G}}$, which play a pivotal role in obtaining our main result.

Proposition 1. $(\mathbf{p}^*, \mathbf{x}^*)$ *is a CE to the market* $\mathcal{M}$ *(a GNE of the game* $\widehat{\mathcal{G}}$*) if it satisfies the system of KKT conditions* (15).

For each buyer n in $\mathcal{N}$

$$\left[\frac{B_n \nabla_{nk} U_n(\mathbf{x}_n, \mathbf{x}^*_{-n})}{\sum_{k' \in \mathcal{K}} \nabla_{nk'} U_n(\mathbf{x}_n, \mathbf{x}^*_{-n}) x_{nk'}} \right]_{\mathbf{x}_n = \mathbf{x}^*_n} - p^*_k + \gamma^*_{nk} = 0, \quad \forall k \in \mathcal{K} \quad (15a)$$

$$p^*_k \left(\sum_{n \in \mathcal{N}} x^*_{nk} - 1 \right) = 0, \gamma^*_{nk} x^*_{nk} = 0, \quad \forall k \in \mathcal{K} \quad (15b)$$

$$p^*_k \geq 0, \gamma^*_{nk} \geq 0, \quad \forall k \in \mathcal{K} \quad (15c)$$

Proof. Appendix A.1 [17]

In the KKT conditions (15), the complementary slackness and dual feasibility conditions related to the budget constraint (6) for each buyer do not appear explicitly. However, they are implicitly captured by the stationarity condition (15a), which allows us to reformulate these conditions as a variational inequality problem. Interestingly, multiplying both sides of (15a) by x_{nk} yields:

$$\left[\frac{B_n \nabla_{nk} U_n(\mathbf{x}_n, \mathbf{x}^*_{-n}) x_{nk}}{\sum_{k' \in \mathcal{K}} \nabla_{nk'} U_n(\mathbf{x}_n, \mathbf{x}^*_{-n}) x_{nk'}} \right]_{\mathbf{x}_n = \mathbf{x}^*_n} - b^*_{nk} = 0, \forall k \in \mathcal{K}. \quad (16)$$

where $b^*_{nk} = p^*_k \cdot x^*_{nk}$. This equation resembles a family of dynamics such as Multiplicative Weights Update [6] and replicator dynamics [46], illustrating how the budget is distributed proportionally to the weighted marginal utilities between resources. We will see later in Sect. 7.2 how this structure can be used to design an equilibrium learning algorithm.

4.1   Variational Inequality (VI) Problem Formulation of Game $\widehat{\mathcal{G}}$

Definition 10. *Consider the Variational Inequality problem $VI(\mathcal{C}, F)$, with F and the (coupled) constraint $\mathcal{C}$ are defined as (17) and (18) respectively*

$$F_{nk}(\mathbf{x}) : \mathbb{R}^{NK} \to \mathbb{R} \ as \ F_{nk}(\mathbf{x}) = \frac{B_n \nabla_{nk} U_n(\mathbf{x})}{\sum_{k' \in \mathcal{K}} \nabla_{nk'} U_n(\mathbf{x}) x_{nk'}} \tag{17}$$

$$and \ F_n(\mathbf{x}) = (F_{nk}(\mathbf{x}))_{k=1}^{K} \ and \ F(\mathbf{x}) = (F_n(\mathbf{x}))_{n=1}^{N}$$

$$\mathcal{C} = \left\{ \mathbf{x} \mid \mathbf{x} \in \mathbb{R}^{NK}, \sum_{n \in \mathcal{N}} x_{nk} \leq 1, \forall k \in \mathcal{K} \right\} \tag{18}$$

Assumption 3. *$F(\mathbf{x})$ is continuous and strictly monotone in $\mathbf{x}$*

Theorem 2. *If the utilities of the buyers in the market $\mathcal{M}$ satisfy Assumptions 1, 2, and 3, then:*

- *The variational equilibrium $\mathbf{x}_{VE}^*$ to the problem $VI(\mathcal{C}, F)$ is unique.*
- *$\mathbf{x}^*$ is a CE allocation if and only if it is a variational equilibrium to $VI(\mathcal{C}, F)$.*
- *If $\mathbf{x}_{VE}^*$ is the solution to $VI(\mathcal{C}, F)$, then the corresponding KKT conditions are satisfied with the optimal Lagrange multiplier vector λ, which corresponds to the CE prices $\mathbf{p}^*$.*

Proof. Appendix A.2 [17]

In the above theorem, the uniqueness of the VE refers only to the allocation $\mathbf{x}_{VE}^*$. Although the allocation is unique, there can be multiple price vectors $\mathbf{p}^*$ that lead to the same allocation. So far, we have demonstrated how the variational inequality problem formulation of the game $\widehat{\mathcal{G}}$ can be derived from the KKT conditions obtained at the GNE. In subsequent sections, we establish several existing results from the literature as corollaries to our findings. Specifically, we investigate scenarios where the buyers' utilities exhibit homogeneity of function degree one, illustrating how these cases are special instances within our broader framework.

5   Homogeneous Utility

Let's delve into a particular market scenario which is extensively explored in the literature, where the utilities of buyers are modeled as CCH. We aim to establish the connection between existing findings in the literature and our results.

Corollary 1. *If each buyer's utility function within the market $\mathcal{M}$ is continuous, concave, and homogeneous of degree one (CCH) with respect to their own decisions, then the following results hold:*

- ***Theorem 7.** [49] The competitive equilibrium pair $(\mathbf{p}^*, \mathbf{x}^*)$ can be determined by solving a variational equilibrium within a coupled-constraint game. In this game, each buyer $n \in \mathcal{N}$ seeks to maximize their utility $\phi_n(\mathbf{x}_n, \mathbf{x}_{-n}) = B_n \log(U_n(\mathbf{x}))$ subject to the coupled constraints: $\sum_{n \in \mathcal{N}} x_{nk} \leq 1, \forall k \in \mathcal{K}$.*
- *Furthermore, in the absence of social influence, where each buyer's utility depends only on their own decision, the competitive equilibrium can be computed by solving an (Eisenberg-Gale) optimization program (19).*

$$\text{Maximize:} \sum_{\mathbf{x}}^{n \in \mathcal{N}} B_n \log(U_n(\mathbf{x}_n)) \quad (19a)$$

$$\text{subject to:} \sum_{n \in \mathcal{N}} x_{nk} \leq 1, \quad \forall k \in \mathcal{K}. \quad (19b)$$

where $\mathbf{x}^*$ represents the equilibrium allocation, while $\mathbf{p}^*$ denotes the Lagrange multiplier vector associated with the constraints (19b).

Proof. Appendix A.3 [17]

In the next section, we examine several properties of the variational inequality problem which serve as the basis for developing the subsequent decentralized learning algorithm.

6   Monotonicity, Stability, and Uniqueness in $\text{VI}(\mathcal{C}, F)$

Definition 11 (Variational stability [34]). *A solution (equilibrium) to $VI(F, C)$ is said to be stable if there exists a neighborhood $N_{bd}(\mathbf{x}^*)$ of $\mathbf{x}^*$ such that*

$$\boxed{\langle F(\mathbf{x}), \mathbf{x} - \mathbf{x}^* \rangle \leq 0 \quad \forall \mathbf{x} \in N_{bd}(\mathbf{x}^*)} \quad (20)$$

with equality if and only if $\mathbf{x} = \mathbf{x}^*$. In particular, if N_{bd} can be taken to be all of C, we say that $\mathbf{x}^*$ is globally variationally stable (or globally stable for short).

Proposition 2. *If the function F in the problem $VI(\mathcal{C}, F)$ satisfies Assumption 3, then the VE for the problem $VI(\mathcal{C}, F)$ is unique and globally stable.*

Proof. If Assumption 3 holds, then the uniqueness follows from Theorem 1.6 [36]. Let $\mathbf{x}^*$ denote the VE of the problem $VI(\mathcal{C}, F)$. Given that F is strictly monotone by Assumption 3, we have:

$$\langle F(\mathbf{x}) - F(\mathbf{x}^*), \mathbf{x} - \mathbf{x}^* \rangle \leq 0$$

Since $\mathbf{x}^*$ is the VE solution of VI$(\mathcal{C}, F)$, by definition it satisfies:

$$\langle F(\mathbf{x}^*), \mathbf{x} - \mathbf{x}^* \rangle \leq 0$$

Subtracting these two inequalities gives us:

$$\langle F(\mathbf{x}), \mathbf{x} - \mathbf{x}^* \rangle \leq 0$$

The monotonicity of $F(\mathbf{x})$ and the stability of the variational equilibrium $\mathbf{x}^*$ can be ensured by analyzing its pseudo-Jacobian. Next, we explore the conditions that guarantee the stability of the variational equilibrium for the VI problem (18). Let $H(\mathbf{x})$ be the block matrix defined as:

$$H(\mathbf{x}) = \begin{bmatrix} [H_1^1] & [H_2^1] & \cdots & [H_N^1] \\ [H_1^2] & [H_2^2] & \cdots & [H_N^2] \\ \vdots & \vdots & \ddots & \vdots \\ [H_1^N] & [H_2^N] & \cdots & [H_N^N] \end{bmatrix} \quad \text{where } H_m^n = \begin{bmatrix} h_{m1}^{n1} & h_{m2}^{n1} & \cdots & h_{mK}^{n1} \\ h_{m1}^{n2} & h_{m2}^{n2} & \cdots & h_{mK}^{n2} \\ \vdots & \vdots & \ddots & \vdots \\ h_{m1}^{nK} & h_{m2}^{nK} & \cdots & h_{mK}^{nK} \end{bmatrix} \quad (21)$$

$$\text{and elements } h_{ml}^{nk} = \frac{1}{2} \frac{\partial F_{nm}}{\partial x_{ml}} \quad (22)$$

where "nk" refers to n^{th} buyer and k^{th} resource

Theorem 3. *If the matrix $\left[H(\mathbf{x}) + H(\mathbf{x})^T \right]$ is negative definite, then $F(\mathbf{x})$ is strictly monotone, and the equilibrium is unique and stable.*

Proof. Appendix A.4 [17].

Next, we analyze the relationship between prices and aggregate excess demand. Specifically, we examine whether the aggregate excess demand function exhibits monotonicity, which plays a crucial role in market stability and equilibrium analysis. The following lemma establishes that under Assumption 3, the aggregate excess demand function is strictly monotone.

Lemma 1. *If the utilities of the buyers in the market $\mathcal{M}$ satisfy Assumption 3, then the aggregate excess demand function $\mathbf{z}(\mathbf{p})$, given prices $\mathbf{p} \in \mathbb{R}_+^K$, is strictly monotone. Specifically, for any $\mathbf{p}^1, \mathbf{p}^2 \in \mathbb{R}_+^K$, the following inequality holds:*

$$\langle \mathbf{z}(\mathbf{p}^1) - \mathbf{z}(\mathbf{p}^2), \mathbf{p}^1 - \mathbf{p}^2 \rangle \leq 0.$$

Proof. Appendix A.5 [17]

Theorem 4. *If the buyers' utilities in market $\mathcal{M}$ satisfy Assumption 2, then $\mathbf{p}^*$ is an equilibrium price vector if and only if*

$$\langle \mathbf{z}(\mathbf{p}), \mathbf{p} - \mathbf{p}^* \rangle \leq 0 \quad \forall \mathbf{p} \in \mathcal{P}. \quad (23)$$

Proof. Given that the buyers' utilities in market $\mathcal{M}$ satisfy Assumption 2, Lemma 1 ensures that:

$$\langle \mathbf{z}(\mathbf{p}^1) - \mathbf{z}(\mathbf{p}^2), \mathbf{p}^1 - \mathbf{p}^2 \rangle \leq 0.$$

Then the claim follows from Theorem 3.1 [16].

7   Decentralized Learning of Competitive Equilibrium

In the previous section, we studied the structural properties of VE within GNEP in the context of market equilibrium. Building on these properties, we now propose two learning algorithms that enable buyers to reach a CE in a decentralized manner.

7.1   Two-Time Scale Stochastic Approximation-Based *tâtonnement*

Our first proposed algorithm is based on the *tâtonnement* approach, where an auctioneer initially sets prices and buyers adjust their demands accordingly. The auctioneer then adapts prices in response to the observed demand, increasing prices when demand exceeds supply and decreasing them vice versa.

In Lemma 1 of the previous section, we demonstrated that the excess demand function is monotone in price and stable at the equilibrium price. This monotonic behavior could have been sufficient to show the convergence of the *tâtonnement* process:

$$\mathbf{p}(t+1) \leftarrow \Pi_{\mathcal{P}} \left[\mathbf{p}(t) + \beta_t \, \mathbf{z}(\mathbf{p}(t)) \right] \qquad \text{(Step8-Algorithm 1)}$$

provided that the game $\mathcal{G}(\mathbf{p}(t))$ is at equilibrium at each round. However, computing the NE of the game $\mathcal{G}(\mathbf{p}(t))$ in response to the prices set by the auctioneer requires an additional algorithm. Fortunately, since the game $\mathcal{G}(\mathbf{p}(t))$ is monotone, it can be solved using existing methods, such as gradient ascent [34]. Despite its theoretical soundness, this approach can be computationally intensive due to the nested loop structure: an inner loop computes the NE of $\mathcal{G}(\mathbf{p}(t))$, while the outer loop involves price adjustments by the auctioneer. To address this challenge, we propose a two-time-scale stochastic approximation-based learning algorithm. In this approach, buyers do not need to reach NE in response to each price update. Instead, they follow a gradient ascent direction with larger steps α_t:

$$x_{nk}(t+1) \leftarrow \left[x_{nk}(t) + \alpha_t \left(F_{nk}(\mathbf{x}(t)) - p_k(t-1) \right) \right]^+ \qquad \text{(Step4-Algorithm1)}$$

whereas Auctioneer adjusts prices with smaller steps β_t, facilitating a more efficient adjustment process and reducing the computational burden on buyers. If the steps size follows the conditions described in Algorithm 1, the algorithm converges to VE of $\mathrm{VI}(\mathcal{C}, F)$ for details see [8,29]

In Algorithm 2

7.2   Trading Post Mechanism Based Learning Algorithm

In the trading post mechanism, each buyer $n \in \mathcal{N}$ places a bid b_{nk} on each type of resource $k \in \mathcal{K}$. Once all buyers have placed their bids, the price of each resource is determined by the sum of the bids: $p_k = \sum_n b_{nk}$. Each buyer n is then allocated the resource of type k in proportion to their bid. The allocation x_{nk} is given by:

Algorithm 1. Two-time scale stochastic approximation-based *tâtonnement*

Require: $\sum_{t=0}^{\infty} \alpha_t = \sum_{t=0}^{\infty} \beta_t = \infty, \sum_{n=0}^{\infty} \alpha_t^2 < \infty, \sum_{n=0}^{\infty} \beta_t^2 < \infty, \frac{\beta_t}{\alpha_t} \to 0$ as $t \to \infty$.

1: **repeat** $t = 1, 2, \ldots,$
2:     **for each** $n \in \mathcal{N}$ **do**
3:         **for each** resource $k \in \mathcal{K}$ **do**
4:             Play $x_{nk}(t+1) \leftarrow [x_{nk}(t) + \alpha_t (F_{nk}(\mathbf{x}(t)) - p_k(t))]^+$
5:         **end for**
6:     **end for**
7:     Auctioneer observes the excess demand for each resource $k \in \mathcal{K}$ $z_k(\mathbf{p}(t)) = \left(\sum_n x_{nk}^*(\mathbf{p}(t)) - 1\right)$
8:     set prices $\mathbf{p}(t+1) \leftarrow \Pi_{\mathcal{P}}[\mathbf{p}(t) + \beta_t \mathbf{z}(\mathbf{p}(t))]$
9: **until** $\|(\mathbf{x}(t) - \mathbf{x}(t-1))\| \leq \epsilon$

$$x_{nk} = \begin{cases} \frac{b_{nk}}{p_k} & \text{if } b_{nk} > 0 \\ 0 & \text{if } b_{nk} = 0 \end{cases} \tag{24}$$

We assume that the buyers are price takers, and they request different amounts of the resources by submitting their bids over the resources. The auctioneer announces the prices of the resources and allocates them according to the trading post mechanism. If all buyers are satisfied with the allocation and prices announced by the auctioneer, the mechanism has reached equilibrium. Otherwise, buyers adjust their bids and resubmit them to the auctioneer. This introduces the challenge of bid dynamics: how do buyers adjust their bids to reach an equilibrium via the trading post mechanism? In this section, we devise bid updating learning schemes, which allow the buyers to reach the desired equilibrium using the trading post mechanism. the buyers adjust the bids

---

Algorithm 2. Trading post mechanism based Learning Algorithm

Require: $\sum_{n=0}^{+\infty} \alpha_t = +\infty, \alpha_t \to 0$ as $t \to +\infty$

1: **repeat** $t = 1, 2, \ldots,$
2:     **for each** $n \in \mathcal{N}$ **do**
3:         **for each** resource $k \in \mathcal{K}$ **do**
4:             Play $b_{nk}(t+1) \leftarrow b_{nk}(t) + \alpha_t b_{nk}(t) (F_{nk}(\mathbf{x}(t)) - p_k(t))$
5:         **end for**
6:     **end for**
7:     **for each** $k \in \mathcal{K}$ **do**
8:         $p_k(t+1) \leftarrow \sum_{n \in \mathcal{N}} b_{nk}(t+1)$
9:         **for each** $n \in \mathcal{N}$ **do**
10:           $x_{nk}(t+1) \leftarrow \frac{b_{nk}(t+1)}{p_k(t+1)}$
11:         **end for**
12:     **end for**
13: **until** $\|(\mathbf{p}(t) - \mathbf{p}(t-1))\| \leq \epsilon$

$$b_{nk}(t+1) \leftarrow b_{nk}(t) + \alpha_t b_{nk}(t)\left(F_{nk}(\mathbf{x}(t)) - p_k(t)\right) \qquad \text{(Step4-Algorithm2)}$$

while resources are allocated according to

$$x_{nk}(t+1) \leftarrow \frac{b_{nk}(t+1)}{\sum_n b_{nk}(t+1)} \qquad \text{(Step8-Algorithm2)}$$

In Algorithm 2, Step 4 and Step 8 collectively resemble the discrete replicator dynamics [24,46], a concept from evolutionary game theory [43]. The stability of associated replicator dynamics can be ensured if the VE is stable. Leveraging this relationship, we demonstrate that the Algorithm 2 converges to the VE.

Theorem 5. *If the function F in the problem $VI(\mathcal{C}, F)$ satisfies Assumption 3, then Algorithm 2 converges to the unique VE of the problem $VI(\mathcal{C}, F)$.*

Proof. Appendix A.6 [17]

8   Numerical Experiments

In this section, we present numerical experiments to validate the proposed learning algorithms. We focus on a Fisher market setting where competition among buyers is modeled using Tullock contests or rent-seeking games [47]. The Tullock contest framework is widely used in economics to capture competitive interactions between multiple agents. It has also found extensive applications in the communication network literature, modeling scenarios such as competition between social media users for visibility on timelines [41], multipath TCP network utility maximization [40], competition among miners in multicryptocurrency blockchain networks [1], and competition between service providers in communication markets to attract users [18]. In the Tullock contest framework, agents expend costly resources in an effort to win a prize, with the probability of winning determined by the contest success function (CSF). The standard form of the CSF is typically expressed as $\rho(x) = \frac{(x_n)^r}{\sum_{n'}(x_{n'})^r}$, where $x_n \in \mathbb{R}_+$ denotes the effort of agent n and r is a parameter. For example, when $r = 1$, the model describes a lottery, while $r \to \infty$ represents an all-pay auction. In our work, we generalize this model by incorporating multiple resources into the CSF. The generalized CSF is defined as

$$U_n(\mathbf{x}_n, \mathbf{x}_{-n}) = \frac{q_n(\mathbf{x}_n)}{\sum_{m \in \mathcal{N}} q_m(\mathbf{x}_m)} \quad \text{where} \quad q_n(\mathbf{x}_n) = \sum_k a_{nk}(x_{nk})^{\rho_{nk}} \qquad (25)$$

where $q_n(\mathbf{x}_n)$ represents the effort function for each agent n. For each buyer n and each good k, the parameters satisfy $0 < \rho_{nk} < 1$ and $0 < a_{nk} < 1$ such that $\sum_k a_{nk} = 1$ for each $n \in \mathcal{N}$. Given fixed resource prices, the multi-resource Tullock rent-seeking game, as defined by the utility functions in (25), is strictly monotone and has a unique, stable variational equilibrium (see Theorem 1 [18]). Moreover, the computation of the pseudo-Jacobian confirms that $F(\mathbf{X})$, as described in (17), is strictly monotone.

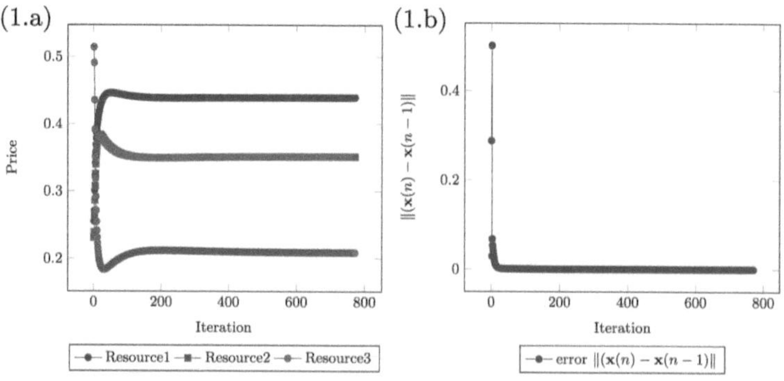

Fig. 1. (a-b) Convergence two-time scale stochastic approximation-based *tâtonnement*.

For numerical simulations, we consider a market scenario involving five buyers and three resources, with parameters ρ and a randomly generated. The competitive equilibrium is computed using Algorithms 1 and 2. In both algorithms, we used step sizes defined as $\alpha_t = \frac{1}{(t+1)^{0.6}}$ and $\beta_t = \frac{1}{(t+1)^{0.9}}$ for Algorithm 1. Figure 1(a–b) illustrates the convergence behavior of the two-time scale stochastic approximation-based *tâtonnement* method for a representative instance, while Fig. 2(a–b) describes the convergence behavior of the trading post mechanism based learning algorithm.

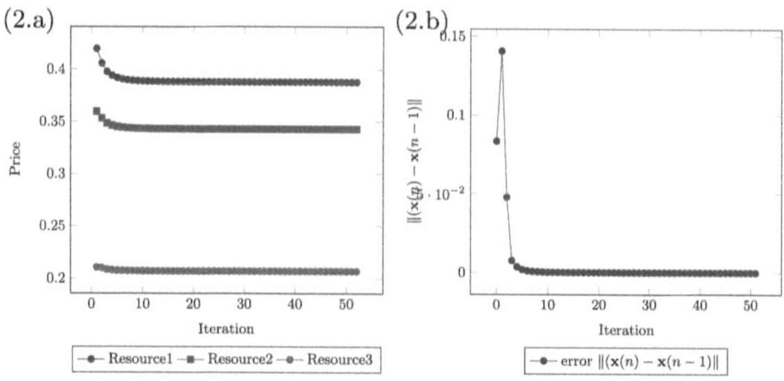

Fig. 2. (a–b) Convergence of trading post mechanism based learning algorithm.

9   Conclusion

In this work, we introduced a novel variational inequality formulation for competitive equilibrium problems within the generalized Fisher market model. Unlike traditional Fisher markets, where buyers' utilities depend solely on their own resource allocations, our formulation considers dependencies on the allocations of their competitors. Our proposed variational inequality framework provides a broader framework for computing competitive equilibrium in generalized Fisher markets, overcoming the constraint of homogeneous buyer utilities that is typical in traditional Fisher markets. We examined various structural properties of this formulation, suggesting avenues for future extensions. In addition, we have developed two decentralized learning algorithms designed to facilitate buyers to achieve competitive equilibrium in a decentralized manner. Moving forward, our future research aims to explore scenarios involving buyers with unknown utility functions.

References

1. Altman, E., et al..: Blockchain competition between miners: a game theoretic perspective. Front. Blockchain **2**, 26 (2020). https://doi.org/10.3389/fbloc.2019.00026. https://www.frontiersin.org/article/10.3389/fbloc.2019.00026
2. Arrow, K.J., Block, H.D., Hurwicz, L.: On the stability of the competitive equilibrium, II. Econometrica J. Econometric. Soc., 82–109 (1959)
3. Arrow, K.J., Debreu, G.: Existence of an equilibrium for a competitive economy. Econometrica J. Econometric. Soc., 265–290 (1954)
4. Arrow, K.J., Hurwicz, L.: On the stability of the competitive equilibrium, I. Econometrica J. Econometric. Soc., 522–552 (1958)
5. Avigdor-Elgrabli, N., Rabani, Y., Yadgar, G.: Convergence of tâtonnement in fisher markets. arXiv preprint arXiv:1401.6637 (2014)
6. Bailey, J.P., Piliouras, G.: Multiplicative weights update in zero-sum games. In: Proceedings of the 2018 ACM Conference on Economics and Computation, pp. 321–338 (2018)
7. Birnbaum, B., Devanur, N.R., Xiao, L.: Distributed algorithms via gradient descent for fisher markets. In: Proceedings of the 12th ACM Conference on Electronic Commerce, pp. 127–136 (2011)
8. Bistritz, I., Bambos, N.: Online learning for load balancing of unknown monotone resource allocation games. In: International Conference on Machine Learning, pp. 968–979. PMLR (2021)
9. Brainard, W.C., Scarf, H.E.: How to compute equilibrium prices in 1891. Am. J. Econ. Sociol. **64**(1), 57–83 (2005)
10. Brânzei, S., Devanur, N., Rabani, Y.: Proportional dynamics in exchange economies. In: Proceedings of the 22nd ACM Conference on Economics and Computation, pp. 180–201 (2021)
11. Chen, X., Dai, D., Du, Y., Teng, S.H.: Settling the complexity of Arrow-Debreu equilibria in markets with additively separable utilities. In: 2009 50th Annual IEEE Symposium on Foundations of Computer Science, pp. 273–282. IEEE (2009)
12. Cheung, Y.K., Cole, R., Devanur, N.: Tatonnement beyond gross substitutes? Gradient descent to the rescue. In: Proceedings of the Forty-Fifth Annual ACM Symposium on Theory of computing, pp. 191–200 (2013)
13. Cheung, Y.K., Cole, R., Tao, Y.: Dynamics of distributed updating in Fisher markets. In: Proceedings of the 2018 ACM Conference on Economics and Computation, pp. 351–368 (2018)
14. Cheung, Y.K., Hoefer, M., Nakhe, P.: Tracing equilibrium in dynamic markets via distributed adaptation. arXiv preprint arXiv:1804.08017 (2018)

15. Cheung, Y.K., Leonardos, S., Piliouras, G.: Learning in markets: greed leads to chaos but following the price is right. arXiv preprint arXiv:2103.08529 (2021)
16. Dafermos, S.: Exchange price equilibria and variational inequalities. Math. Program. **46**(1), 391–402 (1990)
17. Datar, M.: On stability and learning of competitive equilibrium in generalized Fisher market models: a variational inequality approach. arXiv preprint arXiv:2501.07265 (2025)
18. Datar, M., Altman, E., Cadre, H.L.: Strategic resource pricing and allocation in a 5G network slicing Stackelberg game. IEEE Trans. Netw. Serv. Manage. **20**(1), 502–520 (2023). https://doi.org/10.1109/TNSM.2022.3216588
19. Datar, M., Modina, N., El, R., Altman, E.: Fisher market model based resource allocation for 5G network slicing. arXiv preprint arXiv:2307.16585 (2023)
20. Debreu, G.: A social equilibrium existence theorem. Proc. Natl. Acad. Sci. **38**(10), 886–893 (1952)
21. Eisenberg, E.: Aggregation of utility functions. Manage. Sci. **7**(4), 337–350 (1961)
22. Eisenberg, E., Gale, D.: Consensus of subjective probabilities: the Pari-Mutuel method. Ann. Math. Stat. **30**(1), 165–168 (1959)
23. Facchinei, F., Fischer, A., Piccialli, V.: On generalized Nash games and variational inequalities. Oper. Res. Lett. **35**(2), 159–164 (2007)
24. Falniowski, F., Mertikopoulos, P.: On the discrete-time origins of replicator dynamics: from convergence to instability and chaos. arXiv preprint arXiv:2402.09824 (2024)
25. Feldman, M., Lai, K., Zhang, L.: The proportional-share allocation market for computational resources. IEEE Trans. Parallel Distrib. Syst. **20**(8), 1075–1088 (2008)
26. Gao, Y., Kroer, C.: Infinite-dimensional fisher markets and tractable fair division. Oper. Res. **71**(2), 688–707 (2023)
27. Gao, Y., Peysakhovich, A., Kroer, C.: Online market equilibrium with application to fair division. Adv. Neural. Inf. Process. Syst. **34**, 27305–27318 (2021)
28. Goktas, D., Zhao, J., Greenwald, A.: Tâtonnement in homothetic Fisher markets. arXiv preprint arXiv:2306.04890 (2023)
29. Hong, M., Wai, H.T., Wang, Z., Yang, Z.: A two-timescale stochastic algorithm framework for bilevel optimization: complexity analysis and application to actor-critic. SIAM J. Optim. **33**(1), 147–180 (2023)
30. Jain, K., Vazirani, V.V.: Eisenberg-gale markets: algorithms and structural properties. In: Proceedings of the Thirty-Ninth Annual ACM Symposium on Theory of Computing, pp. 364–373 (2007)
31. Jalota, D., Ye, Y.: Stochastic online Fisher markets: static pricing limits and adaptive enhancements. arXiv preprint arXiv:2205.00825 (2022)
32. Kelly, F.: Charging and rate control for elastic traffic. Eur. Trans. Telecommun. **8**(1), 33–37 (1997)
33. McKenzie, L.W.: On the existence of general equilibrium for a competitive market. Econometrica **27**(1), 54–71 (1959). http://www.jstor.org/stable/1907777
34. Mertikopoulos, P., Zhou, Z.: Learning in games with continuous action sets and unknown payoff functions. Math. Program. **173**, 465–507 (2018). https://doi.org/10.1007/s10107-018-1254-8
35. Modina, N., Datar, M., El-Azouzi, R., de Pellegrini, F.: Multi resource allocation for network slices with multi-level fairness. In: IEEE International Conference on Communications, ICC 2022, pp. 4872–4877 (2022). https://doi.org/10.1109/ICC45855.2022.9838759
36. Nagurney, A.: Network Economics. Wiley Online Library (2009)

37. Nan, T., Gao, Y., Kroer, C.: Fast and interpretable dynamics for fisher markets via block-coordinate updates. arXiv preprint arXiv:2303.00506 (2023)
38. Nesterov, Y., Shikhman, V.: Computation of fisher-gale equilibrium by auction. J. Oper. Res. Soc. China **6**(3), 349–389 (2018)
39. Nguyen, D.T., Le, L.B., Bhargava, V.K.: A market-based framework for multi-resource allocation in fog computing. IEEE/ACM Trans. Netw. **27**(3), 1151–1164 (2019). https://doi.org/10.1109/TNET.2019.2912077
40. Raj Pokhrel, S., Williamson, C.: A rent-seeking framework for multipath TCP. SIGMETRICS Perform. Eval. Rev. **48**(3), 63–70 (2021). https://doi.org/10.1145/3453953.3453968
41. Reiffers-Masson, A., Hayel, Y., Altman, E.: Game theory approach for modeling competition over visibility on social networks. In: Proceedings of the IEEE COMSNETS, pp. 1–6 (2014). https://doi.org/10.1109/COMSNETS.2014.6734939
42. Rosen, J.B.: Existence and uniqueness of equilibrium points for concave n-person games. Econometrica J. Econometric. Soc. **33**(3), 520–534 (1965)
43. Sandholm, W.H.: Population Games and Evolutionary Dynamics. The MIT Press (2010). http://www.jstor.org/stable/j.ctt5hhbq5
44. Scarf, H.: Some examples of global instability of the competitive equilibrium. Int. Econ. Rev. **1**(3), 157–172 (1960). http://www.jstor.org/stable/2556215
45. Shapley, L., Shubik, M.: Trade using one commodity as a means of payment. J. Polit. Econ. **85**(5) (1977)
46. Sylvain, S.: Replicator dynamics: old and new. J. Dyn. Games **7**(4), 365–386 (2020). https://doi.org/10.3934/jdg.2020028. https://www.aimsciences.org/article/id/639745c1-5cd8-4849-9303-9e77835f2a0b
47. Tullock, G.: Rent Seeking, no. 383. Edward Elgar Publishing (March undated). https://ideas.repec.org/b/elg/eebook/383.html
48. Walras, L.: Éléments d'économie politique pure, ou. Théorie de la richesse sociale. F. Rouge (1896)
49. Zhao, J., Goktas, D., Greenwald, A.: Fisher markets with social influence. In: Proceedings of the AAAI Conference on Artificial Intelligence, vol. 37, pp. 5900–5909 (2023)

Deception in Oligopoly Games
via Adaptive Nash Seeking Systems

Michael Tang[1]($\boxtimes$), Miroslav Krstic[2], and Jorge Poveda[1]

[1] Department of Electrical and Computer Engineering, University of California San Diego, La Jolla, CA, USA
{myt001,jipoveda}@ucsd.edu
[2] Department of Mechanical and Aerospace Engineering, University of California San Diego, La Jolla, CA, USA
mkrstic@ucsd.edu

Abstract. In the theory of multi-agent systems, deception refers to the strategic manipulation of information to influence the behavior of other agents, ultimately altering the long-term dynamics of the entire system. Recently, this concept has been examined in the context of model-free Nash equilibrium seeking (NES) algorithms for noncooperative games [16]. Specifically, it was demonstrated that players can exploit knowledge of other players' exploration signals to drive the system toward a "deceptive" Nash equilibrium, while maintaining the stability of the closed-loop system. To extend this insight beyond the duopoly case, in this paper we conduct a comprehensive study of deception mechanisms in N-player oligopoly markets. By leveraging the structure of these games and employing stability techniques for nonlinear dynamical systems, we provide game-theoretic insights into deception and derive specialized results, including stability conditions. These results allow players to systematically adjust their NES dynamics by tuning gains and signal amplitudes, all while ensuring closed-loop stability. Additionally, we introduce novel sufficient conditions to demonstrate that the (practically) stable equilibrium point of the deceptive dynamics corresponds to a true Nash equilibrium of a different game, which we term the "deceptive game." Our results show that, under the proposed adaptive dynamics with deception, a victim firm may develop a distorted perception of its competitors' product appeal, which could lead to setting suboptimal prices.

Keywords: Nash equilibrium seeking · Deception · Oligopoly

1 Introduction

1.1 Motivation

The study of multi-agent systems (MAS) is gaining increasing significance, particularly in engineering fields such as smart grids, robotics, and machine learning.

Supported by NSF

V. Aggarwal et al. (Eds.): GameNets 2025, LNICST 657, pp. 61–74, 2026.
https://doi.org/10.1007/978-3-032-12915-4_4

Game theory offers a robust framework for analyzing the strategic interactions between rational decision-makers in such systems. However, traditional game-theoretic concepts, such as Nash equilibrium [11], may need to be revisited in scenarios where agents have access to *privileged information*. In the context of learning in games [23], such asymmetry of information can be exploited to manipulate the system's long-term behavior, leading to outcomes that benefit some agents while disadvantaging others. For instance, in the context of Nash equilibrium seeking in non-cooperative games [1,5], privileged agents can exploit knowledge of other agents' exploration policies to interfere with their learning processes, without altering their own learning capabilities. When this interference maintains the overall system's stability, it can cause the naive agents to converge to incorrect steady-state models or beliefs . This phenomenon, known as *deception in games*, has received significant attention during the last years due to its potential implications in the context of cyber-security and resilient decision making in socio-technical systems. Algorithmic deception has been studied across various domains, including robotics and aerospace control [3,4,6]. Similarly, studies such as [17] propose algorithms for robots to decide when to deceive, as illustrated in hide-and-seek experiments. While deception can aid robots in achieving particular goals in non-competitive environments, it has also been explored in competitive scenarios, such as signaling games [8]. These concepts are further explored in works investigating deception in multi-agent systems, offering strategies to counter deceptive signals and attacks [14]. Deception has also been studied in the context of biological systems [15] and societal systems [10].

In this paper, we focus on studying deception in Nash equilibrium-seeking (NES) problems within non-cooperative games. In these scenarios, a finite number of agents, or players, seek to maximize their individual profits, which depend not only on their own actions but also on the actions of others. Given the challenge associated with computation of Nash equilibria [11] in noncooperative games, the study of NES algorithms has become a very hot research topic. Various algorithms have been designed, including distributed [20–22], semi-decentralized [2,24] and hybrid [18,19] algorithms. However, in some cases, the agents do not have precise knowledge of their cost functions, and hence they must rely on adaptive seeking dynamics that incorporate exploration and exploitation strategies. To address this, extremum-seeking based NES dynamics were introduced in [5] and have been extended to stochastic settings [9], systems with delays [12], nonsmooth algorithms [13], etc. In this setting, agents with privileged knowledge of the exploration policy used by others can manipulate their own exploration policy to induce false beliefs in the other agents, making them take actions that are detrimental for them. Such type of deception was recently introduced and studied in [16] for a general class of games, establishing conditions that preserve stability in the overall system. In particular, it was shown that when players in a non-cooperative game implement the model-free Nash equilibrium seeking (NES) scheme from [5], a player who gains insight into another player's exploration policy can manipulate the Nash equilibrium to their advantage. The proposed deception mechanism involves an additive and dynamic modification to the deceiver's action update, incorporating the victim's exploration frequency. This modification is adjusted using first or second-order dynamics. In the context of duopoly games, deceptive players have been shown to manipulate the victim's perception of their sales function. Using an averaging and singular perturbation approach, it was further shown that the proposed deception mechanisms preserve stability in non-cooperative games with general nonlinear payoffs, including strongly monotone games. While the results in [16] were the first to establish dynamic deception through model-free NES dynamics, their general applicability is constrained by certain assumptions. For example, the "stability-preserving set" described in [16], a key element in the singular perturbation analysis, is only guaranteed to cover a small neighborhood around a specific point. Additionally, although the work in [16] relaxes the diagonal dominance condition from [5], it does so at the cost of requiring all players to use identical gains and amplitudes in their NES dynamics.

1.2   Our Contributions

In this paper, we introduce several new results that relax some of the previous assumptions considered in the literature [16], and, additionally, we introduce new results and computations in the context of general N-player N-player oligopoly markets, such as those studied in [5]. Furthermore, we exploit the structure of the oligopoly market to derive sharper stability results and characterizations that quantify the influence of deception in this context. We also provide a broader estimate for the stability-preserving set in the nominal average dynamics and offer results that determine when the new equilibrium point under deception is truly a Nash equilibrium, rather than just an equilibrium, for the deceptive game. This framework further allows us to consider a more general class of NES dynamics, where players are permitted to use different gains and amplitudes in their update laws. The effectiveness of these results are also demonstrated through numerical simulations.

2   System Model and Oligopoly Formulation

In this section, we describe the types of games considered in this paper, as well as the model-free deception dynamics.

2.1   NES for the Oligopoly

Consider an N-player noncooperative game, where player i implements action $x_i \in \mathbb{R}$ and aims to unilaterally minimize their cost function $J_i : \mathbb{R}^N \to \mathbb{R}$. We use $[N] := \{1, 2, ..., N\}$ to denote the set of players, and we let $x = [x_1, ..., x_N]^\top$ denote the vector of players' actions. Similarly we use $x_{-i} \in \mathbb{R}^{N-1}$ to denote the vector of all players' actions except for the action of player i. Given real-valued cost functions $J_i(x_i, x_{-i}) : \mathbb{R}^N \to \mathbb{R}$, for all i, a policy $x^* \in \mathbb{R}^N$ is called a *Nash equilibrium* if it satisfies

$$x_i^* = \arg\min_{x_i} J_i(x_i, x_{-i}^*), \quad \forall\, i \in [N]. \tag{1}$$

We define the *pseudogradient* of the game to be $\mathcal{G}(x) := [\nabla_1 J_1(x), ..., \nabla_N J_N(x)]^\top$ where $\nabla_i J_i(x)$ is the partial derivative of $J_i(x)$ with respect to x_i. Given $v \in \mathbb{R}^N$ we use $\text{diag}(v) \in \mathbb{R}^{N \times N}$ to denote the diagonal matrix with i-th diagonal element given by v_i. Since we focus on oligopoly games where each player i controls the price x_i of their own product, the cost functions of interest take the form [5]:

$$J_i(x(t)) = -s_i(x(t))(x_i(t) - m_i) \tag{2}$$

where m_i is the marginal cost of the product generated by the ith player, and s_i is their sales function, which is given by

$$s_i(x(t)) = \frac{R_\|}{R_i}\left(S_d - \frac{x_i(t)}{\overline{R}_i} + \sum_{j \neq i}^N \frac{x_j(t)}{R_j}\right). \tag{3}$$

Here, S_d is the total consumer demand and R_i represents the resistance" that consumers have towards buying the product offered by firm i. In other words, the desirability of product i is inversely proportional to R_i. The quantities $R_\|$ and $\overline{R}_i$ are given by

$$\frac{1}{R_\|} = \sum_{k=1}^N \frac{1}{R_k}, \quad \text{and} \quad \frac{1}{\overline{R}_i} = \sum_{k \neq i}^N \frac{1}{R_k}. \tag{4}$$

As in [5], the sales function is motivated by an electrical circuit analogy, illustrated in Fig. 1.

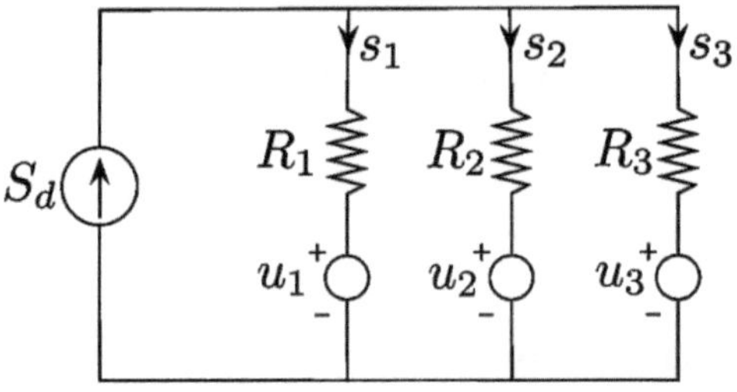

Fig. 1. Market-circuit analogy borrowed from [5], which models the sales s_1, s_2, s_3 of a three-player oligopoly as currents in a 3-resistor parallel circuit.

In Fig. 1, the total demand S_d can be thought of as a current generator, the prices x_i are voltage sources, and R_i is the resistance towards product i. It is also important to note that $s_i(x)(x_i - m_i)$ represents the profit of firm i, but we define J_i as (2) since, without loss of generality, we see J_i as a *cost* to be *minimized* by the ith player.

To converge to a neighborhood of a "standard" Nash equilibrium by only using measurements of their cost J_i, players can implement the following model-free NES dynamics introduced in [5]:

$$x_i(t) = u_i(t) + a_i \sin(\omega_i t) \tag{5a}$$

$$\dot{u}_i(t) = -\frac{2k_i}{a_i} J_i(x(t)) \sin(\omega_i t), \tag{5b}$$

where the gains $a_i, k_i > 0$ are positive tunable parameters, and the frequencies $\omega_i \in \mathbb{R}_{>0}$ are selected to satisfy the following assumption:

Assumption 1. The frequencies satisfy $\omega_i \neq \omega_j$ for $i \neq j$, and $\omega_i = \omega \overline{\omega}_i$, where $\omega \in \mathbb{R}_{>0}$ and $\overline{\omega}_i \in \mathbb{Q}_{>0}$, $\forall i \in [N]$.

It is easy to verify that the costs J_i can be represented in the quadratic form

$$J_i(x) = \frac{1}{2} x^\top Q_i x + b_i^\top x + \frac{R_\| S_d m_i}{R_i}, \tag{6}$$

where $Q_i \in \mathbb{R}^{N \times N}$ and $b_i \in \mathbb{R}^N$ have entries given by

$$[Q_i]_{jk} = \begin{cases} \dfrac{2R_\|}{R_i \overline{R}_i}, & \text{if } j = k = i \\ -\dfrac{R_\|}{R_j R_k}, & \text{if } j \neq k \text{ and either } j = i \text{ or } k = i \\ 0, & \text{else} \end{cases} \tag{7a}$$

$$[b_i]_k = \begin{cases} -\dfrac{m_i R_\|}{R_i \overline{R}_i} - \dfrac{S_d R_\|}{R_i}, & \text{if } k = i \\ \dfrac{m_i R_\|}{R_i R_k}, & \text{else} \end{cases} \tag{7b}$$

Here, $[Q_i]_{jk}$ and $[b_i]_k$ denote the (j,k) entry of Q_i and k-th entry of b_i respectively. It follows immediately that the pseudogradient of the oligopoly can be represented in the form $\mathcal{G}(x) = \mathcal{Q}x + \mathcal{B}$, where $\mathcal{Q} \in \mathcal{R}^{N \times N}$ and $\mathcal{B} \in \mathbb{R}^N$ satisfy $[\mathcal{Q}]_{i:} = [Q_i]_{i:}$ and $[\mathcal{B}]_i = [b_i]_i$ for all i. Here, $[E]_{i:}$ denotes row i of matrix E.

2.2   Deception in the Oligopoly

To incorporate deception into the NES dynamics (5), in this paper we consider the following modified model-free NES algorithm:

Definition 1. *Player $i \in [N]$ is said to be deceptive towards a set of players $\mathcal{D}_i \subset [N] \setminus \{i\}$ if its actions are updated via the following rule:*

$$x_i(t) = u_i(t) + a_i \sin(\omega_i t) + \delta_i(t) \sum_{k \in \mathcal{D}_i} a_k \sin(\omega_k t) \tag{8a}$$

$$\dot{u}_i(t) = -\frac{2k_i}{a_i} J_i(x(t)) \sin(\omega_i t) \tag{8b}$$

where $\delta_i(t)$ is a tuning deceptive gain that satisfies $\sup_{t \geq 0} |\delta_i(t)| > 0$.

In addition to knowing the frequency ω_i, any player who wants to deceive player i must also know the amplitude a_i. While this seem more restrictive than the deception considered in [16], which only required knowledge of ω_i, it is in fact less restrictive since the NES strategy in [16] assumed $a_k = a$ for all $k \in [N]$.

In our setting, we assume there are n deceptive players, and the set of deceptive player is given by $\mathcal{D} = \{z_1, ..., z_n\}$. We say player $i \in \mathcal{D}$ is deceiving $n_i \in [N]$ players in $\mathcal{D}_i := \{d_{i,1}, ..., d_{i,n_i}\}$ if the parameter δ_i is updated according to:

$$\dot{\delta}_i = \varepsilon \varepsilon_i (J_i(x) - J_i^{\text{ref}}), \quad \varepsilon_i > 0, \quad i \in \mathcal{D}, \tag{9}$$

where J_i^{ref} is player i's desired reference cost. For non-deceptive players, we have that $\delta_i := 0$. The full model-free NES dynamics can thus be stated as follows for all players $i \in [N]$:

$$x_i = \begin{cases} u_i + a_i \sin(\omega_i t) + \delta_i \sum_{j \in \mathcal{D}_i} a_j \sin(\omega_j t) & \text{if } i \in \mathcal{D} \\ u_i + a_i \sin(\omega_i t) & \text{else} \end{cases} \tag{10a}$$

$$\dot{u}_i = -\frac{2k_i}{a_i} J_i(x) \sin(\omega_i t), \tag{10b}$$

Now that the overall game dynamics have been established, we will present our main results.

3   Main Results

3.1   Stability

Let $\mathcal{K}_j$ represent the set of players who are deceptive to player j, i.e. $\mathcal{K}_j = \{i \in \mathcal{D} : j \in \mathcal{D}_i\}$. Moreover, let $\delta = [\delta_{z_1}, ..., \delta_{z_n}]^\top$. We define $\overline{\mathcal{Q}}(\delta) \in \mathbb{R}^{N \times N}, \overline{\mathcal{B}}(\delta) \in \mathbb{R}^N$ with entries given by

$$[\overline{\mathcal{Q}}(\delta)]_{i:} = [\mathcal{Q}]_{i:} + \sum_{k \in \mathcal{K}_i} \delta_k [Q_i]_{k:} \tag{11a}$$

$$[\overline{\mathcal{B}}(\delta)]_i = [\mathcal{B}]_i + \sum_{k \in \mathcal{K}_i} \delta_k \frac{m_i R_\|}{R_i R_k}. \tag{11b}$$

These quantities essentially represent the "perturbed" pseudogradient that results from deception, which will become more intuitive when we obtain the averaged system in the stability proof. Before we proceed to the stability analysis, we define the *stability-preserving set*:

$$\Delta = \{\delta \in \mathbb{R}^n : -K\overline{\mathcal{Q}}(\delta) \text{ is Hurwitz}\} \tag{12}$$

where $K = \text{diag}([k_1, ..., k_N]^\top)$. We can then present our first result, which provides a somewhat useful "lower bound" on Δ:

Lemma 1. *If $|\delta| < 1$, then $\delta \in \Delta$.*

Proof. By (7a) we already know $[Q_i]_{kj} = 0$ for $k \in \mathcal{K}_i$ and $j \neq i$, thus for fixed i we have

$$\sum_{j \neq i}^{N} |[\overline{\mathcal{Q}}(\delta)]_{ij}| = \sum_{j \neq i}^{N} \frac{R_{\|}}{R_i R_j} = \frac{R_{\|}}{R_i \overline{R}_i}. \tag{13}$$

and

$$[\overline{\mathcal{Q}}(\delta)]_{ii} = [\mathcal{Q}]_{ii} + \sum_{k \in \mathcal{K}_i} \delta_k [Q_i]_{ki} \geq [\mathcal{Q}]_{ii} - |\delta| \frac{R_{\|}}{R_i \overline{R}_i} > \frac{R_{\|}}{R_i \overline{R}_i}. \tag{14}$$

The result then follows by the Gershgorin Circle Theorem. $\qquad\square$

This estimate is a significant improvement compared to the results of [16], which only guarantee that Δ contains a neighborhood of the origin. By exploiting the structure of the duopoly, we are now able to say that this neighborhood at least contains the unit ball. To characterize when the deceptive players are able to properly achieve their desired payoffs via deception, we introduce the notion of *attainability* as was presented in [16]:

Definition 2. *A vector* $J^{ref} = [J_{z_1}^{ref}, ..., J_{z_n}^{ref}]^\top$ *is said to be attainable if there exists* $\delta^* \in \Delta$ *such that:*

1. $J_{z_k}(-\overline{\mathcal{Q}}(\delta^*)^{-1}\overline{\mathcal{B}}(\delta^*)) = J_{z_k}^{ref}, \quad \forall\ k \in [n].$
2. *The matrix* $\Lambda(\delta^*) \in \mathbb{R}^{n \times n}$ *with* $[\Lambda(\delta^*)]_{jk} = \nabla_j \xi_k(\delta^*)$ *is Hurwitz, where* $\xi_k :$ $\mathbb{R}^n \to \mathbb{R}$ *is given by* $\xi_k(\delta) := \varepsilon_{z_k} J_{z_k}(-\overline{\mathcal{Q}}(\delta)^{-1}\overline{\mathcal{B}}(\delta)).$

We let $\Omega \subset \mathbb{R}^n$ *denote the set of all attainable vectors* $J^{ref} = [J_{z_1}^{ref}, ..., J_{z_n}^{ref}]^\top.$

With this definition at hand, we can now state the main result of this paper. The following theorem characterizes the stability properties of the NES dynamics with deception:

Theorem 1. *Consider the NES seeking dynamics (9) and (10) with* $J^{ref} \in \Omega$, J_i *of the form (2) and* ω_i *satisfying Assumption 1 for all* $i \in [N]$. *Then there exists* $\varepsilon^* > 0$ *such that for all* $\varepsilon \in (0, \varepsilon^*)$, *there exists* $a^* > 0$ *such that for* $a_1, ..., a_N \in (0, a^*)$ *there exists* $\omega^* > 0$ *such that for all* $\omega > \omega^*$ *the state* $\zeta(t) :=$ $[u(t) \quad \delta(t)]^\top$ *converges exponentially to a* $\mathcal{O}(\frac{1}{\omega} + \max_i a_i)$-*neighborhood of a point* $\zeta^* := [u^* \quad \delta^*]^\top$, *provided* $|\zeta(0) - \zeta^*|$ *is sufficiently small.*

Proof. To analyze the system, let $\mu(t) = x - u$, where x, u are given in (10). In other words, $\mu(t)$ is the vector of sinusoids. We apply the time scale transformation $\tau = \omega t$, and denote $\tilde{\mu}(\tau) = \mu(\tau/\omega)$ and $T = 2\pi \times \text{lcm}\{1/\overline{\omega}_1, 1/\overline{\omega}_2, ..., 1/\overline{\omega}_N\}$. With standard averaging theory [7], we can compute the average dynamics of

68   M. Tang et al.

system (10), whose state we denote as $\tilde{u} \in \mathbb{R}^N$:

$$\frac{\partial \tilde{u}_i}{\partial \tau} = \frac{1}{\omega T} \int_0^T -\frac{2k_i}{a_i} J_i(\tilde{u} + \tilde{\mu}(\tau)) \sin(\overline{\omega}_i \tau) d\tau$$

$$= -\frac{2k_i}{a_i \omega T} \int_0^T \left(J_i(\tilde{u}) + \tilde{\mu}(\tau)^\top \nabla J_i(\tilde{u}) + \frac{1}{2}\tilde{\mu}(\tau)^\top Q_i \tilde{\mu}(\tau) \right) \sin(\overline{\omega}_i \tau) d\tau \quad (15)$$

$$= -\frac{2k_i}{a_i \omega T} \int_0^T \sin(\overline{\omega}_i \tau) \tilde{\mu}(\tau)^\top (Q_i \tilde{u} + b_i) d\tau$$

$$= -\frac{k_i}{\omega} \left([Q_i]_{i:} \tilde{u} + [b_i]_i + \sum_{k \in \mathcal{K}_i} \tilde{\delta}_k ([Q_i]_{k:} \tilde{u} + [b_i]_k) \right). \quad (16)$$

By combining all u_i's, we obtain the average system

$$\frac{\partial \tilde{u}}{\partial \tau} = \frac{1}{\omega} \left(-K\overline{\mathcal{Q}}(\tilde{\delta})\tilde{u} - K\overline{\mathcal{B}}(\tilde{\delta}) \right). \quad (17)$$

We can apply the same technique on (10) for $i \in \mathcal{D}$:

$$\frac{\partial \tilde{\delta}_i}{\partial \tau} = \frac{\varepsilon}{\omega} \frac{1}{T} \int_0^T \varepsilon_i \left(J_i(\tilde{u}) - J_i^{\mathrm{ref}} + \tilde{\mu}(\tau)^\top \nabla J_i(\tilde{u}) + \frac{1}{2}\tilde{\mu}(\tau)^\top Q_i \tilde{\mu}(\tau) \right) d\tau \quad (18)$$

$$= \frac{\varepsilon}{\omega} \varepsilon_i \left(J_i(\tilde{u}) - J_i^{\mathrm{ref}} + \mathcal{P}_i([a_1, ..., a_N]^\top) \right), \quad i \in \mathcal{D}, \quad (19)$$

where $P_i : \mathbb{R}^N \to \mathbb{R}$ is a quadratic function satisfying $\mathcal{P}_i(a) = 0$, and can thus be treated as an $\mathcal{O}(a)$ perturbation on compact sets, where $a = [a_1, ..., a_N]^\top$. We recall that $\mathcal{D} = \{z_1, ..., z_n\}$. By setting $\tau^* = \varepsilon \tau$ and $J^*(\tilde{u}) = [J_{z_1}(\tilde{u}), ..., J_{z_n}(\tilde{u})]^\top$, the entire system can be represented as

$$\begin{bmatrix} \varepsilon \dfrac{\partial \tilde{u}}{\partial \tau^*} \\ \dfrac{\partial \tilde{\delta}}{\partial \tau^*} \end{bmatrix} = \frac{1}{\omega} \begin{bmatrix} -K\overline{\mathcal{Q}}(\tilde{\delta})\tilde{u} - K\overline{\mathcal{B}}(\tilde{\delta}) \\ \mathrm{diag}(\varepsilon_{z_1}, ..., \varepsilon_{z_n}) \left(J^*(\tilde{u}) - J^{\mathrm{ref}} \right) \end{bmatrix} + \mathcal{O}(a). \quad (20)$$

If we disregard the perturbation in (20), the resulting system is a singularly perturbed system with quasi steady state $h(\tilde{\delta}) = -\overline{\mathcal{Q}}(\tilde{\delta})^{-1}\overline{\mathcal{B}}(\tilde{\delta})$ and reduced dynamics given by

$$\frac{\partial \tilde{\delta}}{\partial \tau^*} = \frac{1}{\omega} \mathrm{diag}(\varepsilon_{z_1}, ..., \varepsilon_{z_n}) \left(J^*(-\overline{\mathcal{Q}}(\tilde{\delta})^{-1}\overline{\mathcal{B}}(\tilde{\delta})) - J^{\mathrm{ref}} \right). \quad (21)$$

Since $J^{\mathrm{ref}} \in \Omega$, it follows that (21) has an exponentially stable equilibrium point $\delta^* \in \Delta$. Moreover, by denoting $y = \tilde{u} - h(\tilde{\delta})$, we obtain the boundary layer system

$$\frac{\partial y}{\partial \tau} = -K\overline{\mathcal{Q}}(\tilde{\delta})y \quad (22)$$

where the origin is exponentially stable uniformly in any compact set contained in Δ. Hence the unperturbed system (20) has an exponentially stable equilibrium point $\zeta^* = [u^* \quad \delta^*]^\top$ where $u^* = -\overline{\mathcal{Q}}(\delta^*)^{-1}\overline{\mathcal{B}}(\delta^*)$. By standard robustness results for systems with small additive perturbations, we can find $a^* > 0$ such that for $\max_i a_i \in (0, a^*)$, $\tilde{\zeta}$ converges exponentially to a $\mathcal{O}(\max_i a_i)$ neighborhood of ζ^* provided $|\zeta(0) - \zeta^*|$ sufficiently small. Then, by standard averaging results for ODEs [7, Thm 10.4] we prove the claim for ω sufficiently large. $\quad\square$

Even though this proof is similar to that of the main result in [16], we include it here to account for the generalization of allowing distinct k_i and a_i. While this result is quite useful, one main concern is computing the set Ω. A relatively straightforward method for computing Ω when $|\mathcal{D}| = |\mathcal{D}_{z_1}| = 1$ is presented in [16], but in general it is a challenging problem. One promising approach is to use Lemma 1 to evaluate a "lower bound" for $J_i(-\mathcal{Q}(\delta)^{-1}\mathcal{B}(\delta))$ and then use numerical methods to approximate $\Lambda(\delta)$ for $|\delta| < 1$.

3.2   Intuition Behind Deception

In [16], it was shown that deception via (10) essentially transforms the duopoly into a deceptive game with deceptive costs that manipulate the victim's seeking dynamics into misinterpreting their sales function $s_i(x)$, so it is of interest to generalize this intuition to the N-player oligopoly. We first recall the definition of a *deceptive game* from [16]:

Definition 3. *Given a non-cooperative game $\{J_i\}_{i \in [N]}$, we say that $\{\tilde{J}_i\}_{i \in [N]}$ is a deceptive game if there exists a nonempty subset $\mathcal{D} \subset [N]$ such that for each $i \in \mathcal{D}$ there exists a function $\sigma_i : \mathbb{R}^{N-1} \to \mathbb{R}$, a nonempty set $\mathcal{K}_i \subset [N] \setminus \{i\}$ and scalars $\delta_k \neq 0 \;\; \forall k \in \mathcal{K}_i$, such that $\tilde{J}_i$ satisfies:*

$$\tilde{J}_i(x) = J_i(x) + \sigma_i(x_{-i}) + \sum_{k \in \mathcal{K}_i} \delta_k \int_0^{x_i} \nabla_k J_i(y, x_{-i}) dy, \qquad (23)$$

for all $x \in \mathbb{R}^N$. If $i \notin \mathcal{D}$, then $\tilde{J}_i(x) = J_i(x)$.

In other words, this definition captures the effect of deception by framing the emerging behavior of the system as a standard Nash equilibrium-seeking problem parameterized by costs $\{\tilde{J}_i\}_{i \in [N]}$. That is, the game with costs $\{J_i\}_{i \in [N]}$ under the deceptive NES dynamics (10) will exhibit the same asymptotic behavior as a standard non-cooperative game with costs $\{\tilde{J}_i\}_{i \in [N]}$ and players implementing the deception-free NES dynamics (5). We can then use (23) to compute a deceptive game for the oligopoly market scenario:

$$\tilde{J}_i(x) = J_i(x) + \sigma_i(x_{-i}) - \sum_{k \in \mathcal{K}_i} \delta_k \int_0^{x_i} \frac{R_{\|}}{R_i R_k}(y - m_i) dy \qquad (24)$$

$$= -s_i(x)(x_i - m_i) + \sigma_i(x_{-i}) - \sum_{k \in \mathcal{K}_i} \frac{\delta_k R_{\|} x_i}{2 R_i R_k}(x_i - 2m_i). \qquad (25)$$

If we set

$$\sigma_i(x_{-i}) := -\frac{R_{\|} m_i^2}{2 R_i} \sum_{k \in \mathcal{K}_i} \frac{\delta_k}{R_k} \qquad (26)$$

we finally obtain

$$\tilde{J}_i(x) = -\left(s_i(x) + \frac{R_\| x_i}{2R_i} \sum_{k\in\mathcal{K}_i} \frac{\delta_k}{R_k}\right)(x_i - m_i) + (x_i - m_i)\frac{R_\| m_i}{2R_i} \sum_{k\in\mathcal{K}_i} \frac{\delta_k}{R_k} \tag{27}$$

$$= -\left(s_i(x) + (x_i - m_i)\frac{R_\|}{2R_i} \sum_{k\in\mathcal{K}_i} \frac{\delta_k}{R_k}\right)(x_i - m_i). \tag{28}$$

When comparing (28) with (2), we can observe that player i now has a δ-inflated sales function, which is highly reminiscent of the duopoly analysis from [16]. If we reasonably assume that $x_i > m_i$, then $\frac{R_\|}{2R_i}\sum_{k\in\mathcal{K}_i}\frac{\delta_k}{R_k} > 0$ implies that player i's NES dynamics behave as if their sales are greater than they really are. This will result in player i increasing their price x_i to increase their payoff, even though in reality it might harm their profits. Similarly, if $\frac{R_\|}{2R_i}\sum_{k\in\mathcal{K}_i}\frac{\delta_k}{R_k} < 0$, player i's strategy will behave as if their sales are lower than their true value. This will result in player i decreasing their price x_i, which could potentially harm their profits.

Remark 1. *Another useful observation is the term $\frac{\delta_k}{R_k}$, which indicates that a firm with a more desirable product will wield more influence as a deceiver.*

Although the "deceptive game" view adds some intuition behind how deception affects the players' behavior, one of the main drawbacks is that the variability of σ_i may lead to conflicting interpretations. Hence, we present an alternate and somewhat consistent viewpoint that captures the effect of deception on player i's estimate of their gradient $\nabla_i J_i$. From (23) we have:

$$\nabla_i \tilde{J}_i(x) = \nabla_i J_i(x) + \sum_{k\in\mathcal{K}_i} \delta_k \nabla_k J_i(x)$$

$$= \left([Q_i]_{i:} + \sum_{k\in\mathcal{K}_i} \delta_k [Q_i]_{k:}\right)x + \left([b_i]_i + \sum_{k\in\mathcal{K}_i} \delta_k [b_i]_k\right)$$

$$= [\overline{\mathcal{Q}}(\delta)]_{i:}x + [\overline{\mathcal{B}}(\delta)]_i.$$

However, note that $[\overline{\mathcal{Q}}(\delta)]_{ij} = [Q_i]_{ij}$ for $i \neq j$, and we also have

$$[\overline{\mathcal{Q}}(\delta)]_{ii} = [Q_i]_{ii} + \sum_{k\in\mathcal{K}_i} \delta_k [Q_i]_{ki}$$

$$= \frac{2R_\|}{R_i\overline{R}_i} - \sum_{k\in\mathcal{K}_i} \delta_k \frac{R_\|}{R_i R_k}$$

$$= \frac{R_\|}{R_i}\left(\frac{2}{\overline{R}_i} - \sum_{k\in\mathcal{K}_i} \frac{\delta_k}{R_k}\right) \tag{29}$$

and

$$\left([b_i]_i + \sum_{k\in\mathcal{K}_i} \delta_k [b_i]_k\right) = -\frac{m_i R_{\parallel}}{R_i \overline{R}_i} - \frac{S_d R_{\parallel}}{R_i} + \sum_{k\in\mathcal{K}_i} \delta_k \frac{m_i R_{\parallel}}{R_i R_k}$$

$$= -\frac{m_i R_{\parallel}}{R_i}\left(\frac{1}{\overline{R}_i} - \sum_{k\in\mathcal{K}_i}\frac{\delta_k}{R_k}\right) - \frac{S_d R_{\parallel}}{R_i} \tag{30}$$

Both cases seem to indicate that when player i is being attacked, their NES dynamics "learn" that the total desirability of the other players' products is given by $\frac{1}{\overline{R}_i} - \sum_{k\in\mathcal{K}_i}\frac{\delta_k}{R_k}$ instead of $\frac{1}{\overline{R}_i}$.

This means that whenever $\sum_{k\in\mathcal{K}_i}\frac{\delta_k}{R_k} > 0$ holds, player i believes the other player's products to be less desirable than they really are, which would lead to player i increasing their price x_i. Similarly, when $\sum_{k\in\mathcal{K}_i}\frac{\delta_k}{R_k} < 0$, player i's NES dynamics will overestimate the desirability of the other players' products, leading to player i lowering their price. Alternatively, one can also make the following observation:

$$\frac{1}{\overline{R}_i} - \sum_{k\in\mathcal{K}_i}\frac{\delta_k}{R_k} = \sum_{j\notin\mathcal{K}_i\cup\{i\}}\frac{1}{R_j} + \sum_{k\in\mathcal{K}_i}\frac{1-\delta_k}{R_k} \tag{31}$$

which suggests something slightly more intricate. In particular, although (29) and (30) provide some insight into how the players in $\mathcal{K}_i$ collectively alter the beliefs of player i, equation (31) indicates the degree to which each deceptive player affects player i's estimate of the desirability of that deceptive player's product. Just as we have seen before, the term $\frac{1}{R_k}$ implies that the desirability of a firm's product can amplify their ability to deceive.

So far, we have observed that when firms in an oligopoly implement the deceptive NES strategy (10), the asymptotic behavior aligns with that of a game parameterized by costs $\{\tilde{J}_i\}_{i\in[N]}$ with firms implementing the deception-free NES dynamics (5), but it is also of interest to ask if the new "deceptive" equilibrium point is actually a Nash equilibrium of the deceptive game $\{\tilde{J}_i\}_{i\in[N]}$. The following result provides some sufficient conditions to answer this question. We present the proof for completeness:

Theorem 2. *Consider the $N-$player oligopoly with costs J_i of the form (2). Let $\delta \in \{\delta \in \mathbb{R}^n : 0 < |\delta| < 2 \text{ and } \overline{\mathcal{Q}}(\delta) \text{ is invertible}\}$ and let $\{\tilde{J}_i\}_{i\in[N]}$ be a corresponding deceptive game. Then, the point $u^* = -\overline{\mathcal{Q}}(\delta)^{-1}\overline{\mathcal{B}}(\delta)$ is a Nash equilibrium of the deceptive game $\{\tilde{J}_i\}_{i\in[N]}$.*

Proof. Since the pseudogradient of the deceptive game satisfies $\mathcal{G}(x) = \overline{\mathcal{Q}}(\delta)x + \overline{\mathcal{B}}(\delta)$, it is easy to verify that if $\overline{\mathcal{Q}}(\delta)$ is invertible, the first order condition [1] for u^* to be a Nash equilibrium is satisfied. We also have

$$[\overline{\mathcal{Q}}(\delta)]_{ii} = [\mathcal{Q}]_{ii} + \sum_{k\in\mathcal{K}_i}\delta_k[Q_i]_{ki} \geq [\mathcal{Q}]_{ii} - |\delta|\frac{R_{\parallel}}{R_i\overline{R}_i} > 0, \tag{32}$$

since $|\delta| < 2$. Thus, the second order condition [1] is satisfied, which implies u^* is a Nash equilibrium of the deceptive game $\{\tilde{J}_i\}_{i\in[N]}$. $\qquad\square$

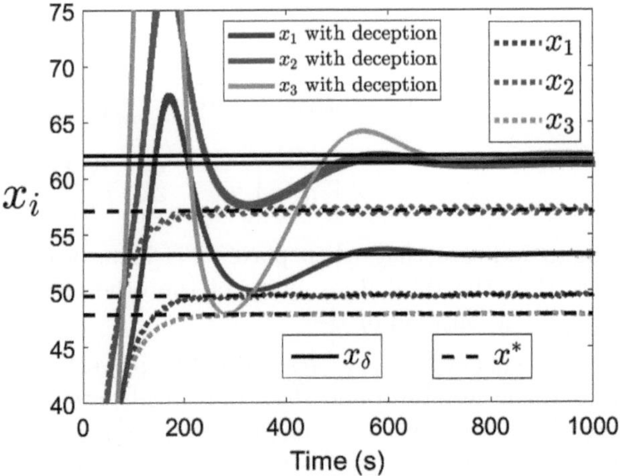

Fig. 2. The price convergence for a three player oligopoly, where we use x^* and x_δ to denote the true Nash equilibrium and the deceptive Nash equilibrium, respectively.

4 Numerical Results

To further illustrate our theoretical results, we present a three-firm oligopoly example with parameters $R_1 = 0.67$, $R_2 = 0.36$, $R_3 = 0.8, m_1 = 20$, $m_2 = 29$, $m_3 = 30$ and $S_d = 100$. It is simple to check that this game has Nash equilibrium $x_0 = [49.55, 57.13, 47.9]^\top$ and steady state costs $J_1(x_0) = -950.7, J_2(x_0) = -1092$, and $J_3(x_0) = -239.2$. For the NES dynamics, the players use $a_1 = 0.04, k_1 = 0.02, \omega_1 = 6346, a_2 = 0.03, k_2 = 0.019, \omega_2 = 4089, a_3 = 0.05$, $k_3 = 0.22$, and $\omega_3 = 6115$. Now we let player 1 be deceptive to player 3, where player 1 tunes δ_1 according to (9) with $\varepsilon = 10^{-4}$, $\varepsilon_1 = 1$ and $J_1^{\text{ref}} = -1200$ (recall that for our algorithm, we treat J_i as a *cost* to be *minimized*). Moreover, we have

$$\overline{Q}(\delta) = \begin{bmatrix} 2.18 & -0.75 & -0.34 \\ -0.75 & 2.76 & -0.63 \\ -0.34 & -0.63 & 2.18 \end{bmatrix} - \delta \begin{bmatrix} 0 & 0 & 0 \\ 0 & 0 & 0 \\ 0 & 0 & 0.34 \end{bmatrix} \tag{33a}$$

$$\overline{B}(\delta) = \begin{bmatrix} -48.82 \\ -90.34 \\ -51.65 \end{bmatrix} + \delta \begin{bmatrix} 0 \\ 0 \\ 10.14 \end{bmatrix} \tag{33b}$$

By numerically solving $J_1(-\overline{Q}(\delta^*)^{-1}\overline{B}(\delta^*)) = J_1^{\text{ref}}$ we obtain $\delta^* = 2.486 \in \Delta$. Moreover, we have $\frac{\partial}{\partial \delta}J_1(-\overline{Q}(\delta)^{-1}\overline{B}(\delta))|_{\delta=\delta^*} = -190 < 0$, so $J_1^{\text{ref}} \in \Omega$. For a more intuitive illustration, we will only plot the *profits* $P_i = -J_i$. As we see in the plots, player 1 is able to force the dynamics to converge to a neighborhood of a point x_δ that achieves $J_1(x_\delta) = J_1^{\text{ref}}$. Moreover, we notice that the deception mechanism causes player 3 to increase their price x_3 significantly, which is consistent with our observations from (28), (29) and (30) since $\delta_1^* > 0$.

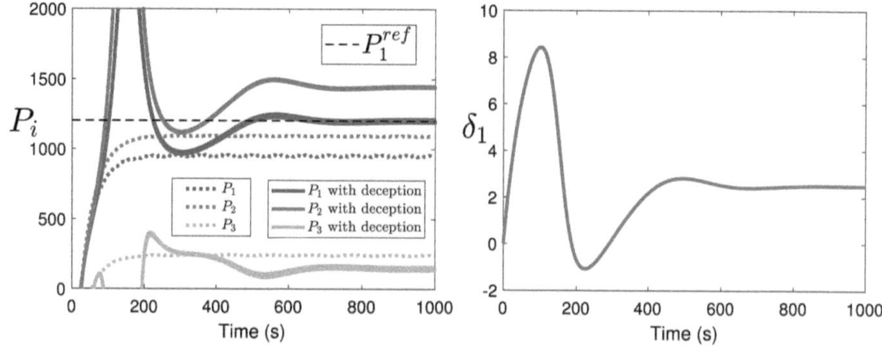

Fig. 3. Left: The profit convergence for a three player oligopoly, where $P_i = -J_i$ and $P_1^{\mathrm{ref}} = -J_1^{\mathrm{ref}}$. Right: The corresponding trajectories of δ_1 when player 1 deceives player 3.

5   Conclusion

In this work, we performed a comprehensive study that applied the deception mechanism from [16] to an N-player *oligopoly market*. By leveraging the structure of the basic two-market duopoly, we establish stability for our proposed deception mechanism in which N players have different gains and exploration amplitudes for their NES dynamics. Moreover, the diagonal dominance property of the duopoly game allows us to derive an improved estimate on the "stability-preserving set" and quantify when the deceptive Nash equilibrium is actually a NE for the corresponding oligopoly class of deceptive games. It was also shown that the deception mechanism can be economically interpreted as an artificial inflation (or deflation) of the desirability of the deceivers' product learned by the victim. Future research directions will characterize how the structure of the interaction graph between players (encoded on how the cost function J_i depends on the actions of the other players) affects the emerging deceptive Nash equilibrium and its stability properties. It is also of interest to study stochastic and hybrid (involving continuous-time and discrete-time dynamics) deception mechanisms.

References

1. Başar, T., Olsder, G.J.: Dynamic Noncooperative Game Theory. SIAM (1998)
2. Belgioioso, G., Grammatico, S.: Semi-decentralized Nash equilibrium seeking in aggregative games with separable coupling constraints and non-differentiable cost functions. IEEE Control Syst. Lett. **1**(2), 400–405 (2017)
3. Davis, A.: Deception in game theory: a survey and multiobjective model. Air Force Institute of Technology Scholar, Theses and Dissertations (2016)
4. Dragan, A., Holladay, R., Srinivasa, S.: Deceptive robot motion: synthesis, analysis and experiments. Auton. Rob. **39**(3), 331–345 (2015). https://doi.org/10.1007/s10514-015-9458-8

5. Frihauf, P., Krstic, M., Basar, T.: Nash equilibrium seeking in noncooperative games. IEEE Trans. Autom. Control **57**(5), 1192–1207 (2012). https://doi.org/10.1109/TAC.2011.2173412

6. Ho, E., Rajagopalan, A., Skvortsov, A., Arulampalam, S., Piraveenan, M.: Game theory in defence applications: a review. Sensors **22**(3), 1032 (2022)

7. Khalil, H.K.: Nonlinear System. Prentice Hall, Upper Saddle River, NJ (2002)

8. Kouzehgar, M., Badamchizadeh, M.A.: Fuzzy signaling game of deception between ant-inspired deceptive robots with interactive learning. Appl. Soft Comput. **75**, 373–387 (2019)

9. Liu, S.J., Krstić, M.: Stochastic Nash equilibrium seeking for games with general nonlinear payoffs. SIAM J. Control. Optim. **49**(4), 1659–1679 (2011). https://doi.org/10.1137/100811738. https://doi.org/10.1137/100811738

10. Mitchell, R.W., Thompson, N.S., et al.: Deception: Perspectives on Human and Nonhuman Deceit. SUNY Press (1986)

11. Nash, J.: Non-cooperative games. Ann. Math.**54**(2), 286–295 (1951). http://www.jstor.org/stable/1969529

12. Oliveira, T.R., Rodrigues, V.H.P., Krstić, M., Başar, T.: Nash equilibrium seeking in quadratic noncooperative games under two delayed information-sharing schemes. J. Optim. Theor. Appl. **191**(2), 700–735 (2021)

13. Poveda, J.I., KrstiÄ, M., BaÅar, T.: Fixed-time Nash equilibrium seeking in time-varying networks. IEEE Trans. Autom. Control **68**(4), 1954–1969 (2023). https://doi.org/10.1109/TAC.2022.3168527

14. Santos, E., Li, D.: On deception detection in multiagent systems. IEEE Trans. Syst. Man Cybern. Part A Syst. Hum. **40**(2), 224–235 (2010). https://doi.org/10.1109/TSMCA.2009.2034862

15. Smith, E.O.: Deception and evolutionary biology. Cult. Anthropol. **2**(1), 50–64 (1987)

16. Tang, M., Javed, U., Chen, X., Krstic, M., Poveda, J.I.: Deception in Nash equilibrium seeking (2024). https://arxiv.org/abs/2407.05168

17. Wagner, A.R., Arkin, R.C.: Acting deceptively: providing robots with the capacity for deception. Int. J. Soc. Robot. **3**, 5–26 (2011)

18. Wang, X.F., Sun, X.M., Teel, A.R., Liu, K.Z.: Distributed robust Nash equilibrium seeking for aggregative games under persistent attacks: a hybrid systems approach. Automatica **122**, 109255 (2020)

19. Xu, W., Wang, Z., Hu, G., Kurths, J.: Hybrid Nash equilibrium seeking under partial-decision information: an adaptive dynamic event-triggered approach. IEEE Trans. Autom. Control **68**(10), 5862–5876 (2023). https://doi.org/10.1109/TAC.2022.3226142

20. Ye, M., Han, Q.L., Ding, L., Xu, S.: Distributed Nash equilibrium seeking in games with partial decision information: a survey. Proc. IEEE **111**(2), 140–157 (2023)

21. Ye, M., Hu, G.: Distributed Nash equilibrium seeking by a consensus based approach. IEEE Trans. Autom. Control **62**(9), 4811–4818 (2017)

22. Yi, P., Pavel, L.: An operator splitting approach for distributed generalized Nash equilibria computation. Automatica **102**, 111–121 (2019). https://doi.org/10.1016/j.automatica.2019.01.008. https://www.sciencedirect.com/science/article/pii/S0005109819300081

23. Young, H.P.: Strategic Learning and Its Limits. OUP Oxford (2004)

24. Zou, S., Lygeros, J.: Semidecentralized zeroth-order algorithms for stochastic generalized Nash equilibrium seeking. IEEE Trans. Autom. Control **68**(2), 1237–1244 (2022)

Mechanisms and Games

Effects of Emotion—Strategy Persistence Mechanism on the Dynamic Evolution of Cooperation

Xin Ge[1]($\boxtimes$), Jian Yang[1], and Lili Li[2]

[1] College of Information Science and Technology, Dalian Maritime University,
Dalian 116026, China
`ge_xin@dlmu.edu.cn`
[2] College of Marine Electrical Engineering, Dalian Maritime University,
Dalian 116026, China

Abstract. In real society, interactions between individuals are accompanied by emotional changes, which in turn affect their decisions. This paper proposes an emotion-strategy persistence mechanism that represents individuals' value orientations through changes in emotions. Intelligent agents are classified into selfish, competitive individuals and mutually beneficial, non-competitive individuals. A positive-negative emotion threshold is introduced to define the emotional states of intelligent agents. A positive emotional state indicates that the intelligent agent is relatively satisfied with the current strategy, leading to persistence in maintaining it. Conversely, the agent is more inclined to change its current strategy. In addition, this paper introduces the concept of emotional sensitivity to measure the amplitude of emotional fluctuations in intelligent agents and introduces strategy duration sensitivity to measure the willingness of intelligent agents to change their current strategy. Extensive simulation experiments show that non-competitive individuals play a decisive role in promoting and emerging cooperative behavior within the group. When the positive-negative emotion threshold is higher and the emotional sensitivity is greater, the level of group cooperation is higher. However, the impact of strategy duration sensitivity on the group cooperation rate exhibits a non-monotonic trend, with an optimal strategy duration sensitivity that maximizes the level of group cooperation.

Keywords: Emotion · strategy persistence time · cooperation rate · Prisoner's dilemma game

1 Introduction

Understanding the persistent and large-scale cooperation among unrelated intelligent individuals is one of the greatest challenges faced by scholars in mathematics and natural sciences in the 21st century. Among the numerous theories and methods, evolutionary game theory [1–3] provides a powerful framework for studying the emergence and maintenance of cooperation among selfish individuals. The conflict between individual selfishness and the maximization of group

V. Aggarwal et al. (Eds.): GameNets 2025, LNICST 657, pp. 77–90, 2026.
https://doi.org/10.1007/978-3-032-12915-4_5

benefits is metaphorically represented by a series of classic game models such as the Prisoner's Dilemma Game [4], the Snowdrift Game [5], and Public Goods Games [6,7]. Building on this foundation, Nowak first proposed the "Five Rules for the Evolution of Cooperation," which include direct reciprocity [8], indirect reciprocity [9], spatial reciprocity [10], group selection [11], and kin selection [12]. Indirect reciprocity refers to the influence of an individual's behavior by the observation and judgment of other members within the population. Prosocial cooperative behavior exhibited by an individual can lead to more cooperation and assistance in the future. Based on this fundamental theory, early researchers proposed a series of mechanisms to promote the emergence of cooperative behavior, such as reputation [13,14], punishment [15,16], incentives [17], conformity [18], learning ability [19], and migration [20].

In recent years, the intrinsic emotions of intelligent agents have emerged as a new dimension for promoting cooperative behavior, gaining favor among researchers in related fields. The pioneering work on emotions in the field of evolutionary game theory was conducted by Attila Szolnoki [21,22] et al., who first proposed quantifying individual value orientations through changes in emotional states. Emotional states depend not only on payoff indicators but also on the heterogeneity of interaction networks, which significantly reduces levels of goodwill-envy. Their research discovered that replacing strategy imitation with emotional state imitation can promote and sustain cooperative behavior within groups. Y. Chao [23] et al. proposed a dual-layer emotional multi-agent reinforcement learning framework, which endows intelligent agents with internal cognitive and emotional capabilities to drive their learning of cooperative behavior. Their research found that emotional evaluation methods, network topologies, and the heterogeneity of intelligent agents significantly impact the learning behavior of these individuals, and that higher levels of cooperation can be achieved in specific environments. Wei Chen [24] et al. viewed emotions as locally accumulative. They used emotions to represent the satisfaction level of intelligent agents with their current strategies. Their research found that non-competitive individuals play a decisive role in promoting the emergence of cooperative behavior. There is an optimal emotional accumulation length that maximizes group cooperation levels. The phenomenon of emotions influencing agent decision-making is already widespread in real society. J.T. Cacioppo [25] et al. believe that the higher dimension of human thinking—rationality—can be awakened by emotions.

To date, in most existing studies exploring the cooperation dilemma among rational individuals based on emotions, the influence of emotions on agent decision-making is direct. That is, agents immediately seek to change their decision-making behavior under emotional stimuli, overly emphasizing the impact of instant emotions on decisions and assuming that the emotional changes are constant across different environments. However, this approach is not particularly realistic. Firstly, emotions are continuous and dynamic, accumulating over time. The emotional state of intelligent agents in social interactions is determined by both their past experiences and current circumstances. Global cumulative emotions can more comprehensively and accurately reflect agent emotional fluctuations and stability over a complete period. Secondly, changing decisions based solely on instant emotions is reckless and irrational, leading to frequent and repeated decision changes. The influence of emotions on decision-making generally occurs by altering satisfaction with the current strategy, thereby affecting the persistence of that strategy. Additionally, the intensity of an agent's emotional response is influenced by both intrinsic traits and changes in the external environment. For example, under stress, people tend to be more sensitive to negative events, whereas in a relaxed and joyful atmosphere, emotional fluctuations in response to similar events may be milder. A constant emotional change magnitude cannot capture the differences in emotional fluctuations in such varied situations.

Based on the above, This paper creatively proposes an emotion-strategy persistence mechanism that represents individuals' value orientations through changes in emotions. Intelligent agents are classified into selfish, competitive individuals and mutually beneficial, non-competitive individuals. For the first time, a positive-negative emotion threshold is introduced to define the emotional states of intelligent agents. When an agent's emotional state is positive and its average payoff is not less than the average payoff of its first-order neighbors, it indicates satisfaction with the current strategy, leading to persistence in the current strategy. Conversely, when the emotional state is negative or the average payoff is less than that of its neighbors, the agent is more inclined to change its current strategy. In addition, this paper creatively introduces the concept of emotional sensitivity to measure the amplitude of emotional fluctuations in intelligent agents and introduces strategy duration sensitivity to measure the willingness of intelligent agents to change their current strategy.

The remainder of this paper is organized as follows: First, the prisoner's dilemma game model based on the emotion-strategy persistence mechanism is elaborated in detail, and the forms in which emotions affect the strategy persistence and updating of intelligent agents are thoroughly discussed. Following this, the third section provides a detailed explanation of the extensive simulation experiments based on the emotion-strategy persistence mechanism. The final section summarizes and reviews the experimental conclusions, identifies the key characteristics that promote the emergence of cooperative behavior under the current model, and mentions possible future research directions.

2 Model

In this section, we first introduce the prisoner's dilemma game model based on the emotion-strategy persistence mechanism. Specifically, this experimental model is established on a two-dimensional lattice network of size $L \times L = 100^2$, following the von-Neumann neighborhood structure. The intelligent agents correspond one-to-one with the nodes in the network. Initially, each intelligent agent x randomly adopts either a cooperation strategy $(S_x = C)$ or a defection strategy $(S_x = D)$ with equal probability. This study uses the Monte-Carlo iteration method to simulate the evolution of cooperative behavior within the group. Each Monte-Carlo step comprises the payoff update phase, emotion update phase, strategy duration update phase, and strategy update phase. After a sufficient number of Monte-Carlo iterations, the system reaches a steady state.

To streamline the experimental process, this study utilizes the degenerate prisoner's dilemma game as the foundational experimental model. The payoff matrix for this model is as follows,

$$M = \begin{bmatrix} 1 & 0 \\ b & 0 \end{bmatrix} \tag{1}$$

The parameter b ranges from 1 to 2, ensuring a conflict between individual and group interests. During the payoff update phase, within any Monte-Carlo time step, each agent x interacts with all its k_x nearest neighbors and obtains their respective payoffs based on the game's payoff matrix. The two-dimensional vector $S_x(t_{MCS}) = (1,0)^T$ represents that the strategy of agent x at t_{MCS} is cooperation, while $S_x(t_{MCS}) = (0,1)^T$ represents that the strategy of agent x at t_{MCS} is defection. Therefore, the equation for the average game payoff $\overline{P_x}(t_{MCS})$ of agent x during one Monte-Carlo iteration is:

$$\overline{P_x}(t_{MCS}) = \frac{\sum_{y \in \Omega_x} S_x(t_{MCS}) M S_y(t_{MCS})^T}{k_x} \tag{2}$$

Here, Ω_x represents the set of nearest neighbors of agent x, and k_x denotes the size of the neighbor set, i.e., the number of neighbors. The equation for the average payoff $\overline{P_{\Omega_x}}(t_{MCS})$ obtained by the nearest neighbors of agent x within t_{MCS} iterations is as follows:

$$\overline{P_{\Omega_x}}(t_{MCS}) = \frac{\sum_{y \in \Omega_x} \sum_{u \in \Omega_y} S_y(t_{MCS}) M S_u(t_{MCS})^T}{k_x k_y} \tag{3}$$

During the emotion update phase, we divide the agents in the group into non-competitive propensity individuals ($NCPI$) and competitive propensity individuals (CPI). The distinction between competitive and non-competitive propensity individuals lies in their value orientations. Competitive propensity individuals are self-interested, always aiming to maximize their own benefits with little or no regard for others' benefits. In contrast, non-competitive propensity individuals not only consider their own benefits but are also more inclined to maximize collective benefits. Initially, each intelligent agent x has a probability ρ of becoming an $NCPI$ and a probability of $1 - \rho$ of becoming a CPI, with this status remaining unchanged throughout subsequent Monte-Carlo iterations.

The emotional mechanism can quantify the value orientation of intelligent agents. During interactions, when the intelligent agent is an $NCPI$, they will feel joy when both parties cooperate, regretful when they exploit the other party as a defector, angry when they are unilaterally betrayed, and show no significant emotional fluctuation when both parties defect. Conversely, when the intelligent agent is a CPI, they will feel regretful during cooperation, regretting not exploiting the other party for personal gain, joy when they successfully exploit the other party, angry when they are unilaterally betrayed, and similarly show no significant emotional fluctuation when both parties defect. The emotional patterns of $NCPI$ and CPI are illustrated in the table below:

Table 1. Emotional Patterns of Intelligent Agents.

	$C_{me} - C_{opponent}$	$C_{me} - D_{opponent}$	$D_{me} - C_{opponent}$	$D_{me} - D_{opponent}$
$NCPI$	Joy	$Anger$	$Regret$	$Neutral$
CPI	$Anger$	Joy	$Regret$	$Neutral$

We have innovatively proposed the concept of emotional sensitivity to measure the amplitude of emotional fluctuations in intelligent agents, denoted as ϑ. A greater emotional sensitivity indicates larger emotional fluctuations, greater influence from external factors, and less emotional stability. When an intelligent agent is in a joyful emotional state, their emotional value increases by the emotional sensitivity ϑ. Conversely, when the intelligent agent is in a state of regret or anger, their emotional value decreases by ϑ. When the intelligent agent is in a neutral emotional state, their emotional value remains unchanged. Therefore, the equation for emotional dynamic changes is given by:

$$\Delta E_{x,t_{MCS}} = \begin{cases} \vartheta, Joy \\ -\vartheta, Regret/Anger \\ 0, Neutral \end{cases} \tag{4}$$

Here, $\Delta E_{x,t_{MCS}}$ represents the change in the emotion of agent x over t_{MCS} iterations. The emotion $E_{x,t_{MCS}}$ of agent x at t_{MCS} results from the accumulation of previous stages, with a value range of $[0, E_{max}]$. The global cumulative emotion equation is given by,

$$E_{x,t_{MCS}} = \begin{cases} 0 & , & E_{x,0} + \sum_{m=0}^{t_{MCS}} \sum_{y \in \Omega_x} \Delta E_{x,m} < 0 \\ E_{x,0} + \sum_{m=0}^{t_{MCS}} \sum_{y \in \Omega_x} \Delta E_{x,m}, & 0 \leq E_{x,0} + \sum_{m=0}^{t_{MCS}} \sum_{y \in \Omega_x} \Delta E_{x,m} \leq E_{max} \\ E_{max} & , & E_{x,0} + \sum_{m=0}^{t_{MCS}} \sum_{y \in \Omega_x} \Delta E_{x,m} > E_{max} \end{cases} \tag{5}$$

Here, $E_{x,0}$ represents the initial emotional value of agent x. To align with the emotional heterogeneity among different individuals in real society, the initial emotion of each agent is set using a uniform distribution, i.e., $E_{x,0} \sim U(0, E_{max})$, with the upper limit of the emotion, set to 30.

To define the quality of the emotion of intelligent agent x, we set a threshold value E_{th} for distinguishing between positive and negative emotions. When the emotion $E_{x,t_{MCS}}$ of agent x at t_{MCS} is greater than or equal to this threshold value E_{th}, i.e., $E_{x,t_{MCS}} \geq E_{th}$, their emotional state is considered positive. Conversely, when $E_{x,t_{MCS}} < E_{th}$, their emotional state is considered negative. Due to the heterogeneity in emotional expectations among different individuals in real society, which means different individuals have varying criteria for defining positive and negative emotions, we consider fitting this using a normal distribution. Therefore, the threshold value $E_{x,th}$ for positive and negative emotions for individual x in the group follows a normal distribution with a mean of E_{th} and a standard deviation σ, i.e., $E_{x,th} \sim N(E_{th}, \sigma^2)$. In order to ensure that the vast majority of the random variable $E_{x,th}$'s values fall within $[0, E_{max}]$, based on the 3σ rule of the normal distribution, $[E_{th} - 3\sigma, E_{th} + 3\sigma]$ must be contained within $[0, E_{max}]$. From this, the formula for σ can be derived as follows,

$$\sigma = \begin{cases} \dfrac{E_{th}}{3}, & 0 \leq E_{th} \leq \dfrac{E_{max}}{2} \\ \dfrac{E_{max} - E_{th}}{3}, & \dfrac{E_{max}}{2} < E_{th} \leq E_{max} \end{cases} \tag{6}$$

In the strategy duration update phase, we introduce the concept of individual strategy persistence time $\tau_x(t_{MCS})$ in our research. This measures the preference of intelligent agent x for their current strategy at t_{MCS}, with a range of $[0, \tau_{max}]$, where τ_{max} is set to 30. The change in $\tau_x(t_{MCS})$ reflects the dynamic adjustment of agent x's preference for their current strategy at t_{MCS}. After each round of Monte-Carlo iteration, the persistence time for agent x's current strategy decreases accordingly. This decrement is independent of their attitude towards the current strategy. The decreasing equation for $\tau_x(t_{MCS})$ can be given as,

$$\tau_x(t_{MCS}) = \begin{cases} 15, & t_{MCS} = 0 \\ max\{0, \tau_x(t_{MCS} - 1) - 1\}, & t_{MCS} > 0 \end{cases} \tag{7}$$

Intelligent agent x will only execute a strategy update when $\tau_x(t_{MCS})$ decreases to 0. Once a strategy update is completed, the strategy persistence time for the next Monte-Carlo iteration will be reset to its initial value, i.e., $\tau_x(t_{MCS} + 1) = 15$.

Furthermore, the emotional state of intelligent agent x at will also affect their strategy persistence time. Specifically, when the emotional state of the intelligent agent is positive, it indicates satisfaction with the current strategy, leading to a greater adherence to the current strategy. Conversely, if the emotional state is negative, the agent is more inclined to switch to a different strategy. Additionally, the relationship between the average payoff $\overline{P_x}(t_{MCS})$ of agent x at t_{MCS} and the average payoff $\overline{P_{\Omega_x}}(t_{MCS})$ obtained by its nearest neighbor set during the iterations will also impact the strategy persistence time. Specifically, when the average payoff $\overline{P_x}(t_{MCS})$ of agent x at t_{MCS} is not less than the average payoff $\overline{P_{\Omega_x}}(t_{MCS})$ obtained by its nearest neighbor set during the iterations, the agent is more satisfied with the current strategy, leading to a greater adherence to the current strategy. Conversely, the agent is more inclined to switch strategies.

Considering the above factors, the iterative equation for $\tau_x(t_{MCS})$ can be written as follows:

$$\tau_x(t_{MCS}) = \begin{cases} min\,\{\tau_x(t_{MCS}) + \Delta\tau, \tau_{max}\}, emotional\ state_x(t_{MCS}) \to positive \\ \qquad\qquad\qquad\qquad \cap\ \overline{P_x}(t_{MCS}) \geq \overline{P_{\Omega_x}}(t_{MCS}) \\ max\,\{0, \tau_x(t_{MCS}) - \Delta\tau\}, \qquad\qquad\qquad\quad other \end{cases}$$

$$(8)$$

Here, $\Delta\tau$ represents the strategy persistence sensitivity, which reflects the willingness of the intelligent agent to change their current strategy.

In the strategy update phase, when the strategy persistence time $\tau_x(t_{MCS})$ of intelligent agent x decreases to 0, a strategy update is executed accordingly. Intelligent agent x will randomly select a neighbor node y from its nearest neighbor set Ω_x and imitate its strategy S_y based on the probability determined by the Fermi rule. The Fermi equation is as follows:

$$W_{(S_x \leftarrow S_y)}(t_{MCS}) = \frac{1}{1 + \exp\left\{ \left[\overline{P_x}(t_{MCS}) - \overline{P_y}(t_{MCS}) \right] / k \right\}} \qquad (9)$$

Here, $\overline{P_x}(t_{MCS})$ and $\overline{P_y}(t_{MCS})$ represent the average payoffs of intelligent agents x and y at t_{MCS}, respectively. The parameter k denotes the influence of the noise factor, representing the uncertainty during the strategy imitation phase. A smaller k indicates that the intelligent agent has a stronger ability to make rational decisions in a noisy environment, while a larger k suggests a tendency towards random strategy selection. In this study, k is set to 0.1.

This study employs the Monte-Carlo iteration method to simulate the evolution of cooperative behavior within a group, approximating the complex interaction dynamics of real society through a large number of randomly sampled simulations. To ensure the group evolves to a final steady state, global iterative evolution is typically executed up to 3×10^4 steps, and the average cooperation rate over the last 1×10^3 steps is taken as the group's steady-state cooperation rate. To eliminate random uncertainties in the experimental results, 10 independent repeated experiments are usually conducted under the same parameter conditions. By averaging the results of these independent experiments, the randomness error can be effectively reduced, enhancing the robustness and credibility of the experimental results. Additionally, the same experimental results can be reproduced in other network topologies, such as ER random networks and SF scale-free networks.

3 Results and Discussion

In this section, we will employ the Monte-Carlo iteration method to simulate the evolution of cooperative behavior within a group, approximating the complex interaction dynamics of real society through a large number of randomly sampled simulations, we will focus on exploring the impact of different proportions of non-competitive individuals ρ, the intensity of social dilemmas–"temptation to

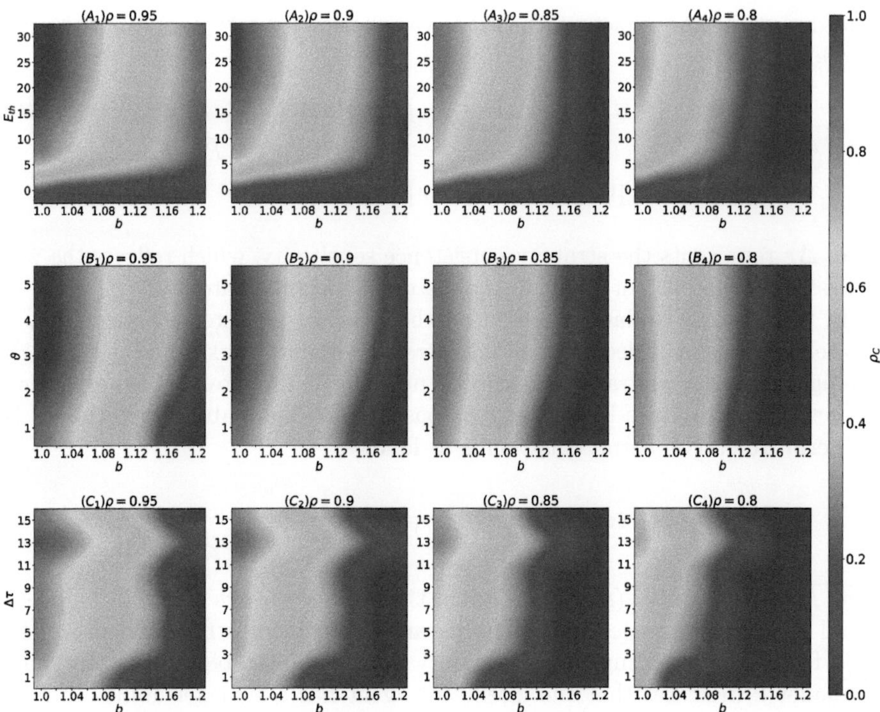

Fig. 1. Heatmaps of the evolution of group cooperation rate ρ_C under different proportions of non-competitive individuals ρ, varying with the positive-negative emotional threshold E_{th}, different emotional sensitivities ϑ, different strategy duration sensitivities $\Delta\tau$ and the "temptation to defect" b. In subfigures (A_1)–(A_4), $\vartheta = 5$, $\Delta\tau = 13$. In subfigures (B_1)–(B_4), $E_{th} = 25$, $\Delta\tau = 13$. In subfigures (C_1)–(C_4), $E_{th} = 25$, $\vartheta = 5$. Respectively, in subfigures (A_1)–(C_1), (A_2)–(C_2), (A_3)–(C_3), (A_4)–(C_4), the proportion ρ of non-competitive individuals is 0.95, 0.9, 0.85, and 0.8.

defect" b, positive-negative emotional threshold E_{th}, emotional sensitivity ϑ, and strategy duration sensitivity $\Delta\tau$ on the evolution of group cooperation.

Figure 1(A_1)–(A_4) shows the evolution of group cooperation rates as E_{th} and b vary. It can be observed that with the increase in b, the group cooperation rate exhibits a monotonically decreasing trend. Particularly in severe social dilemmas ($\rho = 0.9 \cap b > 1.2$, $\rho = 0.85 \cap b > 1.16$, $\rho = 0.8 \cap b > 1.14$), cooperators are driven to extinction under the intense exploitation by defectors. This indicates that the greater the social dilemma, the more difficult it is for cooperative behavior to emerge and be sustained. Conversely, as E_{th} increases, the group cooperation rate shows a significant monotonically increasing trend. This phenomenon is discussed as follows: non-competitive propensity individuals ($NCPI$) play a decisive role in the promotion and emergence of cooperative behavior within the group. An increase in E_{th} means that the threshold for intelligent agents to achieve a positive emotional state is raised. According to

Table 1, when E_{th} is relatively high, $NCPI$ must consistently adhere to cooperative strategies to maintain their current positive emotional state. The positive emotional state, along with higher returns, in turn, leads to further persistence in maintaining the cooperative strategy by $NCPI$, forming a positive feedback loop that significantly promotes cooperative behavior.

In particular, when E_{th} approaches 0, cooperators will ultimately go extinct regardless of the level of social dilemma. This is because, for any node x, $E_{x,t_{MCS}} \geq E_{x,th}$ always holds true, meaning that the persistence of the current strategy entirely depends on the payoff difference. Due to the fact that cooperative and defecting strategies follow an equal probability uniform distribution initially, without loss of generality, when the central node x is a cooperator, its average payoff per round is $\overline{P_x}(t_{MCS}) = \frac{1}{2}$. When the central node y is a defector, its average payoff per round is $\overline{P_y}(t_{MCS}) = \frac{b}{2}$, while the average payoff of the nodes in the first-order neighborhood set is $\overline{P_{\Omega_x}}(t_{MCS}) = \frac{1+b}{4}$. Since $1 < b < 2$, it is easy to see that $\overline{P_x}(t_{MCS}) < \overline{P_{\Omega_x}}(t_{MCS}) < \overline{P_y}(t_{MCS})$. According to Eq. 8, $\tau_x(t_{MCS})$ continuously decreases while $\tau_y(t_{MCS})$ gradually increases, making it difficult for the cooperative strategy to be sustained and causing it to continually shift to the defecting strategy, leading to extinction.

Comparing Fig. 1 subfigures (A_1), (B_1), (C_1), and (D_1), it can be observed that as ρ decreases, ρ_C significantly declines under the same social dilemma conditions. When $b = 1.06$ and $E_{th} = 25$, ρ_C increases by more than 25% when $\rho = 0.95$ compared to $\rho = 0.8$. When $b = 1.14$ and $E_{th} = 25$, ρ_C increases by more than 45% when $\rho = 0.95$ compared to $\rho = 0.8$. This is because the decrease in ρ leads to an increase in the proportion of competitive propensity individuals (CPI). CPI primarily adopt defection and exploitation of opponents as their core strategy, making cooperation nearly impossible within the CPI subgroup. Since CPI are evenly distributed among $NCPI$, the intense exploitation by defectors can disrupt interactions between $NCPI$, hindering the formation of cooperative clusters and thus reducing group cooperation.

Figure 1(B_1)–(B_4) shows the evolution of ρ_C with ϑ and b. It can be observed that as ϑ increases, ρ_C shows a clear upward trend, with the promotional effect being particularly significant when $\rho \geq 0.9 \cap \vartheta \geq 0.3$. For example, when $\rho = 0.95$ and $b = 1.06$, ρ_C increases by more than 15% when $\vartheta = 5$ compared to $\vartheta = 1$. This is because when intelligent agents have large emotional fluctuations, meaning their emotions are relatively unstable, their ability to adjust their current strategy based on emotional mechanisms is further enhanced. When $NCPI$ hold a defection strategy and interact with intelligent agents holding a cooperation strategy, their emotion $E_{x,t_{MCS}}$ can quickly drop below $E_{x,th}$ in a short time. According to Eq. 8, $\tau_x(t_{MCS})$ continuously decreases, further leading them to adjust their strategy towards cooperation based on the Fermi probability determined by Eq. 9, and this adjustment can spread in a chain-like manner to neighboring nodes, effectively promoting the emergence of cooperative behavior within the group. However, as the proportion of non-competitive propensity individuals decreases, the promotional effect of high emotional sensitivity ϑ on

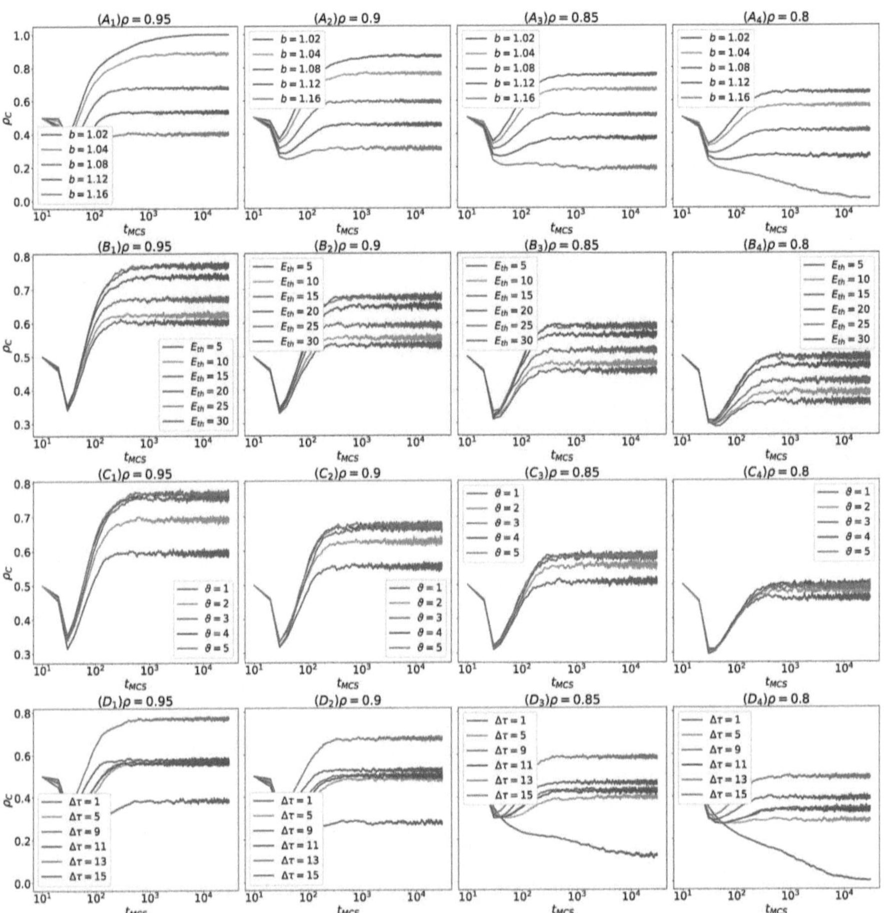

Fig. 2. Evolutionary time series of group cooperation rates ρ_C under different "temptations to defect" b, different positive-negative emotional thresholds E_{th}, different emotional sensitivities ϑ, and different strategy duration sensitivities $\Delta\tau$. In subfigures (A_1)–(A_4), $E_{th} = 25$, $\vartheta = 5$, $\Delta\tau = 13$. In subfigures (B_1)–(B_4), $b = 1.06$, $\vartheta = 5$, $\Delta\tau = 13$. In subfigures (C_1)–(C_4), $b = 1.06$, $E_{th} = 25$, $\Delta\tau = 13$. In subfigures (D_1)–(D_4), $b = 1.06$, $E_{th} = 25$, $\vartheta = 5$. Respectively, in subfigures (A_1)–(D_1), (A_2)–(D_2), (A_3)–(D_3), (A_4)–(D_4), the proportion ρ of non-competitive individuals is 0.95, 0.9, 0.85, and 0.8.

cooperative behavior weakens. For example, when $\rho = 0.8 \cap b = 1.06$, the increase in ρ_C is less than 5% when $\vartheta = 5$ compared to $\vartheta = 1$.

Figure 1(C_1)–(C_4) shows the evolution of ρ_C with $\Delta\tau$ and b. Unlike the linear impact produced by E_{th} and ϑ, as $\Delta\tau$ increases, ρ_C first rises and then falls. This indicates that there is an optimal $\Delta\tau$ that maximizes ρ_C, and changes in social dilemmas (such as ρ and b) do not significantly shift.

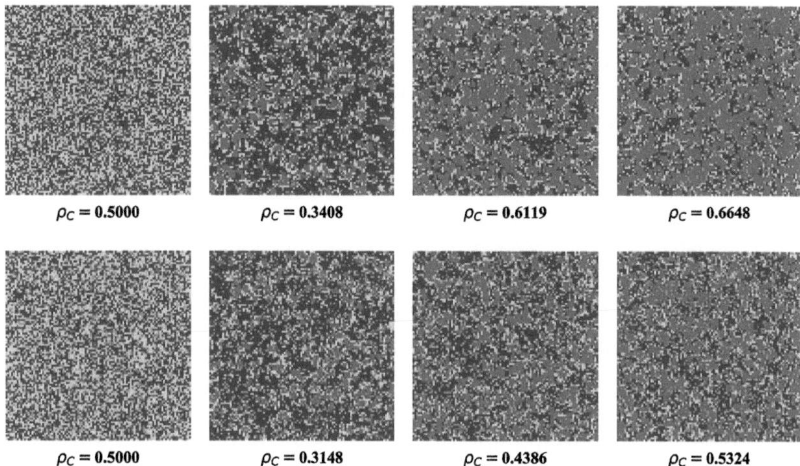

Fig. 3. Snapshots of strategy distributions under different proportions of non-competitive individuals ρ at specific iterative evolution rounds. In the $NCPI$ subgroup, cooperators (defectors) whose individual emotion $E_{x,t_{MCS}}$ exceeds their positive-negative emotional threshold $E_{x,th}$ are marked in red (dark blue), and cooperators (defectors) whose individual emotion $E_{x,t_{MCS}}$ does not reach their positive-negative emotional threshold $E_{x,th}$ are marked in yellow (dark green). In the CPI subgroup, cooperators (defectors) whose individual emotion $E_{x,t_{MCS}}$ exceeds their positive-negative emotional threshold $E_{x,th}$ are marked in orange (light green), and cooperators (defectors) whose individual emotion $E_{x,t_{MCS}}$ does not reach their positive-negative emotional threshold $E_{x,th}$ are marked in pink (grey-blue). All subfigures are vertically layered according to ρ values of 0.9 and 0.8, and horizontally arranged according to Monte-Carlo iterative rounds of 0, 20, 100, and 30,000. Additionally, the group cooperation rate ρ_C corresponding to each snapshot is annotated below each subfigure. In all subfigures, $b = 1.06$, $E_{th} = 25$, $\vartheta = 5$, $\Delta\tau = 13$. (Color figure online)

Figure 2 respectively show the dynamic evolution of ρ_C over time under different b, E_{th}, ϑ and $\Delta\tau$. It can be observed that despite the differences in the social dilemmas faced by intelligent agents, the curves of over Monte-Carlo time steps (t_{MCS}) exhibit similar patterns. We divide the entire Monte-Carlo iteration process into two phases: the Endurance phase (END) ($t_{MCS} \leq 20$) and the Expansion phase (EXP) ($t_{MCS} > 20$). Due to the high payoff temptation generated by defecting strategies exploiting neighboring cooperators, ρ_C first undergoes a rapid decline, referred to as the Endurance phase (END). When ρ_C reaches its lowest point, the emotion-strategy persistence mechanism begins to take effect. Intelligent agents gradually adjust their strategies based on their emotional states, and the emerging cooperative behaviors are maintained and further expanded through the formation of tight cooperative clusters until reaching a steady state, this phase is called the Expansion phase (EXP).

Although all the time series curves exhibit a similar evolutionary trend, in Fig. 2(A_1)–(A_4), as b increases, the lowest cooperation level the group can achieve during END, denoted as ρ_C°, decreases accordingly. In Fig. 2(B_1)–(B_4) and 2(C_1)–(C_4), E_{th} and ϑ have almost no effect on ρ_C°. In Fig. 2(D_1)–(D_4), as $\Delta\tau$ increases, ρ_C° shows a non-monotonic trend, first rising and then falling.

Finally, Fig. 3 and Fig. reffig:Experiment4 respectively explore the spatial distribution snapshots of strategies held by $NCPI/CPI$ with different emotional states under varying ρ and E_{th}. In the $NCPI$ subgroup, cooperators (defectors) with a positive emotional state are marked in red (dark blue), while cooperators (defectors) with a negative emotional state are marked in yellow (dark green). In the CPI subgroup, cooperators (defectors) with a positive emotional state are marked in orange (light green), while cooperators (defectors) with a negative emotional state are marked in pink (gray-blue).

It can be clearly observed that when $E_{th} > 0$, during the Endurance phase (END), defectors with negative emotions in the $NCPI$ subgroup rapidly spread throughout the group and gradually become dominant. However, even in such extremely challenging social dilemmas, cooperative strategies can still be

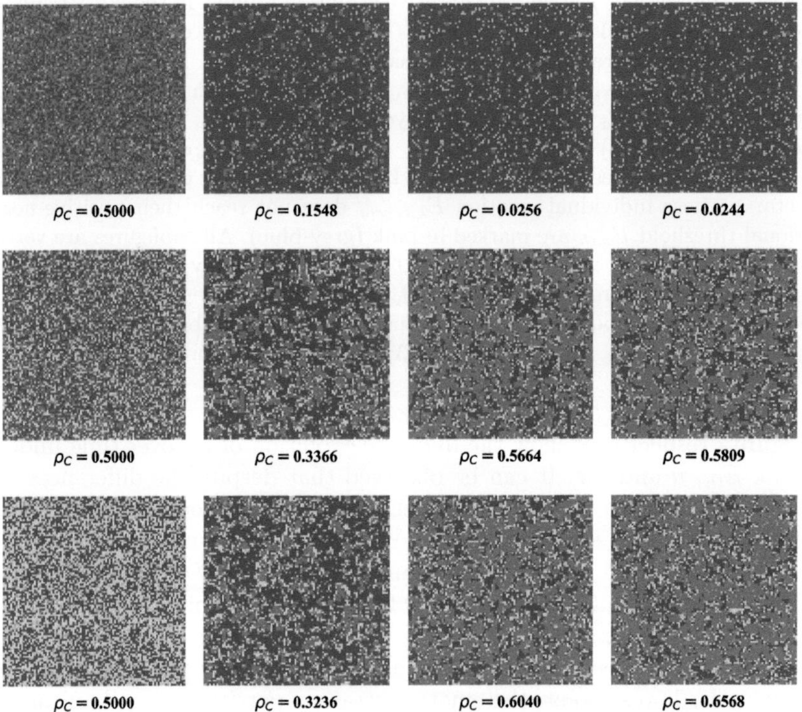

Fig. 4. Snapshots of strategy distributions under different positive-negative emotional threshold E_{th} at specific iterative evolution rounds. The color settings are the same as in Fig. 3. All subfigures are vertically layered according to E_{th} values of 0, 15, and 30, and horizontally arranged according to Monte-Carlo iterative rounds of 0, 20, 100, and 30,000. Additionally, the group cooperation rate ρ_C corresponding to each snapshot is annotated below each subfigure. In all subfigures, $\rho = 0.9$, $b = 1.06$, $\vartheta = 5$, $\Delta\tau = 13$.

maintained by forming tight cooperative clusters. In these clusters, cooperators with positive emotions in the $NCPI$ subgroup dominate, interspersed with a very small number of CPI cooperators with negative emotions, while the edges of the clusters are filled with $NCPI$ cooperators with negative emotions. During the Expansion phase (EXP), the emotion-strategy persistence mechanism starts to play a role. The cooperative clusters gradually expand while being maintained and interconnect with surrounding cooperative clusters, further enhancing their ability to resist defection exploitation and forming a positive feedback loop, greatly promoting the flourishing of cooperative behavior. When $E_{th} \rightarrow 0$ (the first row of Fig. 4), according to previous analytical deductions, the emotional mechanism cannot function, making it difficult for cooperative strategies to be maintained, leading to their continuous conversion to defection strategies and eventual extinction.

4 Conclusion

The emotion-strategy persistence mechanism proposed in this paper significantly promotes the emergence and flourishing of cooperative behavior in the prisoner's dilemma game. We explored in detail how various factors in the model affect the group cooperation rate and analyzed the corresponding causes. We found that the group cooperation rate ρ is higher when the social dilemma intensity–"temptation to defect" b is smaller, the positive-negative emotional threshold E_{th} is higher, and the emotional sensitivity ϑ is greater. However, the impact of strategy duration sensitivity $\Delta\tau$ on ρ_C shows a non-monotonic trend, with an optimal $\hat{\Delta}\tau$ that maximizes ρ_C.

The emotion-strategy persistence mechanism proposed in this paper ameliorates the limitations of previous studies that relied solely on single factor influencing the decision-making of intelligent agents. It provides a new perspective for future researchers to understand the emergence and maintenance of cooperative behavior among selfish individuals in social dilemmas. A possible future research direction is to delve deeper into the emotional mechanism to explore how the spatial distribution of $NCPI$ and CPI subgroups affects the evolution of cooperation.

References

1. Axelrod, R., Hamilton, W.D.: The evolution of cooperation. Science **211**(4489), 1390–1396 (1981)
2. Macy, M.W., Flache, A.: Learning dynamics in social dilemmas. Proc. Nat. Acad. Sci. **99**(Suppl 3), 7229–7236 (2002)
3. Szabó, G., Fath, G.: Evolutionary games on graphs. Phys. Rep. **446**(4–6), 97–216 (2007)
4. Wang, J., Wang, R., Fengyuan, Yu., Wang, Z., Li, Q.: Learning continuous and consistent strategy promotes cooperation in prisoner's dilemma game with mixed strategy. Appl. Math. Comput. **370**, 124887 (2020)

5. Du, W.-B., Cao, X.-B., Hu, M.-B., Wang, W.-X.: Asymmetric cost in snowdrift game on scale-free networks. Europhys. Lett. **87**(6), 60004 (2009)
6. Santos, F.C., Santos, M.D., Pacheco, J.M.: Social diversity promotes the emergence of cooperation in public goods games. Nature **454**(7201), 213–216 (2008)
7. Hauert, C., De Monte, S., Hofbauer, J., Sigmund, K.: Volunteering as Red Queen mechanism for cooperation in public goods games. Science **296**(5570), 1129–1132 (2002)
8. Trivers, R.L.: The evolution of reciprocal altruism. Q. Rev. Biol. **46**(1), 35–57 (1971)
9. Nowak, M.A., Sigmund, K.: Evolution of indirect reciprocity. Nature **437**(7063), 1291–1298 (2005)
10. Nowak, M.A., May, R.M.: Evolutionary games and spatial chaos. Nature **359**(6398), 826–829 (1992)
11. Nunney, L.: Group selection, altruism, and structured-deme models. Am. Nat. **126**(2), 212–230 (1985)
12. Hamilton, W.D.: The genetical evolution of social behaviour. II. J. Theor. Biol. **7**(1), 17–52 (1964)
13. Hilbe, C., Schmid, L., Tkadlec, J., Chatterjee, K., Nowak, M.A.: Indirect reciprocity with private, noisy, and incomplete information. Proc. Nat. Acad. Sci. **115**(48), 12241–12246 (2018)
14. Dong, Y., Sun, S., Xia, C., Perc, M.: Second-order reputation promotes cooperation in the spatial prisoner's dilemma game. IEEE Access **7**, 82532–82540 (2019)
15. Yang, H.-X., Zhi-Xi, W., Rong, Z., Lai, Y.-C.: Peer pressure: enhancement of cooperation through mutual punishment. Phys. Rev. E **91**(2), 022121 (2015)
16. Perc, M., Szolnoki, A.: A double-edged sword: benefits and pitfalls of heterogeneous punishment in evolutionary inspection games. Sci. Rep. **5**(1), 11027 (2015)
17. Yu'e, W., Zhang, Z., Wang, X., Chang, S.: Impact of probabilistic incentives on the evolution of cooperation in complex topologies. Physica A Stat. Mech. Appl. **513**, 307–314 (2019)
18. Lin, J., Huang, C., Dai, Q., Yang, J.: Evolutionary game dynamics of combining the payoff-driven and conformity-driven update rules. Chaos, Solitons Fractals **140**, 110146 (2020)
19. Li, X., Geng, Y., Shen, C., Shi, L.: The influence of heterogeneous learning ability on the evolution of cooperation. Sci. Rep. **9**(1), 13920 (2019)
20. Zhang, L., Li, H., Dai, Q., Yang, J.: Migration based on environment comparison promotes cooperation in evolutionary games. Physica A Stat. Mech. Appl. **595**, 127073 (2022)
21. Szolnoki, A., Xie, N.-G., Wang, C., Perc, M.: Imitating emotions instead of strategies in spatial games elevates social welfare. Europhys. Lett. **96**(3), 38002 (2011)
22. Szolnoki, A., Xie, N.-G., Ye, Y., Perc, M.: Evolution of emotions on networks leads to the evolution of cooperation in social dilemmas. Phys. Rev. E Stat. Nonlinear Soft Matter Phys. **87**(4), 042805 (2013)
23. Chao, Yu., Zhang, M., Ren, F., Tan, G.: Emotional multiagent reinforcement learning in spatial social dilemmas. IEEE Trans. Neural Netw. Learn. Syst. **26**(12), 3083–3096 (2015)
24. Chen, W., Wang, J., Fengyuan, Yu., He, J., Wenshu, X., Wang, R.: Effects of emotion on the evolution of cooperation in a spatial prisoner's dilemma game. Appl. Math. Comput. **411**, 126497 (2021)
25. Cacioppo, J.T., Gardner, W.L.: Emotion. Annu. Rev. Psychol. **50**(1), 191–214 (1999)

Balancing Rationality and Social Influence: Alpha-Rational Nash Equilibrium in Games with Herding

Khushboo Agarwal[1]([✉]), Konstantin Avrachenkov[1], Veeraruna Kavitha[2], and Raghupati Vyas[2]

[1] Inria Sophia Antipolis, 2004 Route des Lucioles, Valbonne 06902, France
khushboo.agarwal@inria.fr, k.avrachenkov@inria.fr
[2] IEOR, IIT Bombay, Powai, Mumbai 400076, India
vkavitha@iitb.ac.in, raghupati.vyas@iitb.ac.in

Abstract. The classical game theory considers rational players and proposes Nash equilibrium (NE) as the solution. However, real-world scenarios rarely feature rational players; instead, players make inconsistent and irrational decisions. Often, irrational players exhibit herding behaviour by simply following the majority.

In this paper, we consider a mean-field game with α-fraction of rational players and the rest being herding-irrational players. For such a game, we introduce a novel concept of equilibrium named α-Rational NE (in short, α-RNE). We extensively analyze the α-RNEs and their implications in games with two actions. Due to herding-irrational players, new equilibria may arise, and some classical NEs may be deleted.

We establish that the rational players are not harmed but benefit from the presence of irrational players. More interestingly, in some examples, the rational players attain higher utility (under α-RNE) than even the social optimal utility (in the classical setting), by leveraging upon the herding behaviour of irrational players.

Surprisingly, the irrational players may also benefit by not being rational. We observe that irrational players do not lose compared to some classical NEs for participation and bandwidth-sharing games. Importantly, in bandwidth-sharing game, the irrational players also receive utility near social optimal utility. Such examples indicate that it may sometimes be 'rational' to be irrational.

Keywords: bounded rationality · game theory · mean-field games

---

The work is supported by: the French National Agency for Research (ANR) via the project n°ANR-22-PEFT-0010 of the France 2030 program PEPR réseaux du futur; DST-INRIA Cefipra project 'Learning In Operations and Networks' (LION); and CSIR, India.

V. Aggarwal et al. (Eds.): GameNets 2025, LNICST 657, pp. 91–107, 2026.
https://doi.org/10.1007/978-3-032-12915-4_6

1   Introduction

Classical game theory explores the interactions between rational and intelligent players. In [14], a player is defined as rational if it consistently makes decisions aligned with its objectives, striving to maximize its utility. Additionally, an intelligent player possesses complete knowledge of the game and can perform computations to identify its optimal strategy. This line of thought is widely acknowledged and serves as a benchmark for analyzing an ideal world.

Nevertheless, contemporary perspectives challenge the strong assumptions regarding rationality and intelligence due to human irrationality and computational limitations. This has sparked interest in understanding actual human behavior, leading to the emergence of fields like behavioural game theory, behavioural economics, and neuro-economics (see [8, 18, 19] respectively). Social experiments play a major role in driving research in these domains.

Several behavioral traits like behavioral probability weighting, cognitive hierarchy model, time-inconsistent planning, impact of extrinsic vs intrinsic motivation, among the players have been studied in [1, 6, 7, 17] recently. In these models, the players are partially aligned towards their utilities. Another strand of literature considers players who do not have the full potential to evaluate their utility functions accurately. More realistic notions of equilibrium considering such bounded-rational players are proposed, for example, quantal response, action-sampling, payoff-sampling, impulse-balance and k-fault tolerant equilibrium (see [10, 15, 20, 21]). A common thread in all these models is that the players exhibit some form of rationality or the other. We differ precisely at this point.

We attempt to model the players who do not even acknowledge the utility function while making choices. In particular, for some $\alpha \in (0, 1]$, we consider two types of players: (i) rational players, constituting an α-fraction of the population, and (ii) *irrational players, who exhibit herding behavior*. The latter group does not optimize the utility function—they simply choose the action taken by the majority. Such behavior is discussed at length in papers like [5, 11, 13, 22] and is also evident in career or fashion choices driven by the trends, and consumers favoring famous brands, etc. In the mentioned papers, either the focus is only on the herding players or they do not consider game theoretic aspects, while we study the resultant of the strategic and 'herding' interactions in a mixture of the population.

Assuming a large number of players, we analyze the game within mean-field framework. Drawing inspiration from the Nash equilibrium (NE) in the classical mean-field games, for a given value of α, *we introduce a novel equilibrium concept termed 'α-Rational NE' (in short, 'α-RNE') for our game, which encompasses both the rational and irrational choices of the players.*

In this paper, we consider games with two actions to obtain initial insights into the new concept of α-RNE. There are numerous examples of important games with two choices (for instance, participation games with participate or not-participate choices, minority games with two restaurants, vaccination games, etc.), which highlight the relevance of the games of interest. Further, we believe the insights derived here can prove to be a stepping stone for extending the notions of this paper to general games (with more actions) in the future.

Notably, we show that the set of α-RNEs does not always coincide with the set of NEs. If rational players dominate the system ($\alpha > 1/2$), the two sets are the same. However, when $\alpha \leq 1/2$, some classical NEs may disappear, and two new equilibria (α or $1 - \alpha$) can emerge. We also provide simple conditions for identifying α-RNEs based on the utility difference function.

After characterizing the α-RNEs, we compare the utilities of rational and herding players at a given α-RNE and assess whether either type is at an advantage or disadvantage relative to the NE. We show that rational players benefit from the presence of herding players, rather than being harmed. This aligns with the observation in [2], where behavioral probability weighting is used to model player behavior, but here we deduce this in the context of herding players.

Interestingly, under α-RNE, *the rational players can receive more utility than the social optimal utility obtained under $\alpha = 1$ case.* Even though the incompetent behaviour of the irrational players never allows them to surpass the social optimal utility, nonetheless, in some cases, the irrational players get utility at par with the rational players. Remarkably, in an example, we observe that *all the players (including irrational players) receive higher utility at α-RNE than they could have received if everyone were rational.* Such instances encourage us to claim that *'it may be rational to be irrational sometimes'.*

Another motivation for α-rational NE comes from the behavioral game dynamics. In fact, we showed in [3] that any limit of turn-by-turn dynamics, involving both myopic rational and herding players, is one of the α-RNEs.

2   New Notion: α-RNE with Herding

In classical game theory, it is assumed that all players are perfectly rational, and then, the widely-known and accepted Nash Equilibrium (NE) is provided as the solution of the game. However, in reality, we rarely encounter such perfectly rational players. Instead, more often than not, players take decisions based on some simple rules. The most common of such rules is the one where players exhibit herding behaviour; for example, in a stock market, players tend to buy the derivative that they believe the majority of the players will purchase, or on a traffic signal, people cross the road when they see others crossing the road, etc.

Our aim in this paper is to propose an appropriate notion of equilibrium that caters to such a mix of rational and irrational (to be more specific, the ones with the herding behaviour) players. Towards this, consider a large population and assume that there are α fraction of rational players, while the remaining population is composed of irrational players, for some $\alpha \in (0, 1]$. Each player has to choose an action from the set of actions, denoted by $\mathcal{A} := \{1, 2, \ldots, n\}$, where $n < \infty$. For each $a \in \mathcal{A}$, let $\mu(a)$ be the fraction of players who choose action a; define $\mu := (\mu(a))_{\{a \in \mathcal{A}\}}$. Similarly, let $\mu^R := (\mu^R(a))_{\{a \in \mathcal{A}\}}$ be the empirical distribution corresponding to (only) rational players.

Define the function $u : \mathcal{A} \times [0, 1]^{|\mathcal{A}|} \to \mathbb{R}$ to represent the utility of players. Thus, each player receives the utility $u(a, \mu)$ if it chooses an action a and the empirical distribution of the actions by the rest of the population is μ. Note that the utility function is the same for all the players and depends upon μ like in mean-field games (see, for example, [9]). As in classical theory, the rational players are capable of performing extensive computations and thus, choose an action that maximizes their utility. Hence, if μ were the empirical distribution of the actions chosen by the entire population[1], the best response (μ^R) of any rational player against μ would satisfy the following:

$$\text{support}(\mu^R) \subseteq \text{Arg} \max_{a \in \mathcal{A}} u(a, \mu), \tag{1}$$

where $\text{support}(\mu) := \{a \in \mathcal{A} : \mu(a) > 0\}$.

On the other hand, irrational players exhibit herding behaviour—they blindly follow others and do not optimize like rational players. One simple way to model the herding behaviour of the irrational players is to assume that such players choose an action that is played the most by rational players, i.e., they choose the action a which satisfies $\mu^R(a) \geq \mu^R(a')$ for all $a' \neq a$. However, since typically irrational players cannot distinguish rational from irrational players, we consider a more realistic way of capturing the herding behavior of the irrational players. We assume that each irrational player chooses an action played by the majority among all other players, including irrational players. To be precise, we assume that each irrational player chooses the following action, against μ:

$$f(\mu) := \min \left\{ i : i \in \text{Arg} \max_{a \in \mathcal{A}} \mu(a) \right\}. \tag{2}$$

In the above, for simplicity and tractability of the analysis, we assume that the action with the smallest index in the set $\text{Arg} \max_{a \in \mathcal{A}} \mu(a)$ is preferred in case of a tie.

Before we proceed further, we provide few important remarks regarding the choices made by herding (irrational) players:

(i) The action chosen by the irrational players as per the rule (2) may not be the best response to μ; it is just a response driven by the herding behaviour of the players. Thus, it is not a rational choice where the players attempt to leverage upon the efforts (or the decisions) of others, as in free-riding (see [12]).

(ii) The second remark is about the possibility of herding players following (only) themselves. In reality, one can have many more variants of irrational behaviors, for example, some players can choose randomly or can have some blind preferences, or can avoid the crowd, etc., and these players might be insignificant in the bigger picture (or in a large population) but can be significant enough to lead (or mis-lead) the herding crowd. Basically, some initial players (whose proportion is negligible at the limit) make some choices and the

---

[1] Note that the game is described in the mean-field framework, therefore, the action chosen by a single player does not affect the outcome of the game (see [9]). Given this, it is appropriate to view μ as the empirical distribution corresponding to the 'entire' population.

herding crowd starts following them, eventually leading to all herding players choosing an action different from the choices of rational players. Alternatively, the rational players might estimate an action to be beneficial in the beginning (like in game dynamics, e.g., [16]), irrationals can follow such rational players and themselves. But, later the rational players can find an alternate action to be beneficial in view of the new empirical measure μ. In all such cases, at the limit, it appears that herding players are following themselves. Such possibilities are formalized in [3] for a special game dynamics among (myopic) rational and herding players (see, for example, [3, Theorems 2, 4(ii.b)]).

Finally, the proportion of players choosing different actions in $\mathcal{A}$ is given by:

$$\mu(a) = \alpha\mu^R(a) + (1 - \alpha)1_{\{a=f(\mu)\}}, \text{ for each } a \in \mathcal{A}. \tag{3}$$

The above relationship is obtained as $\alpha\mu^R(a)$-fraction of rational players choose the action a, and all irrational players choose the same action a only if $a = f(\mu)$ (see (2)).

At this point, one should note that rational players choose an action anticipating the response of the irrational players (as μ depends on $f(\mu)$, see (1) and (3)). Thus, we define a pair (μ, μ^R) to be an equilibrium if it satisfies:

(i) $\mu^R \in$ Best Response(μ);
(ii) the empirical measure (μ) of the population is given by (3), when the corresponding counterpart for rational players is given by μ^R; and
(iii) $f(\mu)$ denotes the majority action as in (2).

The above discussion is formally summarized below:

Definition 1. *For $\alpha \in (0, 1]$, a pair of empirical measures (μ, μ^R) is called an $\alpha - Rational\ Nash\ Equilibrium$, or in short, α-RNE, if it satisfies (1), (2) and (3).*

Observe that the above definition is a natural extension of the NE defined in the classical mean-field games (MFGs), where 'all' players are rational and optimize the utility function $u(\cdot; \mu)$ (see [9]). Thus, (1) is satisfied by μ in MFGs at the NE (not by μ^R), i.e., support$(\mu) \subseteq \text{Arg max}_{a \in \mathcal{A}} u(a, \mu)$. Due to the presence of herding-players, we will see that an α-RNE need not be a classical NE.

In the coming, we delve deep into the new notion for the game with two actions, where we derive several interesting insights. Further, we also derive the simple conditions to identify the α-RNEs.

3   Game with Two Actions

Let us consider that players can choose either action 1 or 2, i.e., $\mathcal{A} = \{1, 2\}$. For this setting, we propose simpler notations as follows: (i) let z be the proportion of players who choose $a = 1$ and thus, $\mu = (z, 1 - z)$ and (ii) let y be the proportion of rational players (among rational players) who choose $a = 1$ and thus, $\mu^R = (y, 1 - y)$. As a result, we write the utility function $u(\cdot, \mu)$ as $u(\cdot, z)$.

Finally, the α-RNE is given by $(\mu, \mu^R) \equiv (z, y)$ which satisfy the following:

$$z = \alpha y + (1 - \alpha)1_{\{z \geq \frac{1}{2}\}}, \tag{4}$$

$$\text{support}(\mu^R) \subseteq \text{Arg} \max_{a \in \mathcal{A}} u(a, z). \tag{5}$$

Note that in the underlying case with two actions, $f(\mu) = 1$ only if $z \geq 1/2$. Therefore, (2) and (3) together lead to (4) given above.

Now, by (4), α-RNE can be represented only in terms of the proportion z. Denote the set of α-RNEs by $\mathcal{N}_\alpha$. Then, one can easily verify that the set $\mathcal{N}_\alpha$ has the following structure (recall $\alpha \in (0, 1]$):

$$\mathcal{N}_\alpha = \{z : (z, y^*(z)) \text{ is an } \alpha\text{-RNE}\}, \text{ for } y^*(z) := \begin{cases} \frac{z}{\alpha}, & \text{if } z < \frac{1}{2}, \\ 1 - \frac{1-z}{\alpha}, & \text{if } z \geq \frac{1}{2}. \end{cases} \tag{6}$$

In the above, $y^*(z)$ is provided by solving (4). Thus, by virtue of the above structure, it is sufficient to solve for (5) alone, instead of solving for (4) and (5) simultaneously. Now, observe that $\text{Arg} \max_{a \in \mathcal{A}} u(a, z)$ can be simply recognized by comparing the utilities $u(1, z)$ and $u(2, z)$ in the underlying case. This motivates us to define the following *utility difference function*:

$$h(z) := u(1, z) - u(2, z). \tag{7}$$

The idea is to identify the α-RNEs using the zeros of h, i.e., from the set:

$$\mathcal{Z}^h := \{z^* \in [0, 1] : h(z^*) = 0\}. \tag{8}$$

3.1 Identification of Equilibria

For the sake of reference, we first provide characterization of the set of classical NEs of MFGs with two actions. The proofs of the next result and the upcoming ones are provided in Appendix A.

Theorem 1 (Identification of MFG-NEs). *Suppose* $\mathcal{A} = \{1, 2\}$. *Then, the set of classical NEs:*

$$\mathcal{N}_1 \subseteq \mathcal{Z}^h \cup \{0, 1\}. \tag{9}$$

For the converse, we have:

(i) $\mathcal{Z}^h \subseteq \mathcal{N}_1$,
(ii) $0 \in \mathcal{N}_1$ *only if* $h(0) \leq 0$, *and*
(iii) $1 \in \mathcal{N}_1$ *only if* $h(1) \geq 0$. $\qquad\qquad\square$

The above result provides simple conditions for identifying classical NEs. It states that every zero of h is a NE. Further, 0 and 1 are also NEs if $h(0) < 0$ and $h(1) > 0$, respectively. Next, we identify the set of α-RNEs in terms of $\mathcal{N}_1$.

Theorem 2 (Identification of α-RNEs). *Suppose* $\mathcal{A} = \{1, 2\}$. *Let* $O_{a,b} := \{z : a < z < b\}$ *denote the open interval. If* $\alpha > 1/2$, *then* $\mathcal{N}_\alpha = \mathcal{N}_1$. *Else (i.e., if* $\alpha \leq 1/2$), *the following statements hold:*

(i) $\mathcal{N}_\alpha \subseteq \mathcal{N}_1 \cup \{\alpha, 1-\alpha\} \backslash O_{\alpha,1-\alpha}$, and
(ii) conversely,
   (a) $\mathcal{N}_1 \backslash O_{\alpha,1-\alpha} \subseteq \mathcal{N}_\alpha$,
   (b) $(1-\alpha) \in \mathcal{N}_\alpha$ if and only if $h(1-\alpha) \leq 0$, and
   (c) For $\alpha < 1/2$, $\alpha \in \mathcal{N}_\alpha$ if and only if $h(\alpha) \geq 0$. $\square$

Interestingly, the above theorem asserts that *the presence of irrational players has no effect on the set of equilibria ($\mathcal{N}_\alpha = \mathcal{N}_1$) when rational players outnumber irrational players ($\alpha > 1/2$).*

More interestingly, the situation drastically differs when $\alpha \leq 1/2$. Firstly, two new equilibria can arise, namely α and $1-\alpha$, see Theorem 2(i), under the conditions specified in (ii.b) and (ii.c), respectively. Secondly, not every zero of h can be an α-RNE—the zeroes which are only in the interval $[0,\alpha] \cup [1-\alpha, 1]$ are allowed. Thus, *some classical NEs are deleted and new equilibria are added when the irrational players form the majority.*

Next, for any equilibrium, it is natural to ask if the equilibrium is attainable through some dynamics. In classical setups, best-response dynamics, fictitious play, etc. are known to converge to the NE (under certain conditions). In our mixed-behavioral setup, the turn-by-turn dynamics studied in [3] converges to some/all α-RNEs. In particular, it has been shown in [3, Theorems 1, 3, 4] that when myopic-rational and herding players play a game with two actions one after the other, in a random order and only once, then the empirical distribution of players choosing different actions converges to points that satisfy all the conditions of α-RNE. Thus, such dynamics provides a natural foundation for the new concept of α-RNE.

3.2 Comparison of Utilities

In our framework, both rational and irrational players participate in the game. Therefore, first and foremost, one would like to know whether the utility of rational players diminishes due to the presence of irrational players. Subsequently, one might be interested in knowing if the irrational players suffer due to their herding behaviour, when compared with the utility they could have obtained if they were rational.

Further, it is known that NE often results in players gaining lesser utility than the social optimal utility. So happens because the NE provides stability only against unilateral deviations. However, if multiple players deviate from NE, higher utility can possibly be achieved. Considering this, it is plausible that players' utility may be closer to the social optimal utility at α-RNE, than at NE, since irrational players collectively deviate from NE. If this anticipation holds, it suggests a rational inclination towards irrationality. We formally investigate all these aspects below.

Denote the expected utility of a rational player at $z_\alpha^* \in \mathcal{N}_\alpha$ by $u_\alpha^R(z_\alpha^*)$, for $0 < \alpha \leq 1$, and observe:

$$u_\alpha^R(z_\alpha^*) = y^*(z_\alpha^*)u(1, z_\alpha^*) + (1 - y^*(z_\alpha^*))u(2, z_\alpha^*). \tag{10}$$

In the above, $y^*(z_\alpha^*)$ is the probability of a rational player choosing action 1. Similarly, denote the expected utility for an irrational player by $u_\alpha^I(z_\alpha^*)$, and note that it is given by:

$$u_\alpha^I(z_\alpha^*) = 1_{\{z_\alpha^* \geq \frac{1}{2}\}} u(1, z_\alpha^*) + \left(1 - 1_{\{z_\alpha^* \geq \frac{1}{2}\}}\right) u(2, z_\alpha^*). \tag{11}$$

Recall that our motive is to compare the utilities of the players under α-RNE and classical NE. Keeping this in mind, we aim to investigate if, under α-RNE, players can achieve utility that is comparable to the social optimal utility (u^S) under the classical setting $(\alpha = 1)$. Thus, define:

$$u^S := \sup_{z \in [0,1]} \left(zu(1, z) + (1 - z)u(2, z)\right). \tag{12}$$

We begin with comparing the utilities for a rational and irrational player under α-RNEs. Further, we compare the utilities with the social optimal utility.

Proposition 1. *For any $\alpha \in (0, 1)$, $u_\alpha^I(z_\alpha^*) \leq u_\alpha^R(z_\alpha^*)$ and $u_\alpha^I(z_\alpha^*) \leq u^S$, for all $z_\alpha^* \in \mathcal{N}_\alpha$.* □

The above result asserts that rational players always obtain more utility than irrational players. Additionally, the irrational players can never achieve higher utility than the social optimal utility (u^S).

Recall from Theorem 2 that some new equilibria may get added or classical NEs may be deleted in the presence of irrational players. The next result states that if new equilibria (namely, α and $1 - \alpha$) are not added (i.e., $\mathcal{N}_\alpha \subseteq \mathcal{N}_1$), then both the rational players and more importantly, the irrational players attain exactly as much as a rational player gets in the classical setting.

Proposition 2. *For any $\alpha \in (0, 1]$, when $\mathcal{N}_\alpha \subseteq \mathcal{N}_1$, then $u^S \geq u_\alpha^R(z_\alpha^*) = u_\alpha^I(z_\alpha^*) = u_1^R(z_\alpha^*)$ for all $z_\alpha^* \in \mathcal{N}_\alpha$.* □

Thus, for example, if more rational players are present in the system ($\alpha > 1/2$), then they are able to manipulate the irrational players in such a way that no player loses anything. Further, by the above result, it is clear that no player (not even a rational player) receives more than the social optimal utility (u^S), when $\mathcal{N}_\alpha \subseteq \mathcal{N}_1$.

Now, observe that the above result comments on all α-RNEs, except $z_\alpha^* \in \{\alpha, 1 - \alpha\}$ such that $z_\alpha^* \in \mathcal{N}_\alpha$ but $z_\alpha^* \notin \mathcal{Z}^h$. Thus, if $\mathcal{N}_1 \subseteq \mathcal{N}_\alpha$, then according to Proposition 1, it is evident that the irrational players definitely receive strictly less utility than the rational players at α-RNE. However, several interesting possibilities arise at $z_\alpha^* \in \{\alpha, 1 - \alpha\}$ under said conditions:

(i) the rational players may outperform the utility attainable in social optimization (when all players are rational and their actions are governed by a central controller), i.e., $u_\alpha^R(z_\alpha^*) > u^S$. This holds for all the examples discussed in the subsequent section;

(ii) the irrational players may experience no change or a loss $(u_\alpha^I(z_\alpha^*) < u_1^R(z_1^*))$ or a gain $(u_\alpha^I(z_\alpha^*) > u_1^R(z_1^*))$ when compared to some classical NE $(z_1^* \in \mathcal{N}_1)$. The first two scenarios occur for the non-atomic routing game, while the latter applies to the other two games discussed in the coming section;

(iii) interestingly, we shall see in the bandwidth sharing game that both rational and irrational players benefit at α-RNE such that for all $z_1^* \in \mathcal{N}_1$:

$$u_\alpha^R(z_\alpha^*) > u_1^R(z_1^*) \text{ and } u_\alpha^I(z_\alpha^*) > u_1^R(z_1^*).$$

Clearly, the utility of rational and irrational players surpasses and approaches closer to the social optimal utility (u^S) respectively. Thus, in such cases, we may declare that 'it is rational to be irrational'.

4 Examples

4.1 Non-Atomic Routing Game

Consider a non-atomic routing game, which is a slight modification of Pigou's network game [14]. One can travel from source (S) to destination (T) via hub 1 or 2. The users must opt for either the path via hub 1 or hub 2 to minimize their travel time.

It takes γz hour(s) to travel from S to T, for some $\gamma \in (1, \infty)$, while the travel time via hub 2 is just 1 hour. Consider that α-fraction of users are rational, and the rest adhere to the majority's choice (as in (2)). Rational users base their decisions on optimizing the following utility function:

$$u(a, z) = (-\gamma z)\,1_{\{a=1\}} + (-1)\,1_{\{a=2\}}, \tag{13}$$

where z is the proportion of users travelling via hub 1.

Next, we provide the set of α-RNEs for the above game. The proof is omitted as it directly follows from Theorem 2.

Corollary 1. *Consider the non-atomic routing game and define $\Delta := 1/\gamma$. Then, the set of α-RNEs is given below in two regimes:*

(i) when $\Delta \le \frac{1}{2}$:

$$\mathcal{N}_\alpha = \begin{cases} \{\alpha, 1-\alpha\}, & \text{if } \alpha \le \Delta, \\ \{\Delta, 1-\alpha\}, & \text{if } \Delta < \alpha \le \frac{1}{2}, \\ \{\Delta\}, & \text{if } \alpha > \frac{1}{2}; \end{cases}$$

(ii) when $\Delta > \frac{1}{2}$:

$$\mathcal{N}_\alpha = \begin{cases} \{\alpha, 1-\alpha\}, & \text{if } \alpha \le 1-\Delta, \\ \{\Delta, \alpha\}, & \text{if } 1-\Delta < \alpha < \frac{1}{2}, \\ \{\Delta\}, & \text{if } \alpha \ge \frac{1}{2}. \end{cases}$$

$\square$

At first, note that the classical NE is unique and equals Δ. A new equilibrium emerges when $\alpha > \min\{\Delta, 1 - \Delta\}$. Otherwise, the classical NE is removed, and two new equilibria emerge.

Thus, under classical setting ($\alpha = 1$), Δ-fraction of users choose to travel through hub 1. However, if we consider the game with the rational and irrational users, then the congestion on the path via hub 1 can either remain the same (as before), or it can decrease to α-level, or increase to $(1 - \alpha)$-level. Even at times when congestion is lesser, the irrational users are at a loss in this game as[2] $u_\alpha^I(z_\alpha^*) \leq u_1^R(\Delta)$, for all $z_\alpha^* \in \mathcal{N}_\alpha$.

Rational users exploit the presence of irrational users and benefit in multiple ways:

(i) rational users take an equal or less amount of time to travel, compared to irrational users (as $u_\alpha^R(z_\alpha^*) \geq u_\alpha^I(z_\alpha^*)$ for any $z_\alpha^* \in \mathcal{N}_\alpha$, by Proposition 1).
(ii) *rational users take lesser or equal amount of time to travel than under all-rational case* (as[3] $u_\alpha^R(z_\alpha^*) \geq u_1^R(\Delta)$, for all $z_\alpha^* \in \mathcal{N}_\alpha$).
(iii) the utility $u_\alpha^R(\alpha)$ is strictly decreasing in α. Thus, if α emerges as the α-RNE, then lower α (more herding players) implies that rational players take less time to reach the destination. In fact, if $\alpha < (1 - \Delta/4)\,\Delta$, then rational users receive more utility at α than the social optimal utility ($u^S = \Delta/4 - 1$).

4.2   Participation Game and Mechanism Design

Motivated by [4], we consider the game where each player has to decide whether to participate or not in an activity. Let us designate $a = 1$ as the action indicating participation and $a = 2$ as the action of non-participation in the activity. Thus, z denotes the proportion of participants.

Each non-participant gets a (perceived) utility equal to 1. To increase participation, the game designer provides a fixed utility $C < 1$ to each participant, and additionally, it offers a reward of $P > 0$, which is equally distributed among all the participants. Hence, the utility function can be expressed as follows:

$$u(a, z) = \left(C + \frac{P}{z}1_{\{z>0\}}\right)1_{\{a=1\}} + 1_{\{a=2\}}. \tag{14}$$

For the above game, the set of α-RNEs depends on the value of P. We consider two disjoint regimes: (i) $P \geq 1 - C$ and (ii) $P < 1 - C$, and present the results for the respective regimes below. The proofs again follow from Theorem 2.

Corollary 2. *Consider the participation game with $P \geq 1 - C$. Then, we have:*

(i) when $\alpha \in [1/2, 1]$, $\mathcal{N}_\alpha = \mathcal{N}_1 = \{0, 1\}$, and

---

[2] Here, $u_\alpha^I(z_\alpha^*) = -1$ for $z_\alpha^* \in \{\Delta, \alpha\}$. Further, $u_\alpha^I(1 - \alpha) = -(1-\alpha)/\Delta < u_1^R(\Delta)$; to verify this, note the conditions when $1 - \alpha \in \mathcal{N}_\alpha$ from Corollary 1.

[3] Here, $u_1^R(\Delta) = -1 = u_\alpha^R(z_\alpha^*)$ for $z_\alpha^* \in \{\Delta, 1 - \alpha\}$. Further, $u_\alpha^R(\alpha) = -\alpha/\Delta > u_1^R(\Delta)$; to verify this, note the conditions when $\alpha \in \mathcal{N}_\alpha$ from Corollary 1.

(ii) when $\alpha \in (0, {}^1\!/_2)$, $\mathcal{N}_\alpha = \mathcal{N}_1 \cup \{\alpha\}$.

$\square$

Under classical NE, dichotomy occurs: either everyone participates or no one participates. This situation may be undesirable for the designer as the chances of zero participation are 50%. Interestingly, when irrational players also play the game and constitute the majority, the designer can exploit the inherent herding behavior of irrationals and possibly induce α-level of participation. Thus, the likelihood of non-zero participation increases due to herding.

Further, the rational players benefit when $\mu = (\alpha, 1 - \alpha)$ is the α-RNE, as they receive higher[4] utility ($u_\alpha^R(\alpha) = C + P/\alpha$) than the social optimal utility ($u^S = 1 + P$), see (12).

Corollary 3. *Consider the participation game with $P < 1 - C$. Then, we have:*

(i) when $\alpha \in ({}^1\!/_2, 1]$, $\mathcal{N}_\alpha = \mathcal{N}_1 = \left\{ 0, \frac{P}{1-C} \right\}$,

(ii) when $\alpha = {}^1\!/_2$,

$$\mathcal{N}_\alpha = \begin{cases} \mathcal{N}_1 \cup \{\frac{1}{2}\}, & \text{if } P < \frac{1-C}{2}, \\ \mathcal{N}_1, & \text{otherwise, and,} \end{cases}$$

(iii) when $\alpha \in (0, {}^1\!/_2)$, define $P_1 := \alpha(1 - C)$ and $P_2 := (1 - \alpha)(1 - C)$. Then:

$$\mathcal{N}_\alpha = \begin{cases} \mathcal{N}_1 \cup \{1 - \alpha\}, & \text{if } 0 < P \leq P_1, \\ \{0, 1, \alpha, 1 - \alpha\}, & \text{if } P_1 < P < P_2, \\ \mathcal{N}_1 \cup \{\alpha\}, & \text{if } P_2 \leq P < 1 - C. \end{cases}$$

$\square$

As observed before, here also, either new equilibria are added, or some classical NEs are deleted when $\alpha \leq {}^1\!/_2$. As one can anticipate, lesser rewards imply lesser utility for the players. When $P < 1 - C$, rational players get lesser utility (at $\alpha, 1 - \alpha$) than the social optimal utility; recall previously, $u_\alpha^R(\alpha) > u^S$.

Importantly, note that *lesser reward means higher participation* under the realistic setting with $\alpha < {}^1\!/_2$. To be precise, $(1 - \alpha)$-level (more than 50%) of participation can occur when $P < P_2$ (also compare it with Corollary 2). This happens because rational players tend to lose interest in participation with low reward, so they choose $a = 2$; irrational players (which form the majority) then choose $a = 1$ due to herding.

In all, less reward proves detrimental for the players but advantageous for the game designer.

---

[4] Given $P \geq 1 - C$. Therefore, $\Delta := \frac{P}{1-C} > 1$. Now, observe $u_1^R(\alpha) - u^S = C - 1 - P + \frac{P}{\alpha} > 0$, only if $\alpha < \frac{1}{1 + \frac{1-C}{P}} = \frac{\Delta}{1+\Delta}$. Since $\alpha \in \mathcal{N}_\alpha$ when $\alpha < \frac{1}{2}$, and $\frac{\Delta}{1+\Delta} > \frac{1}{2}$, therefore, $u_1^R(\alpha) > u^S$.

4.3   Bandwidth Sharing Game – Is It Rational to Be Irrational?

Consider a communication network where players share the bandwidth to transmit their signals/information. The players can either transmit at the maximum capacity (which equals 1) of the shared channel, or they can transmit at a lower level, which equals $1/2$. We refer to the two actions as $a = 1$ and $a = 2$, respectively. In the first case, the communication of others can get interfered with, while in the latter case, no disruption occurs. The overall utility derived by any player depends upon its maximum capacity discounted by the overall interference caused by the opponents, and hence, the utility function is as follows:

$$u(a, z) = \left(1_{\{a=1\}} + \frac{1}{2}1_{\{a=2\}}\right)(1 - z). \tag{15}$$

The above game is a simplified version of the bandwidth sharing game discussed in [14] for classical strategic form setup; here we have also modified it for the mean-field setting. Now, we will provide the set of α-RNEs for this game, which can be derived by Theorem 2.

Corollary 4. *Consider the bandwidth-sharing game. The set of α-RNEs is as below:*

(i) when $\alpha \in [1/2, 1]$, $\mathcal{N}_1 = \mathcal{N}_\alpha = \{1\}$, and
(ii) when $\alpha \in (0, 1/2)$, $\mathcal{N}_\alpha = \mathcal{N}_1 \cup \{\alpha\}$.

$\square$

It is easy to solve the social optimization problem (12) for this game: $u^S = 1/2$, which is realized when no one transmits at capacity 1.

When there are only rational players (i.e., $\alpha = 1$), clearly from (15), the unique classical NE equals $z_1^* = 1$ and the corresponding utility $u_1^R(1) = 0$. Now, consider $\alpha < 1/2$. Then, by (10), (11), one can calculate that $u_\alpha^R(\alpha) = 1 - \alpha$ and $u_\alpha^I(\alpha) = 1/2\,(1 - \alpha)$.

Interestingly, the rational players have strictly improved their utility compared to the scenario with all rational players, as $u_1^R(1) < u_\alpha^R(\alpha)$. More interestingly, the utility of irrational players is also higher than that of the rational players under classical NE, as $u_1^R(1) < u_\alpha^I(\alpha)$. *Thus, in this case, it is 'rational' to be irrational!*

Moreover, as α approaches 0, $u_\alpha^I(\alpha) \to u^S$. This is a surprising outcome—at a selfish equilibrium, the players are achieving near social optimal utilities. Notably, the existence of a small fraction of rational players and a large fraction of herding players achieves this feat.

As said before, $u_1^R(z_1^*) \le u^S$ for all $z_1^* \in \mathcal{N}_1$. However, here, $u^S < u_\alpha^R(\alpha)$ due to the presence of irrational players. Conclusively, the introduction of irrationality can be beneficial in some cases.

5   Conclusions

This paper studies the mean-field game involving α-fraction of rational and $(1 - \alpha)$-fraction of irrational players. While rational players adhere to classical game theory principles, irrational players exhibit herding behavior by blindly choosing the action chosen by the majority. We introduce a novel equilibrium concept, termed α-Rational Nash equilibrium (α-RNE), which extends the NE for the classical mean-field games by capturing the responses of the irrational players.

The analysis in this paper focuses on the games with two actions, which captures many yes/no, this/that like scenarios encountered in daily lives.

Our findings reveal that the presence of irrational players can alter the set of equilibria compared to the set of classical NEs. New equilibria may emerge, while some classical equilibria may disappear when more irrational players are in the system. Otherwise, the set of equilibria does not change. We also provide easy conditions to identify α-RNEs for such games.

The price of anarchy (PoA) is known to be significant in many classical games, and arises due to the rational behaviour of the players involved. With the inclusion of 'herding-irrational' players, an immediate interesting question is about the way the PoA manifests. And as one may anticipate, we found some games for which the PoA reduces (in fact to zero) as the fraction of rational players decreases.

Future Directions: A key next step is to extend the notion of this paper to more general games, in particular, to games with more than two actions. One can also attempt to formulate an appropriate Stackelberg game, whose outcome matches with the equilibria introduced here. In [3], one special kind of dynamics is studied which converges to a subset of α-RNEs. It will be interesting to consider other behavioral learning dynamics and investigate the properties of their stationary points. Another promising direction would be to examine elaborate mechanism design scenarios involving herding players.

A   Appendix

Note: *Only in this section, we refer* $\mathrm{Arg\,max}_{a \in \mathcal{A}}\, u(a, z)$ *as* $\mathcal{A}_u$, *in short.*

Proof of Theorem 1: Before we start the proof, note that when $\alpha = 1$, (4) implies $z = y$. By (5), for any z to be in $\mathcal{N}_1$, following should hold:

$$\mathrm{support}(\mu) \subseteq \mathcal{A}_u, \text{ for } \mu = (z, 1 - z). \tag{16}$$

Now, consider any $z \in \mathcal{N}_1$. Then, three different cases arise based on the value of $h(z)$. Suppose $h(z) > 0$. By (7), $\mathcal{A}_u = \{1\}$. Under (16), $\mathrm{support}(\mu) = \{1\}$ (since $z \in \mathcal{N}_1$); thus, $z = 1$. Similarly, one can show that $z = 0$ if $h(z) < 0$. Lastly, suppose $h(z) = 0$. Then, $\mathcal{A}_u = \{1, 2\}$, again by (7). Since $z \in \mathcal{N}_1$, therefore, under (16), either $\mathrm{support}(\mu) = \{1\}$ or $\{2\}$ or $\{1, 2\}$. In the first two cases, $z = 1, 0$ respectively as above. In the last case, $z \in (0, 1)$. Combining all the implications from above, we get (9).

We now prove the claims for the converse of (9). Suppose $z \in \mathcal{Z}^h \cap (0,1)$. Then, support($\mu$) = $\{1,2\}$ = $\mathcal{A}_u$. Thus, $z \in \mathcal{N}_1$. Next, suppose $z = 0$. Then, support(μ) = $\{2\}$. If $h(0) \leq 0$, then $\mathcal{A}_u = \{1,2\}$ or $\{2\}$; thus, $0 \in \mathcal{N}_1$. However, if $h(0) > 0$, then $\mathcal{A}_u = \{1\}$. Clearly, it contradicts (16) and thus, $0 \notin \mathcal{N}_1$ in this case. One can similarly prove the claim for $z = 1$. Conclusively, (i)-(iii) hold. $\square$

Proof of Theorem 2: We divide the proof into two cases.

Case 1. when $\alpha > \frac{1}{2}$

Claim 1: $\mathcal{N}_\alpha \subseteq \mathcal{N}_1$

Suppose $z \in \mathcal{N}_\alpha$. Firstly, let $h(z) > 0$. By (7), $\mathcal{A}_u = \{1\}$. Under (5), support(μ^R) = $\{1\}$; thus, $y^*(z) = 1$. By (6), $z = 1$ (as $\alpha > \frac{1}{2}$). Thus, $z = 1 \in \mathcal{N}_1$, as $\{1\} \subseteq \mathcal{N}_1$ (see Theorem 1). Similarly, one can show that $z = 0 \in \mathcal{N}_1$ when $h(z) < 0$. Further, if $h(z) = 0$, then, $z \in \mathcal{Z}^h$. By Theorem 1(i), it is clear that $z \in \mathcal{N}_1$. In all, $\mathcal{N}_\alpha \subseteq \mathcal{N}_1$.

Claim 2: $\mathcal{N}_1 \subseteq \mathcal{N}_\alpha$

Let $z \in \mathcal{N}_1$. Then by (9), either $z \in \mathcal{Z}^h$ or $z \in \{0,1\}$. Say $z \in \mathcal{Z}^h \cap [0, \frac{1}{2})$. Here, $y^*(z) = \frac{z}{\alpha}$; observe $y^*(z) = 0$ if $z = 0$ and $y^*(z) \in (0,1)$ otherwise. Thus, support(μ^R) = $\{2\}$ or $\{1,2\} \subseteq \mathcal{A}_u$, as $z \in \mathcal{Z}^h$. By Definition 1, $z \in \mathcal{N}_\alpha$. One can prove in a similar manner that any $z \in \mathcal{Z}_\alpha^h \cap [\frac{1}{2}, 1)$ is also in $\mathcal{N}_\alpha$.

Now, say $z = 0$. Observe $y^*(0) = 0$. Thus, support(μ^R) = $\{2\}$. Recall $z = 0 \in \mathcal{N}_1$ only if $h(0) \leq 0$, by Theorem 1(ii). Thus, $\mathcal{A}_u = \{1,2\}$ or $\{2\}$. Then, as above, $z \in \mathcal{N}_\alpha$. The proof similarly follows when $z = 1$. Hence, $\mathcal{N}_1 \subseteq \mathcal{N}_\alpha$.

Conclusively, $\mathcal{N}_1 = \mathcal{N}_\alpha$.

Case 2. when $\alpha \leq \frac{1}{2}$

(i) Say $z \in \mathcal{N}_\alpha$. Then, z satisfies (5). Now, we divide the proof based on the values of $h(z)$.

Firstly, let $h(z) > 0$. Then, as in the case with $\alpha > \frac{1}{2}$, $y^*(z) = 1$. By (6), either $z = \alpha$ if $\alpha < \frac{1}{2}$ or $z = 1$. Observe that $\alpha \notin \mathcal{N}_1$ and $\{1\} \subseteq \mathcal{N}_1$. This implies that $z \in \mathcal{N}_1 \cup \{\alpha, 1 - \alpha\} \backslash (\alpha, 1 - \alpha)$. Similarly, one can prove (??) when $h(z) < 0$. At last, let $h(z) = 0$. Then, $\mathcal{A}_u = \{1,2\}$, again by (7). Under (5), three possibilities arise:

- support(μ^R) = $\{1\}$: here, $z = \alpha$ if $\alpha < \frac{1}{2}$ or $z = 1$, as when $h(z) > 0$.
- support(μ^R) = $\{2\}$: here, $z = 1 - \alpha$ if $\alpha \leq \frac{1}{2}$ or $z = 0$, as when $h(z) < 0$.
- support(μ^R) = $\{1,2\}$: here, $y^* \in (0,1)$. This implies that either $z < \alpha$ and $z < \frac{1}{2}$, or $z > 1 - \alpha$ and $z \geq \frac{1}{2}$.

In all three cases, one can easily see that $z \in \mathcal{N}_1 \cup \{\alpha, 1 - \alpha\} \backslash (\alpha, 1 - \alpha)$. Conclusively, (i) holds.

(ii.a) Suppose $z \in \mathcal{N}_1 \backslash (\alpha, 1 - \alpha)$. Then by (9), $z \in \mathcal{Z}^h \backslash (\alpha, 1 - \alpha)$ or $z \in \{0,1\}$.

Firstly, say $z \in \mathcal{Z}^h \backslash (\alpha, 1 - \alpha)$ such that $z < \frac{1}{2}$. Here, $y^*(z) = \frac{z}{\alpha}$; observe $y^*(z) = 1$ if $z = \alpha$ and $y^*(z) < 1$ otherwise. Thus, support(μ^R) = $\{1\}$ or $\{1,2\}$; in either case, support(μ^R) $\subseteq \mathcal{A}_u$, as $z \in \mathcal{Z}^h$. This implies that z satisfies

(5). By Definition 1, $z \in \mathcal{N}_\alpha$. One can prove in a similar manner that any $z \in \mathcal{Z}^h \cap \left[\frac{1}{2}, 1\right) \setminus (\alpha, 1-\alpha)$ is also in $\mathcal{N}_\alpha$.

When $z = 0$ or 1, the claim holds exactly as in the case with $\alpha > 1/2$.

(ii.b) Let $\alpha < 1/2$. Say $\alpha \in \mathcal{N}_\alpha$. Then, $y^*(\alpha) = 1$, and hence support$(\mu^R) = \{1\} \subseteq \mathcal{A}_u$ only if $h(\alpha) \geq 0$. Conversely, say $h(\alpha) \geq 0$. Then, $\mathcal{A}_u = \{1,2\}$ or $\{1\}$. It is now easy to observe that $\alpha \in \mathcal{N}_\alpha$ as $y^*(\alpha) = 1$ ensures (5) is satisfied.

(ii.c) The proof follows as in part (ii.c). $\qquad\square$

Proof of Proposition 1: Firstly, consider $z^* \in \mathcal{N}_\alpha \cap \mathcal{Z}^h$. Then, by definition of $\mathcal{Z}^h$, $u(1, z^*) = u(2, z^*)$. Thus, note from (10), (11) that $u_\alpha^R(z^*) = u(1, z^*) = u_\alpha^I(z^*)$. Secondly, consider $z^* = 0 \in \mathcal{N}_\alpha \setminus \mathcal{Z}^h$. Then, $y^*(0) = 0$, and thus, $u_\alpha^R(0) = u(2, 0) = u_\alpha^I(0)$. One can similarly prove that $u_\alpha^R(1) = u(1, 1) = u_\alpha^I(1)$, when $1 \in \mathcal{N}_\alpha \setminus \mathcal{Z}^h$.

Next, suppose $z^* = \alpha \in \mathcal{N}_\alpha \setminus \mathcal{Z}^h$. Then, by Theorem 2, $h(\alpha) > 0$, i.e., $u(1, \alpha) > u(2, \alpha)$, and $\alpha < \frac{1}{2}$. The latter implies that $y^*(\alpha) = 1$; thus:

$$u_\alpha^R(\alpha) = u(1, \alpha) > u(2, \alpha) = u_\alpha^I(\alpha).$$

Lastly, one can similarly prove the claim for $1 - \alpha \in \mathcal{N}_\alpha \setminus \mathcal{Z}^h$.

Define $f(z) := zu(1, z) + (1 - z)u(2, z)$ for all $z \in [0, 1]$. Consider any $z^* \in \mathcal{N}_\alpha$, then, $u^S = \sup_{z \in [0,1]} f(z) = \max\left\{\sup_{z \in [0,1] - \{z^*\}} f(z), f(z^*)\right\} \geq f(z^*) \geq u_\alpha^I(z^*)$, see (12). $\qquad\square$

Proof of Proposition 2: Suppose $\alpha > \frac{1}{2}$. By Theorem 2, $\mathcal{N}_\alpha = \mathcal{N}_1$. Further, $u^S \geq u_\alpha^R(z^*) - u_\alpha^I(z^*)$, for each $z^* \in \mathcal{N}_\alpha$, see proof of Proposition 1. From (10):

$$u_1^R(z^*) = \begin{cases} u(2, z^*), & \text{if } z^* = 0 \in \mathcal{N}_\alpha \setminus \mathcal{Z}^h, \\ u(1, z^*), & \text{otherwise.} \end{cases}$$

Then, observe $u_1^R(z^*) = u_\alpha^I(z^*)$, again from the proof of Proposition 1. This completes the proof for $\alpha > \frac{1}{2}$.

Next, consider $\alpha \leq \frac{1}{2}$. Then, $\mathcal{N}_\alpha \subseteq \mathcal{N}_1$ only if $\alpha, 1 - \alpha \notin \mathcal{N}_\alpha$, see Theorem 2. Thus, the proof follows as in case with $\alpha > \frac{1}{2}$. $\qquad\square$

References

1. Abdallah, M., Cason, T., Bagchi, S., Sundaram, S.: The effect of behavioral probability weighting in a sequential defender-attacker game. In: 2020 59th IEEE Conference on Decision and Control (CDC), pp. 3255–3260 (2020)
2. Abdallah, M., Naghizadeh, P., Hota, A.R., Cason, T., Bagchi, S., Sundaram, S.: The impacts of behavioral probability weighting on security investments in interdependent systems. In: 2019 American Control Conference (ACC), pp. 5260–5265. IEEE (2019)
3. Agarwal, K., Avrachenkov, K., Vyas, R., Kavitha, V.: Two choice behavioral game dynamics with myopic-rational and herding players. In: Proceedings of the ACM on Measurement and Analysis of Computing Systems (2025). https://inria.hal.science/hal-04883482
4. Agarwal, K., Kavitha, V.: Single-out fake posts: participation game and its design. In: 2023 American Control Conference (ACC), pp. 2344–2350. IEEE (2023)
5. Banerjee, A.V.: A simple model of herd behavior. Q. J. Econ. **107**(3), 797–817 (1992)
6. Bénabou, R., Tirole, J.: Intrinsic and extrinsic motivation. Rev. Econ. Stud. **70**(3), 489–520 (2003)
7. Bonau, S.: A case for behavioural game theory. J. Game Theory **6**(1), 7–14 (2017)
8. Camerer, C.F.: Behavioral game theory: Experiments in strategic interaction. Princeton university press (2011)
9. Carmona, R., Delarue, F.: Probabilistic Theory of Mean Field Games with Applications I-II. Springer (2018)
10. Eliaz, K.: Fault tolerant implementation. Rev. Econ. Stud. **69**(3), 589–610 (2002)
11. Eyster, E., Rabin, M.: Rational and naive herding (2009)
12. Feldman, M., Chuang, J.: Overcoming free-riding behavior in peer-to-peer systems. ACM Sigecom Exchanges **5**(4), 41–50 (2005)
13. Morone, A., Samanidou, E.: A simple note on herd behaviour. J. Evol. Econ. **18**, 639–646 (2008)
14. Narahari, Y.: Game Theory and Mechanism Design, vol. 4. World Scientific (2014)
15. Noti, G.: From behavioral theories to econometrics: inferring preferences of human agents from data on repeated interactions. In: Proceedings of the AAAI Conference on Artificial Intelligence, vol. 35, pp. 5637–5646 (2021)
16. Sandholm, W.H.: Population Games and Evolutionary Dynamics. MIT Press (2010)
17. Sanjab, A., Saad, W., Başar, T.: Prospect theory for enhanced cyber-physical security of drone delivery systems: a network interdiction game. In: 2017 IEEE International Conference on Communications (ICC), pp. 1–6 (2017)
18. Schultz, W.: Introduction. neuroeconomics: the promise and the profit. Philosop. Trans. Royal Soc. B: Biolog. Sci. **363**(1511), 3767–3769 (2008)
19. Thaler, R.H.: From cashews to nudges: the evolution of behavioral economics. Am. Econ. Rev. **108**(6), 1265–1287 (2018)

20. Vasal, D., Berry, R.: Alpha-robust equilibrium in anonymous games. Available at SSRN 3643821 (2020)
21. Vasal, D., Berry, R.: Fault tolerant equilibria in anonymous games: best response correspondences and fixed points. arXiv preprint arXiv:2005.06812 (2020)
22. Verginer, L., Vaccario, G., Ronzani, P.: The robotic herd: Using human-bot interactions to explore irrational herding. SocArXiv (2023)

Incentive Mechanisms with Sequential Voluntary Participation

Ziyuan Huang and Mingyan Liu$^{(\boxtimes)}$

University of Michigan, Ann Arbor, MI 48109, USA
{ziyuanh,mingyan}@umich.edu

Abstract. Network games have been commonly used as a formalism to study the provisioning of public goods, and mechanism design as a tool to induce socially desirable effort from agents. When the type of public goods is non-excludable, i.e., an agent can opt out of the mechanism and yet continue to benefit from actions of those who remain in the mechanism, existing literature has shown the difficulty of designing transfer mechanisms that simultaneously achieve social optimality, weak budget balance, and voluntary participation. This challenge stems from the fact that the participation of some agents creates excessive positive externality, thereby reducing the incentive for others to voluntarily opt in. To get around this difficulty, we consider instead a sequential model whereby agents are invited in some order σ to commit to the mechanism, with each agent's commitment contingent on the decisions of those preceding it and in anticipation of those following it. This gives rise to the notion of sequential participation referred to as σ-voluntary participation (σ-**VP**), which is a full-participation outcome under the given order. We show that satisfying the conventional voluntary participation condition is equivalent to satisfying σ-**VP** for all orderings σ. Furthermore, we demonstrate via examples that it is possible to simultaneously achieve social optimality, weak budget balance, and full participation in the sense of σ-**VP**, especially in large systems.

Keywords: Mechanism design · IInterdependent security games · Network games · Voluntary participation

1 Introduction

Network game as a formalism is often used to study the provision and allocation of public goods among interacting agents, whereby the effort exerted (or investment made) by one agent carries (positive or negative) externality for those connected to it, see e.g., [3]. As a sub-field, the family of *interdependent security* (IDS) games is a special class of network games that treats the investment/effort in security measures as the public good and adopts utility functions that capture the positive externality in security investment, such as total (weighted) effort model [1,14] and weakest link model [4,8,20]. This paper will focus on this spe-

© ICST Institute for Computer Sciences, Social Informatics and Telecommunications Engineering 2026
Published by Springer Nature Switzerland AG 2026. All Rights Reserved
V. Aggarwal et al. (Eds.): GameNets 2025, LNICST 657, pp. 108–123, 2026.
https://doi.org/10.1007/978-3-032-12915-4_7

cial class of IDS games as our utility functions follow the common assumptions made in this literature.

Strategic decision making in such a networked setting can be complex and inefficient: if an agent can benefit from neighboring agents' high effort, or if one's investment is seen to mostly benefit others, then there may exist incentives to under-invest, leading to a form of free-riding. This is often observed both in theory (in the form of an inefficient Nash equilibrium compared to socially optimal – maximizing sum of utilities – effort levels) and in practice (e.g., under-investment in public libraries and clean air). In response, a mechanism design approach is often used to induce self-interested agents to act in a more socially responsible manner. One of the most commonly used type of mechanisms is the *transfer mechanism* or *tax-based mechanisms*, whereby agents' incentives are realigned with a social-optimal objective through taxation and subsidization; the use of taxes and subsidies effectively revises the agents' utility functions and induces a new game. The agents are typically assumed to satisfy two assumptions:

(IC) that they act selfishly, i.e., individually utility maximizing given others' actions; this is also referred to as incentive compatibility (IC);
(IR) that the agents are individually rational (IR) in determining whether to participate in the mechanism (i.e., those who participate receive higher utility than their outside options would yield).

The efficacy of the mechanism is then assessed by examining the equilibrium (typically a Nash equilibrium) of this mechanism-induced game. The goal of the mechanism design is to achieve the following set of properties at the equilibrium (and sometimes off equilibrium as well) of the induced game:

(SO) that the action or effort profile at equilibrium achieves social optimality;
(BB) or (WBB) that the mechanism is fiscally feasible at equilibrium; when the mechanism is budget neutral, i.e., sum of all taxes equal sum of all subsidies, we say the mechanism is (strongly) budget balanced; the mechanism is said to be weakly budget balanced if it runs a finite surplus at equilibrium.
(VP) that all agents would voluntarily participate in the mechanism.

Literature has explored various transfer mechanisms in IDS games and network games more generally. Examples include [11] that links the transfers (taxes or subsidies) to agents' investments; [5] that proposes rebates and penalties associated with the mechanism outcome; [10] that incorporates a message-passing system, and [7] that bases the transfers on certain screening/auditing results. Two prototypical mechanisms emerged from this literature that formed the basis for many other variants and extensions: the pivotal mechanism and the externality mechanism [2,6]. These mechanisms are often shown to simultaneously satisfy all the properties/conditions listed above, see e.g., [16].

Of particular interest to our study is the notion of voluntary participation. In a typical mechanism cited above, this (**VP**) property is satisfied by ensuring that all agents' utility inside the mechanism is no less than outside, whereby the outside option is either normalized to zero (e.g., a transceiver not participating in a power control mechanism does not get access to the wireless channel [19]), or assumed to be disconnected from the system inside the mechanism (e.g., an agent becomes isolated and exerts an effort aimed at optimizing its utility that is no longer a function of other agents actions). This treatment of the (**VP**) property is appropriate when the public good under study is *excludable* (or sometimes referred to as a *club good*), in the sense that by opting out an agent is excluded from benefiting from others' actions.

However, when a public good is *non-excludable* (i.e., a real public good as opposed to a club good), then an agent's outside option is more complicated. In particular, when an agent who has opted out of the mechanism but nonetheless remains connected to those who have opted in, and therefore can continue to benefit from the latter's actions induced by the mechanism, the comparison is no longer straightforward. In particular, an impossibility result was presented in [12], which serves to highlight the challenge in achieving **SO**, **WBB**, and **VP** simultaneously when the public good is non-excludable. An intuitive way of understanding such negative results is to consider a system of N agents, where there may exist some agent whose equilibrium effort, if it participates in the mechanism, is insignificant (as a result of their high cost of effort as well as connectivity to others), and who relies on, benefits from, and gets taxed to pay for some other agents' more significant effort. When N becomes large, such an agent is more likely to exist. Note that this agent can opt out with very little impact on the resulting new equilibrium effort of the remaining $N - 1$ agents. Thus by opting out it enjoys virtually the same benefit, while not paying taxes. As a result, to prevent this agent from opting out, the mechanism needs to offer a subsidy instead. As N grows, the number of such agents is also likely to grow, leading to a (growing) budget deficit.

In this paper, we consider instead a sequential model whereby agents are sequentially invited in some order σ to commit to the mechanism, with each agent's commitment contingent on the decisions of those preceding it and in anticipation of those following it. This gives rise to the notion of sequential participation referred to as σ-voluntary participation (σ-**VP**), which is a full-participation outcome under this sequential structure. We show that satisfying the conventional voluntary participation condition is equivalent to satisfying σ-**VP** for all orderings σ. Furthermore, we demonstrate via examples that it is possible (and easier) to simultaneously achieve **SO**, **WBB**, and full participation in the sense of σ-**VP** than in the conventional **VP**, especially in large systems.

Our main contributions are summarized as follows:

1. We highlight the critical role of partial participation in shaping mechanism outcomes, an aspect often overlooked in the mechanism literature. We analyze the outcome of the mechanism-induced game, defined as the (equilibrium effort profile, participation set) pair.

2. We propose σ-voluntary participation based on a sequential participation game and explore its relationship with conventional **VP** in Theorem 1.

3. We propose a procedure for constructing a transfer mechanism that satisfies **SO** and σ-**VP** and derive conditions and task-dependent heuristics that satisfy **WBB**. We evaluate this approach for the negative (impossibility) examples given in [12,13], showing its capability of guaranteeing all three properties, especially with large numbers of agents.

The remainder of the paper is organized as follows. In Sect. 2, we formulate the problem and reproduce the impossibility result from [12,13] to explain the failure of classical transfer mechanisms and motivate our method. In Sect. 3.2, we formally state σ-voluntary participation and analyze its performance over widely adopted interdependent games. We conclude the paper in Sect. 4.

2   The Model and Preliminaries

Consider a collection of N interconnected agents indexed by $i \in [N]$ where $[N] := \{1, 2, \ldots, N\}$. Each agent chooses an effort level $x_i \geq 0$. Denote $\mathbf{x} := \{x_i\}_{i=1}^{N}$ as the effort profile of the N agents and $\mathbf{x}_{-i} := \{x_j\}_{j \neq i}$ as the effort profile of all but the i-th agent. Each agent is associated with a utility function $u_i^o : \mathbb{R}_+^N \to \mathbb{R}$ where $u_i^o(\mathbf{x})$ numerically encodes its valuation of the effort profile $\mathbf{x}$. Assume $u_i^o(\cdot)$ is differentiable and strictly concave, $\forall i$, and $\frac{\partial u_i^o}{\partial x_j} \geq 0$, $\forall j \neq i$. The latter reflects the positive externality of agent j's effort on agent i's utility. Let $\mathbf{u}^o := \{u_i^o(\cdot)\}_{i=1}^{N}$ denote the profile of these utilities in the absence of a mechanism (also referred to as *outside utilities*). We assume all agents are utility maximizing and the Nash equilibrium of the game with utility profile $\mathbf{u}^o$ is $\hat{\mathbf{x}}^o$.[1]

2.1   Transfer Mechanism

A transfer mechanism or tax-based mechanism $\mathbb{M}$ induces a game $\mathbf{G}^{\mathcal{V}}$ among the N agents where a subset of participants $\mathcal{V} \subseteq [N]$ subscribe to (participate in) a transfer that effectively revises their utility functions. Specifically, the transfer (function) $\mathbf{t} := \{t_i\}_{i=1}^{N}$, where $t_i : \mathbb{R}_+^N \times 2^{[N]} \to \mathbb{R}$, $2^{[N]}$ denoting the power set of $[N]$, is a function of the effort profile $\mathbf{x}$ and the state of participation (given by the subset of participants). We require that $t_i(\cdot, \mathcal{V}) \equiv 0$, $\forall i \notin \mathcal{V}$, indicating that opt-out agents are not subject to the transfers. This transfer modifies the utility function as a *commodity numeraire*, in what will be referred to as the *modified* utility or *inside* utility $u_i^{\mathcal{V}}$:

$$u_i^{\mathcal{V}}(\mathbf{x}) := u_i^o(\mathbf{x}) + t_i(\mathbf{x}, \mathcal{V}), \quad \forall i \in [N]. \tag{1}$$

While we refer to this as a transfer mechanism, depending on its sign, $\mathbf{t}$ is either a tax or a subsidy: when $t_i(\mathbf{x}, \mathcal{V}) < 0$, agent i is *taxed* by participating

---

[1] Because the characterization of equilibrium is not the primary focus of this paper, for ease of exposition, we will assume $\hat{\mathbf{x}}^o$ exists and is unique.

as $u_i^{\mathcal{V}}(\mathbf{x}) < u_i^o(\mathbf{x})$; when $t_i(\mathbf{x}, \mathcal{V}) > 0$, agent i is *subsidized* by participating as $u_i^{\mathcal{V}}(\mathbf{x}) > u_i^o(\mathbf{x})$. Let $\mathbf{u}^{\mathcal{V}} := \{u_i^{\mathcal{V}}(\cdot)\}_{i=1}^N$ denote the modified utility profile with the set of participants $\mathcal{V}$. The outcome of the game induced by the mechanism should be consistent with the IC and IR properties mentioned in Sect. 1, formally defined as follows.

Definition 1 ($\mathcal{V}$-Incentive-Compatible Profile (IC($\mathcal{V}$))). *For any set of participants $\mathcal{V} \subseteq [N]$, the $\mathcal{V}$-incentive-compatible profile is the effort profile $\hat{\mathbf{x}}$ satisfying*

$$\hat{x}_i = \arg\max_{x_i \geq 0} u_i^{\mathcal{V}}(x_i, \hat{\mathbf{x}}_{-i}), \ \forall i \in \mathcal{V},$$
$$\hat{x}_i = \arg\max_{x_i \geq 0} u_i^o(x_i, \hat{\mathbf{x}}_{-i}), \ \forall i \notin \mathcal{V}. \tag{2}$$

This $\mathcal{V}$-incentive-compatible profile will be denoted concisely as **IC($\mathcal{V}$)**.

Definition 2 (Individual Rationality). *A subset $\mathcal{V} \subseteq [N]$ satisfies individual rationality if*

$$u_i^{\mathcal{V}}(\mathbf{IC}(\mathcal{V})) \geq u_i^o(\mathbf{IC}(\mathcal{V} \setminus \{i\})), \ \forall i \in \mathcal{V}, \tag{3}$$

$$u_i^o(\mathbf{IC}(\mathcal{V})) \geq u_i^{\mathcal{V} \cup \{i\}}(\mathbf{IC}(\mathcal{V} \cup \{i\})), \ \forall i \notin \mathcal{V}. \tag{4}$$

The above definition guarantees that no participant in $\mathcal{V}$ has the incentive to unilaterally exit, and no agent outside $\mathcal{V}$ has the incentive to unilaterally join.

Definition 3 (Mechanism Outcome). *The outcome of the mechanism is the Nash equilibrium of the game induced by the mechanism, and is given by the pair $(\overline{\mathbf{x}}, \overline{\mathcal{V}})$ where $\overline{\mathbf{x}} = \mathbf{IC}(\overline{\mathcal{V}})$, and $\overline{\mathcal{V}}$ satisfies individual rationality.*

It is worth noting that in much of the existing literature, the effort profile $\overline{\mathbf{x}}$ alone defines the outcome of such a mechanism, with the assumption that there is full participation, i.e., it is explicitly or implicitly assumed that $\mathcal{V} = [N]$. We do not make such an assumption and therefore the set $\mathcal{V}$ is part of the outcome ($\mathcal{V}$ is not necessarily unique).

As mentioned in the introduction, the goal of a mechanism is typically to induce a game such that its outcome enjoys the set of desirable properties; these are described next. The first is social optimality (**SO**). We say the mechanism outcome $(\overline{\mathbf{x}}, \overline{\mathcal{V}})$ achieves *social optimality* (**SO**) if $\overline{\mathbf{x}} = \hat{\mathbf{x}}^s$ where

$$\hat{\mathbf{x}}^s := \arg\max_{\mathbf{x} \in \mathbb{R}_+^N} \sum_{i=1}^N u_i^o(\mathbf{x}). \tag{5}$$

Notably, this property is independent of $\overline{\mathcal{V}}$ and may indeed hold even if the outcome involves partial participation ($\mathcal{V} \neq [N]$).

One way to achieve (5) using a transfer mechanism is to ensure that total transfers equal zero at equilibrium. In general, the total transfer at the equilibrium should be non-positive, so the mechanism does not run a deficit:

$$\sum_{i \in \mathcal{V}} t_i(\overline{\mathbf{x}}, \overline{\mathcal{V}}) \leq 0. \tag{6}$$

This happens when the total taxes collected are no less than the total subsidies offered, in which case we say the mechanism outcome is *weakly budget balanced* (**WBB**). When equality holds, the outcome is (strongly) *budget balanced* (**BB**). Finally, the outcome $(\overline{\mathbf{x}}, \overline{\mathcal{V}})$ satisfies *voluntary participation* (**VP**) if $\overline{\mathcal{V}} = [N]$.

We end this section by noting that much of the mechanism design literature is on eliciting truthful utility information from the agents through message passing. For instance, the VickreyClarkeGroves (VCG) mechanism has been shown to induce truthful revelation [16]. In this study, however, we will instead focus on the simultaneous attainment of the list of desirable properties outlined earlier. As shown in the next section, transfer mechanisms in general fail to satisfy **SO**, **VP**, and **WBB** simultaneously, when agents are assumed **IC** and **IR**. This is true even when the mechanism designer has full information of the agents' utility. For this reason, for the remainder of this paper, we will assume that the mechanism designer has full information of the agents' utilities.

2.2   An Impossibility Result

As mentioned earlier, an example was given in [12,13] to demonstrate that no transfer mechanism satisfies **WBB**, **VP**, and (a limited version of) **SO** simultaneously. We reproduce this negative example below.

Example 1. Consider a total-effort utility model

$$u_i^o(\mathbf{x}) = -\exp(-\sum_{j=1}^{N} x_j) - c_i x_i, \quad \forall i \in [N],$$

with $c_1 < c_2 < \cdots < c_N$ such that $c_1 < \frac{c_2}{N-1}$. It is known from [4,20] that $\hat{\mathbf{x}}^o = [-\ln c_1, 0, 0, \ldots, 0]^T$ – the most cost-efficient agent is the only one making a positive effort. In contrast, the socially optimal profile is $\hat{\mathbf{x}}^s = [-\ln(c_1/N), 0, 0, \ldots, 0]^T$, whereby the most cost-efficient agent is incentivized (subsidized) to make a higher effort.

Consider a transfer mechanism $\mathbb{M}$ with transfer $\mathbf{t}$. If the mechanism satisfies **VP**, we need to ensure every agent i's inside utility under $\mathbf{IC}([N])$ is no less than its outside utility under $\mathbf{IC}([N] \setminus \{i\})$. An additional requirement is imposed that the equilibrium effort of the remaining $N - 1$ participants, as a result of the induced game and in best response to the effort x_i exerted by the outsider, maximizes the social welfare among themselves, $\sum_{j \neq i} u_j^o(x_i, \mathbf{x}_{-i})$.[2].

Under such requirement, when $i = 1$ (agent 1 opting out), the KKT condition of agent 1's self-utility maximization implies

$$\left(\sum_{i=2}^{N} x_i > -\ln c_1 \,\&\, x_1 = 0\right) \quad \text{or} \quad \sum_{i=1}^{N} x_i = -\ln c_1. \tag{7}$$

---

[2] This is the definition of "exit equilibrium" introduced in [12,13].

At the same time, the other agents' best response in the mechanism-induced game can be alternatively (and much more easily) computed by

$$\max_{x_2,\ldots,x_N \geq 0} \; -(N-1)\exp(-\sum_{j=1}^{N} x_j) - \sum_{i=2}^{N} c_i x_i,$$

whose KKT condition implies, $\forall 2 \leq i \leq N$,

$$\left(\sum_{j \neq i} x_j > -\ln\frac{c_i}{N-1} \,\&\, x_i = 0 \right) \quad \text{or} \quad \sum_{j \neq i} x_j = -\ln\frac{c_i}{N-1}. \tag{8}$$

Combining and solving (7) and (8), we obtain $[-\ln c_1, 0\ldots,0]^T$ as $c_1 < \frac{c_2}{N-1}$, $\forall i \geq 2$, which is exactly the Nash equilibrium at anarchy. In other words, this implies $\mathbf{IC}([N]\setminus\{1\}) = \hat{\mathbf{x}}^o$. For agent 1 to voluntarily participate,

$$u_1^{[N]}(\mathbf{x}^s) = u_1^o(\hat{\mathbf{x}}^s) + t_1(\hat{\mathbf{x}}^s, [N]) \geq u_1^o(\mathbf{IC}([N]\setminus\{1\})) = u_1^o(\hat{\mathbf{x}}^o)$$
$$\iff t_1(\hat{\mathbf{x}}^s, [N]) \geq c_1\left(\ln N - \frac{N-1}{N}\right).$$

Similarly, when agent $i \geq 2$ opts out, we obtain $\mathbf{IC}([N]\setminus\{i\}) = [-\ln(c_1/(N-1)), 0, 0, \ldots, 0]^T$. For agent i to voluntarily participate, we need

$$u_i^{[N]}(\mathbf{x}^s) = u_i^o(\hat{\mathbf{x}}^s) + t_i(\hat{\mathbf{x}}^s, [N]) \geq u_i^o(\mathbf{IC}([N]\setminus\{i\}))$$
$$\iff t_i(\hat{\mathbf{x}}^s, [N]) \geq -\frac{c_1}{N(N-1)}, \quad \forall i \in [N].$$

To maintain participation incentives of all N agents, the total budget is therefore bounded below by

$$\sum_{i=1}^{N} t_i(\hat{\mathbf{x}}^s, [N]) \geq c_1(\ln N - 1).$$

This is positive whenever $N > 1$, implying that the mechanism designer has to pay a net positive subsidy, leading to a budget deficit that grows in N. $\qquad\square$

The reason for the failure in Example 1 is that an outsider can still benefit from the more socially responsible actions of the participants. This is due to both the positive externality and the non-excludable nature of the public goods.

3   A Sequential Participation Mechanism

We now propose a different notion of participation property based on a sequential game and demonstrate its potential in circumventing the impossibility result.

3.1 Sequential Voluntary Participation

Let $\sigma : [N] \to [N]$ be a permutation of $[N]$ and Σ_N be the set of all permutations over $[N]$. Consider a full-information sequential game (denoted as $\tilde{\mathbf{G}}$) with $N + 1$ steps where agent $\sigma(1)$ announces its participation decision $p_{\sigma(1)} \in \{0, 1\}$, followed by agent $\sigma(2)$, and so on. At the last stage, all agents who have declared participation ($p_i = 1$) stay in the mechanism $\mathbb{M}$, while others maximize their outside utility, each group best-responding to the other. In other words, the last-stage outcome is exactly $\mathbf{IC}(\{i|p_i = 1, \forall i\})$. We assume that agents will commit to their decisions once announced (or that the mechanism designer is able to enforce participation once an agent has committed).

Definition 4 (σ-Voluntary Participation (σ-VP)). *The mechanism $\mathbb{M}$ satisfies σ-voluntary participation (σ-VP) if $p_i = 1$, $\forall i \in [N]$, is part of a subgame perfect equilibrium (SPE) of the game $\tilde{\mathbf{G}}$. If all agents participating is the* unique *subgame perfect equilibrium, we say the mechanism satisfies* strict σ-VP.

Our goal is to establish whether it is in general possible to design a mechanism that satisfies **SO**, **WBB**, and σ-**VP** (instead of **VP**). While checking **VP** only requires transfer functions defined over participation sets of size $N - 1$, i.e., $t_j(\cdot, [N] \setminus \{i\}), \forall j \neq i, \forall i \in [N]$, checking σ-**VP** requires a larger set of transfer functions to be defined because a future agent may opt out if an earlier agent does so. For this reason, we begin by defining this larger set of transfer functions.

Let $\mathbb{M}$ be a conventional simultaneous-move mechanism with transfer functions $\mathbf{t}$.[3] Denote by $\upsilon_{<i} := \{\sigma(j) : j < i\}$ the set of agents ranked before $\sigma(i)$ in σ with $\sigma_{<1} := \emptyset$ and the collection $\mathcal{T}_i := \{\mathcal{V} \subset [N] : \sigma(i) \in \mathcal{V},\ \sigma(j) \notin \mathcal{V},\ \forall j > i\}$ of all proper subsets of $[N]$ containing $\sigma(i)$ but no agents ranked after $\sigma(i)$. Let $\tilde{\mathbb{M}}$ be a sequential mechanism with a given ordering σ and transfer $\tilde{\mathbf{t}}$ derived from $\mathbf{t}$ as follows, $\forall \mathcal{V} \subseteq [N]$:

$$\tilde{t}_{\sigma(i)}(\mathbf{x}, \mathcal{V}) := t_{\sigma(i)}(\mathbf{x}, \mathcal{V}) +$$

$$\begin{cases} u^o_{\sigma(i)}(\mathbf{IC}(\sigma_{<i})) - u^o_{\sigma(i)}(\mathbf{IC}([N] \setminus \{\sigma(i)\})) & \mathcal{V} = [N] \\ u^o_{\sigma(i)}(\mathbf{IC}(\mathcal{V} \setminus \{\sigma(i)\})) - u^o_{\sigma(i)}(\mathbf{IC}(\mathcal{V})) - t_{\sigma(i)}(\mathbf{IC}(\mathcal{V}), \mathcal{V}) - \varepsilon & \mathcal{V} \in \mathcal{T}_i \\ 0 & \mathcal{V} \notin \mathcal{T}_i,\ \mathcal{V} \neq [N] \end{cases}$$

$$(9)$$

where $\mathbf{IC}(\mathcal{V})$ is under the original, $\mathbb{M}$-induced game, and $\varepsilon > 0$ is a small number (for tie-breaking purposes).[4]. Denote the inside utility of the $\tilde{\mathbb{M}}$-induced game as $\tilde{u}_i^{\mathcal{V}}(\cdot) := u_i^o(\cdot) + \tilde{t}_i(\cdot, \mathcal{V})$. We will also write $\tilde{\mathbb{M}}$ as $\tilde{\mathbb{M}}_\sigma$ to emphasize its dependence on the ordering. The following lemma follows directly from the observation that $\tilde{\mathbf{t}} - \mathbf{t}$ is independent of the effort profile $\mathbf{x}$.

---

[3] As noted earlier, a conventional $\mathbb{M}$ does not specify transfer functions for all possible participation sets, which we need to derive the new sequential mechanism. For our purpose, the missing original transfers may be defined arbitrarily.

[4] We note that (9) is not a unique design of transfers; there exist alternatives that maintain the same total budget under full participation.

116   Z. Huang and M. Liu

Lemma 1. *The incentive compatible profile under the $\tilde{\mathbb{M}}_\sigma$- and $\mathbb{M}$-induced games with participation set $\mathcal{V}$ are the same, $\forall \mathcal{V} \subseteq [N]$.*

Lemma 1 implies that $\tilde{\mathbb{M}}_\sigma$ as constructed in (9) has the nice property that its equilibrium effort profile is inherently the same as the simultaneous-move mechanism from which it is derived. In light of this, we will not further distinguish between the two and simply denote the incentive-compatible profile under both $\tilde{\mathbb{M}}$ and $\mathbb{M}$ as $\mathbf{IC}(\mathcal{V})$ for simplicity, for given participation set $\mathcal{V}$.

Lemma 2. *In the $\tilde{\mathbb{M}}_\sigma$-induced game, agent $\sigma(i)$'s best response, provided that at least one of its predecessors opts out, is to also opt out, $\forall i \geq 2$.*

Proof. We prove this by induction on the index i. For each i, consider the set $\mathcal{W}_i := \{\mathcal{V} \subset \sigma([i]) : \sigma(i) \in \mathcal{V} \text{ and } \exists j < i, \sigma(j) \notin \mathcal{V}\}$. Note $\mathcal{T}_N = \mathcal{W}_N$. Using (9), we have $\forall \mathcal{V} \in \mathcal{T}_N$,

$$\tilde{u}^\mathcal{V}_{\sigma(N)}(\mathbf{IC}(\mathcal{V})) = u^o_{\sigma(N)}(\mathbf{IC}(\mathcal{V} \setminus \{\sigma(N)\})) - \varepsilon < u^o_{\sigma(N)}(\mathbf{IC}(\mathcal{V} \setminus \{\sigma(N)\})).$$

Thus, whenever a predecessor opts out, agent $\sigma(N)$ would also opt out. Assume agent $\sigma(i)$'s best response is to opt out given its predecessors' participation falling in $\mathcal{W}_i$, $\forall i \geq k+1$. Consider agent $\sigma(k)$ and any $\mathcal{V} \in \mathcal{W}_k$. If agent $\sigma(k)$ opts out, the induction hypothesis implies that all its followers would opt out. Thus, its outside utility is $u^o_{\sigma(k)}(\mathbf{IC}(\mathcal{V} \setminus \{\sigma(k)\}))$. If agent $\sigma(k)$ opts in, $\tilde{u}^\mathcal{V}_{\sigma(k)}(\mathbf{IC}(\mathcal{V})) = u^o_{\sigma(k)}(\mathbf{IC}(\mathcal{V} \setminus \{\sigma(k)\})) - \varepsilon$. Thus, agent $\sigma(k)$'s best response is to opt out. This completes the induction step. $\square$

Lemma 2 suggests that the fact that its successors will all follow suit constitutes a credible threat to prevent $\sigma(i)$ from opting out. This holds regardless of the original mechanism $\mathbb{M}$ and the ordering σ. It is a direct consequence of the design of the transfer function for participation sets in $\mathcal{T}_i$ that discourages participation whenever a predecessor opts out.

Theorem 1. $\mathbb{M}$ *satisfies* ***VP*** *if and only if* $\forall \sigma \in \Sigma_N$, $\tilde{\mathbb{M}}_\sigma$ *satisfies strict σ-**VP**.*

Proof. First, consider the forward direction. For the last agent in σ, when all its predecessors participate, its best response is to participate as well, since

$$\begin{aligned}
\tilde{u}^{[N]}_{\sigma(N)}(\mathbf{IC}([N])) &= u^o_{\sigma(N)}(\mathbf{IC}([N])) + \tilde{t}_{\sigma(N)}(\mathbf{IC}([N]), [N]) \\
&= u^o_{\sigma(N)}(\mathbf{IC}([N])) + t_{\sigma(N)}(\mathbf{IC}([N]), [N]) + u^o_{\sigma(N)}(\mathbf{IC}(\sigma_{<N})) \\
&\quad - u^o_{\sigma(N)}(\mathbf{IC}([N] \setminus \{\sigma(N)\})) \geq u^o_{\sigma(N)}(\mathbf{IC}(\sigma_{<N})),
\end{aligned} \qquad (10)$$

where the second equality is due to the definition of $\tilde{t}_{\sigma(i)}$ in (9) and the inequality is due to the **VP** of $\mathbb{M}$: $u^{[N]}_{\sigma(N)}(\mathbf{IC}([N])) = u^o_{\sigma(N)}(\mathbf{IC}([N])) + t_{\sigma(N)}(\mathbf{IC}([N]), [N]) \geq u^o_{\sigma(N)}(\mathbf{IC}([N] \setminus \{\sigma(N)\}))$, with tie-breaking in favor of participation.

Consider the induction hypothesis that agent $\sigma(i)$ will participate given all its predecessors participate for all $i \geq k+1$. Consider now agent $\sigma(k)$. If all agents in $\sigma([k])$ participate, then by the induction hypothesis, all agents from $\sigma(k+1)$ to $\sigma(N)$ will also participate, in which case agent $\sigma(k)$ has a utility of $\tilde{u}_{\sigma(k)}^{[N]}(\mathbf{IC}([N]))$. If agent $\sigma(k)$ opts out, then by Lemma 2 all its successors will opt out, yielding the utility $u_{\sigma(k)}^{o}(\mathbf{IC}(\sigma_{<k}))$. As in (10), plugging in the definition of $\tilde{t}_{\sigma(k)}$ and by the **VP** property of $\mathbb{M}$ on agent $\sigma(k)$ results in the conclusion that agent $\sigma(k)$ will participate if all its predecessors do. Thus everyone participating is an SPE. This SPE is unique by construction, implying strict σ-**VP**.

For the reverse direction, consider an arbitrary σ. The strict σ-**VP** property implies that agent $\sigma(N)$ is better off participating than opting out, i.e.,

$$\tilde{u}_{\sigma(N)}^{[N]}(\mathbf{IC}([N])) = u_{\sigma(N)}^{[N]}(\mathbf{IC}([N])) + u_{\sigma(N)}^{o}(\mathbf{IC}(\sigma_{<N})) - u_{\sigma(N)}^{o}(\mathbf{IC}([N] \setminus \{\sigma(N)\}))$$
$$= u_{\sigma(N)}^{[N]}(\mathbf{IC}([N])) \geq u_{\sigma(N)}^{o}(\mathbf{IC}([N] \setminus \{\sigma(N)\})),$$

since $\sigma_{<N} = [N] \setminus \{\sigma(N)\}$. The inequality says that under $\mathbb{M}$ agent $\sigma(N)$ has no incentive to opt out (tie-breaking in favor of participation). As σ is arbitrary, $\sigma(N)$ can be any agent; thus no agent has an incentive to opt out, proving the **VP** property of $\mathbb{M}$. $\qquad\square$

By Lemma 1, $\mathbb{M}$ and $\tilde{\mathbb{M}}_\sigma$ yield the same mechanism outcome $(\mathbf{IC}([N]), [N])$ when $\mathbb{M}$ (resp. $\tilde{\mathbb{M}}$) satisfies **VP** (resp. σ-**VP**). This directly leads to following.

Corollary 1. $\mathbb{M}$ *satisfies* ***SO*** *and* ***VP*** *if and only if* $\forall \sigma \in \Sigma_N$, $\tilde{\mathbb{M}}$ *satisfies* ***SO*** *and strict* σ-***VP***.

On the other hand, $\mathbb{M}$ and $\tilde{\mathbb{M}}$ generally differ in their budget. As will be shown in Sects. 3.3 and 3.4, there are cases where $\mathbb{M}$ runs a budget deficit while $\tilde{\mathbb{M}}_\sigma$ earns a nonzero profit for some ordering σ.

Theorem 1 and Corollary 1 shed some interesting light on why the original **VP** condition is hard to satisfy, especially when **SO** and **WBB** are also required. The reverse direction in the theorem involves a universal qualifier over all permutations σ. That is, the simultaneous satisfaction of these three properties can only hold if σ-**VP** is satisfied under *all* possible permutations. If, however, we take the sequential view (and adopt a sequential mechanism), then we only need one such permutation to satisfy these properties.

3.2   The Sequential Mechanism

This subsection attempts to find a sequential mechanism that satisfies all three properties by first identifying a simultaneous-move mechanism $\mathbb{M}$ satisfying **SO** and **VP**, and then obtaining $\tilde{\mathbb{M}}_\sigma$ using (9) and an appropriate ordering σ.

Consider a standard Pivotal mechanism $\mathbb{M}$ [13], where the taxes are given by

$$t_i(\mathbf{x}, [N]) = \sum_{j \neq i} u_j^o(\mathbf{x}) - \sum_{j \in [N]} u_j^o(\hat{\mathbf{x}}^s) + u_i^o(\mathbf{IC}([N] \setminus \{i\})), \ \forall i \in [N], \quad (11)$$

$$t_i(\mathbf{x}, [N] \setminus \{k\}) = \sum_{j \neq i,k} u_j^o(\mathbf{x}) - \sum_{j \neq k} u_j^o(\hat{\mathbf{x}}^{s,[N] \setminus \{k\}}), \ \forall k, i \in [N]. \quad (12)$$

where $\hat{\mathbf{x}}^{s,\mathcal{V}}$ denotes the equilibrium to the following system

$$\hat{x}_i^{s,\mathcal{V}} = \arg\max_{x_i \geq 0} \sum_{j \in \mathcal{V}} u_j^o(x_i, \hat{x}_{-i}^{s,\mathcal{V}}), \quad \forall i \in \mathcal{V},$$

$$\hat{x}_i^{s,\mathcal{V}} = \arg\max_{x_i \geq 0} u_i^o(x_i, \hat{x}_{-i}^{s,\mathcal{V}}), \quad \forall i \notin \mathcal{V},$$

i.e., agents in $\mathcal{V}$ act socially optimally and in best response to the rest under the game induced by $\mathbb{M}$ with participation set $\mathbf{V}$. This is exactly the "exit equilibrium" introduced in Example 1 and [12,13]. Such mechanisms are known to guarantee **SO** and **VP** simultaneously [16].

However, they usually fail to satisfy **WBB**, especially for a large number of agents, for reasons discussed in Example 1 and [10,12]. Below we show that changing the requirement to (strict) σ-**VP** for some σ may allow the mechanism to extract more taxes and consequently satisfy **WBB**.

Take some permutation $\sigma \in \Sigma_N$ and construct $\tilde{\mathbb{M}}$ with transfer functions $\tilde{t}$ based on the Pivotal mechanism $\mathbb{M}$ following (9). $\tilde{\mathbb{M}}$ readily satisfies **SO** and strict σ-**VP** by Corollary 1. Denote the total budget of the mechanism as $B(\sigma)$, and

$$B(\sigma) = \sum_{i=1}^{N} \tilde{t}_i(\hat{\mathbf{x}}^s, [N]) = \sum_{i=1}^{N} u_{\sigma(i)}^o(\mathbf{IC}(\sigma_{<i})) - \sum_{i=1}^{N} u_{\sigma(i)}^o(\hat{\mathbf{x}}^s). \tag{13}$$

$B(\sigma)$ represents the net utility that the mechanism offers the agents as subsidies. The mechanism satisfies **WBB** if $B(\sigma) \leq 0$. The mechanism with the minimum deficit (or the highest revenue) corresponds to the solution to the problem;

$$\min_{\sigma \in \Sigma_N} \sum_{i=1}^{N} u_{\sigma(i)}^o(\mathbf{IC}(\sigma_{<i})). \tag{14}$$

The optimal permutation σ^* always exists due to the finite solution space. The question thus becomes whether it is possible for the mechanism to satisfy $B(\sigma^*) \leq 0$. While finding σ^* is in general a NP-hard problem as the search space is of order $N!$, it is possible to find sufficient conditions for the solution to (14) to be negative. Whether such conditions are computationally easier to verify remains an direction of future research. We also conjecture that there exist problem-dependent heuristics that yield σ satisfying **WBB**. We next present how to construct such heuristics for the negative (impossibility) examples given in [12,13] and show that the resulting sequential mechanism generates positive revenue while maintaining **SO** and σ-**VP**.

3.3   An Example with Heterogeneous Agents

Example 2. Recall the setting in Example 1 with agents' unit costs $c_1 < c_2 < \cdots < c_N$. The construction below works with or without the additional constraint $c_1 < \frac{c_2}{N-1}$. We show that there exists a sequential mechanism that satisfies **SO**,

σ-**VP**, and **WBB** simultaneously. Use the mechanism constructed in Sect. 3.2 with the permutation $\sigma(i) = N + 1 - i$, $\forall i \in [N]$. Corollary 1 implies that it already satisfies **SO** and σ-**VP**. We will show **WBB** by proving $B(\sigma) < 0$.

If $c_1 \leq \frac{c_2}{N-1}$, agent 1 is the most cost-efficient agent and the only agent exerting positive effort in the Nash equilibrium. Thus under the mechanism, $\mathbf{IC}(\sigma_{<i}) = \hat{\mathbf{x}}^o$, $\forall i \leq N$, where the last agent, opted in or out, serves as the single positive investor. Thus, the total budget is $B(\sigma) = \sum_{i=1}^{N} u_i^o(\hat{\mathbf{x}}^o) - \sum_{i=1}^{N} u_i^o(\hat{\mathbf{x}}^s) \leq 0$ by social optimality.

Consider the case when $c_1 > \frac{c_2}{N-1}$. Let $k \in [N]$ be the smallest index such that $c_{\sigma(k)}/k < c_1$. It must hold that $2 \leq k \leq N - 1$ because the function $k \mapsto c_{\sigma(k)}/k$ is monotonically decreasing. Thus, $\mathbf{IC}(\sigma_{<i}) = \hat{\mathbf{x}}^o$, $\forall i \leq k$, while $\mathbf{IC}(\sigma_{<i}) = \ln\left(\frac{c_{\sigma(i-1)}}{i-1}\right) \mathbf{e}_{i-1}$, $\forall i > k$ where $\mathbf{e}_{i-1}$ is the $(i-1)$-th Euclidean basis of dimension N. Then, the total budget is

$$B(\sigma) = \sum_{i=1}^{k} \left[u_{\sigma(i)}^o(\hat{\mathbf{x}}^o) - u_{\sigma(i)}^o(\hat{\mathbf{x}}^s) \right] + \sum_{i=k+1}^{N} \left[u_{\sigma(i)}^o(\mathbf{IC}(\sigma_{<i})) - u_{\sigma(i)}^o(\hat{\mathbf{x}}^s) \right]$$

$$= -c_1 k \frac{N}{N-1} + \sum_{i=k+1}^{N} \left(-\frac{c_{\sigma(i-1)}}{i-1} + \frac{c_1}{N} \right) < 0, \tag{15}$$

where the last inequality is because each term in the summation is negative. Notice that the inequality holds regardless of the values of k. Thus, the mechanism satisfies **WBB**. $\qquad\square$

The intuition is that the most "powerful" (cost-efficient in this example) agent makes its decision after observing all other agents' participation choices. A cost-efficient agent typically exerts higher investment in social optimality than at the Nash equilibrium, thus whether such agents participate in the mechanism greatly impacts the social optimality of the outcome. Accordingly, by placing such agents at the end of the sequence, we create a credible threat to the earlier, less powerful agents that the mechanism outcome could be unfavorable if insufficient taxes are collected, thereby ensuring their participation which in turn incentivizes the participation of successive agents. This highlights the significance of the permutation σ in the success of the mechanism.

Compared to Example 1, the above construction shows the possibility of maintaining **SO**, σ-**VP**, and **WBB** simultaneously by arranging the agents in decreasing order of their unit cost of effort. Interestingly, the total budget (15) is upper bounded by the negative term $-c_1 k \frac{N}{N-1}$ which is strictly less than $-2c_1$. This means the mechanism can always obtain net profit regardless of the number of agents in the system. In the same setting as Example 1, however, transfer mechanisms satisfying **SO** and **VP** necessarily run into budget deficit for all N when $c_1 < \frac{c_2}{N-1}$.[5]

---

[5] [9] studied the complementary case when $c_1 > \frac{c_2}{N-1}$ and concluded that transfer mechanisms run into deficit whenever $N > c_1 e$.

3.4 An Example with Homogeneous Agents

In this example, we illustrate the efficacy and robustness of such a mechanism by analyzing a homogeneous system where all permutations are equivalent.

Example 3. Let the agent's utility function be defined as follows

$$u_i^o(\mathbf{x}) = -\left(\sum_{i=1}^{N} \exp(-\gamma x_i)\right)^{1/\gamma} - cx_i, \quad \forall i = 1, 2, \ldots, N,$$

where $\gamma > 0$ is a constant. This formulation was introduced in [13] as a smooth approximation to the weakest-link interdependency: $u_i(\mathbf{x}) \approx -\exp(-\min_j x_j) - cx_i$. The approximation accuracy increases in γ. [13] showed that a standard simultaneous-move mechanism runs into budget deficit whenever $N > e^\gamma 2^{1-\gamma}$.

By symmetry, we have $\hat{\mathbf{x}}^o = \left(\frac{1}{\gamma} \ln \frac{N^{1-\gamma}}{c^\gamma}\right) \mathbf{1}_N$ where $\mathbf{1}_N$ is the N-size vector of all 1's. Each agent's utility under Nash equilibrium is the same and equals $u_i^o(\hat{\mathbf{x}}^o) = -cN - \frac{c}{\gamma} \ln \frac{N^{1-\gamma}}{c^\gamma}$. Similarly, we solve the social optimality problem and obtain $\hat{\mathbf{x}}^s = \left(\frac{1}{\gamma} \ln \frac{N}{c^\gamma}\right) \mathbf{1}_N$. Each agent's socially optimal utility is $u_i^o(\hat{\mathbf{x}}^s) = -c - \frac{c}{\gamma} \ln \frac{N}{c^\gamma}$. Since permutation does not matter, we will simply let $\sigma(i) = i$, $\forall i \in [N]$. Fix any $k = 2, \ldots, N$. The effort profile $\mathbf{IC}(\sigma_{<k})$ is determined by the following system

$$(k-1)\exp(-\gamma x_i)\left(\sum_{i=1}^{N}\exp(-\gamma x_i)\right)^{\frac{1}{\gamma}-1} = c, \qquad \forall i < k$$

$$\exp(-\gamma x_i)\left(\sum_{i=1}^{N}\exp(-\gamma x_i)\right)^{\frac{1}{\gamma}-1} = c, \qquad \forall i \geq k.$$

by symmetry, the opt-in (resp. opt-out) agents share the same effort levels. Thus,

$$\mathbf{IC}(\sigma_{<k}) = \mathbf{x} \iff x_i = \begin{cases} \frac{1}{\gamma} \ln \frac{(k-1)(N-k+2)^{1-\gamma}}{c^\gamma} & i < k \\ \frac{1}{\gamma} \ln \frac{(N-k+2)^{1-\gamma}}{c^\gamma} & i \geq k \end{cases}$$

The utilities of the opt-out agents are

$$u_i^o(\mathbf{IC}(\sigma_{<k})) = -c(N-k+2) - \frac{c}{\gamma} \ln \frac{(N-k+2)^{1-\gamma}}{c^\gamma}.$$

Then, the total budget given by the sequential mechanism is

$$B(\sigma) = u_1(\hat{\mathbf{x}}^o) - u_1(\hat{\mathbf{x}}^s) + \sum_{i=2}^{N} \left(u_i(\mathbf{IC}(\sigma_{<i})) - u_i(\hat{\mathbf{x}}^s) \right)$$

$$= c(\ln N - N + 1) + c\sum_{i=2}^{N} \left(\frac{1}{\gamma} \ln \frac{N}{(N-i+2)^{1-\gamma}} - N + i - 1 \right)$$

$$\overset{(1)}{\cong} \left(1 + \frac{N-1}{\gamma} \right) \ln N - \frac{1-\gamma}{\gamma} \sum_{i=2}^{N} \ln(N-i+2) - \left(\frac{1}{2}N^2 + \frac{1}{2}N - 1 \right)$$

$$\overset{(2)}{\leq} O(N \ln N) - O(N^2),$$

where (1) hides the common positive multiplier c and (2) translates each term into its asymptotic growth rate in N. Since $N \ln N = o(N^2)$, we conclude that the total budget is negative for N large enough, implying **BB** or **WBB** when the number of agents increases. $\qquad\square$

4   Discussion and Conclusion

In this paper, we proposed a sequential voluntary participation property for transfer mechanisms and demonstrated that it is easier to satisfy together with social optimality and weak budget balance. This is in contrast to the results in [12,13] where no transfer mechanism can satisfy voluntary participation, social optimality, and weak budget balance simultaneously. In the process of doing so, we introduced the concept of sequential voluntary participation, which was shown to be a relaxed version of voluntary participation studied in the literature.

Unlike the classical definition of voluntary participation, the sequential participation property relies heavily on the knowledge of agents' utilities in order to design the order of the report sequence to extract the appropriate amount of taxes. It remains an open question whether a similar partial-information mechanism exists that satisfies the revelation principle as well.

There is an interesting relationship between the problem studied here and the family of coalitional games. Coalitional games study the stability of coalitions formed among agents and the joint actions each coalition takes by utility redistribution [17]. A coalition is called *grand coalition* when it consists of all agents in the game [16]. Much of the coalition game literature focuses on characterizing stable coalitions instead of how they could naturally arise from a non-cooperative system. From this perspective, transfer mechanisms satisfying voluntary participation describe a way to implement the grand coalition.

The idea of leveraging future threats to influence agents' behaviors has been widely exploited in the literature of *intertemporal incentives*. Intertemporal incentive mechanisms work by linking future benefits or cooperation to the agents' current actions. For example, in cybersecurity agreements, [15] utilizes intertemporal incentives to motivate firms to share their private assessments of each other's actions with the understanding that future cooperation will depend on their prior disclosure behavior. Although the rationale is similar, intertemporal incentives are typically studied in repeated games with discounted utilities, whereas our sequential mechanism constructs the threats within a finite-stage sequential game context.

The game perspective of voluntary participation was first introduced by [18] where the mechanism outcome was generated by a two-stage model: agents *simultaneously* decide to participate or not in the first stage and best respond to each other with each utility modified according to their participation choices in the second stage. This view of voluntary participation serves as a motivation for sequential voluntary participation proposed in this paper.

References

1. Allouch, N.: On the private provision of public goods on networks. J. Econ. Theor. **157**, 527–552 (2015). https://doi.org/10.1016/j.jet.2015.01.007. https://www.sciencedirect.com/science/article/pii/S0022053115000095
2. Clarke, E.H.: Multipart pricing of public goods. Pub. Choice **11**, 17–33 (1971). https://www.jstor.org/stable/30022651
3. Galeotti, A., Goyal, S., Jackson, M.O., Vega-Redondo, F., Yariv, L.: Network games. Rev. Econ. Stud. **77**(1), 218–244 (2010). https://www.jstor.org/stable/40587626
4. Grossklags, J., Christin, N., Chuang, J.: Secure or insure?: a game-theoretic analysis of information security games. In: Proceedings of the 17th international conference on World Wide Web, Beijing China, April 2008, pp. 209–218. ACM (2008). https://doi.org/10.1145/1367497.1367526. https://dl.acm.org/doi/10.1145/1367497.1367526
5. Grossklags, J., Radosavac, S., Cardenas, A.A., Chuang, J.: Nudge: intermediaries' role in interdependent network security (2010)
6. Hurwicz, L.: Outcome functions yielding Walrasian and Lindahl allocations at Nash equilibrium points. Rev. Econ. Stud. **46**(2), 217–225 (1979). https://doi.org/10.2307/2297046. https://www.jstor.org/stable/2297046
7. Khalili, M.M., Naghizadeh, P., Liu, M.: Designing cyber insurance policies: the role of pre-screening and security interdependence. IEEE Trans. Inf. Forensics Secur. **13**(9), 2226–2239 (2018). https://doi.org/10.1109/TIFS.2018.2812205
8. Laszka, A., Felegyhazi, M., Buttyan, L.: A survey of interdependent information security games. ACM Comput. Surv. **47**(2), 23:1–23:38 (2014). https://doi.org/10.1145/2635673
9. Naghizadeh, P., Liu, M.: Budget balance or voluntary participation? Incentivizing investments in interdependent security games. In: 2014 52nd Annual Allerton Conference on Communication, Control, and Computing (Allerton), Monticello, IL, USA, September 2014, pp. 1102–1109. IEEE (2014). https://doi.org/10.1109/ALLERTON.2014.7028578. http://ieeexplore.ieee.org/document/7028578/
10. Naghizadeh, P., Liu, M.: Closing the price of anarchy gap in the interdependent security game. arXiv arXiv:1308.0979 [cs], August 2014. https://doi.org/10.48550/arXiv.1308.0979
11. Naghizadeh, P., Liu, M.: Voluntary participation in cyber-insurance markets. In: Workshop on the Economics of Information Security (WEIS), State College, Pennsylvania, USA, pp. 23–24, June 2014

12. Naghizadeh, P., Liu, M.: Exit equilibrium: towards understanding voluntary participation in security games. In: The 35th Annual IEEE International Conference on Computer Communications, IEEE INFOCOM 2016, , San Francisco, CA, USA, April 2016, pp. 1–9. IEEE (2016). https://doi.org/10.1109/INFOCOM.2016.7524353. http://ieeexplore.ieee.org/document/7524353/
13. Naghizadeh, P., Liu, M.: Opting out of incentive mechanisms: a study of security as a non-excludable public good. Trans. Info. For. Sec. **11**(12), 2790–2803 (2016). https://doi.org/10.1109/TIFS.2016.2599005
14. Naghizadeh, P., Liu, M.: Provision of public goods on networks: on existence, uniqueness, and centralities. arXiv arXiv:1604.08910 [cs], May 2016. https://doi.org/10.48550/arXiv.1604.08910
15. Naghizadeh, P., Liu, M.: Using private and public assessments in security information sharing agreements, January 2020. http://arxiv.org/abs/1604.04871. arXiv:1604.04871
16. Nisan, N., Roughgarden, T., Tardos, E., V. Vazirani, V.: Algorithmic Game Theory. Cambridge University Press, New York (2007)
17. Osborne, M.J., Rubinstein, A.: A Course in Game Theory. MIT Press, Cambridge, Mass (1994)
18. Saijo, T., Yamato, T.: A voluntary participation game with a non-excludable public good. J. Econ. Theor. **84**(2), 227–242 (1999). https://doi.org/10.1006/jeth.1998.2476. https://www.sciencedirect.com/science/article/pii/S0022053198924760
19. Saraydar, C., Mandayam, N., Goodman, D.: Efficient power control via pricing in wireless data networks. IEEE Trans. Commun. **50**(2), 291–303 (2002). https://doi.org/10.1109/26.983324. http://ieeexplore.ieee.org/document/983324/
20. Varian, H.: System reliability and free riding. In: Camp, L.J., Lewis, S. (eds.) Economics of Information Security. Advances in Information Security, pp. 1–15. Springer, Boston (2004). https://doi.org/10.1007/1-4020-8090-5_1

Interval Scheduling Games

Vipin Ravindran Vijayalakshmi[1], Marc Schröder[2], and Tami Tamir[3(✉)]

[1] Berlin, Germany
[2] School of Business and Economics, Maastricht University,
Maastricht, The Netherlands
`m.schroder@maastrichtuniversity.nl`
[3] School of Computer Science, Reichman University, Herzliya, Israel
`tami@runi.ac.il`

Abstract. We consider a game-theoretic variant of an interval scheduling problem. Every job is associated with a length, a weight, and a color. Each player controls all the jobs of a specific color, and needs to decide on a processing interval for each of its jobs. Jobs of the same color can be processed simultaneously by the machine. A job is covered if the machine is configured to its color during its whole processing interval. The goal of the machine is to maximize the sum of weights of all covered jobs, and the goal of each player is to place its jobs such that the sum of weights of covered jobs from its color is maximized. The study of this game is motivated by several applications like antenna scheduling for wireless networks.

We first show that given a strategy profile of the players, the machine scheduling problem can be solved in polynomial time. We then study the game from the players' point of view. We analyze the existence of Nash equilibria, its computation, and inefficiency. We distinguish between instances of the classical interval scheduling problem, in which every player controls a single job, and instances in which color sets may include multiple jobs.

Keywords: Interval scheduling · Scheduling games · Equilibrium inefficiency

1 Introduction

Scheduling problems and game-theory are a fruitful and well studied combination. The machine scheduling problem that we consider in this paper is motivated by the beam selection problem on a base station [23,26]. Antennas in modern 5G base stations are designed to dynamically steer their beams to focus transmission signals towards specific users using a technique known as beam forming. Beam forming maximizes data throughput between the base station and the user equip-

---

V. R. Vijayalakshmi—Independent researcher.

© ICST Institute for Computer Sciences, Social Informatics and Telecommunications Engineering 2026
Published by Springer Nature Switzerland AG 2026. All Rights Reserved
V. Aggarwal et al. (Eds.): GameNets 2025, LNICST 657, pp. 124–142, 2026.
https://doi.org/10.1007/978-3-032-12915-4_8

ment while minimizing the radio interference. Base stations serve multiple users by allocating time intervals during which it directs its beam toward each user. However, base station antennas often suffer the restriction that only a subset of beams can be activated at any given point in time [23,26]. The resource scheduler in a base station must choose these time intervals effectively to maximize overall network performance, especially in environments with multiple users competing for access to the radio resource, e.g., at a football stadium, by deciding when and for how long the radio resources are scheduled for a user. Beam forming techniques have become an integral part of 5G wireless communication and this gives rise to the optimization problem of deciding which beam is active at which point in time, having implications for the set of users that can be serviced.

We model this scheduling problem by means of a generalization of the classic interval scheduling problem [21]. In the classic interval scheduling problem, we are given a machine and processing intervals for jobs so that the machine has to decide which jobs are rejected and which jobs are processed, subject to no two processed jobs having overlapping processing intervals. In our generalization, at each point in time the machine has to be configured to a certain color, a color can be thought of as a single beam direction in the beam selection problem, so that all jobs of this color can be serviced simultaneously. A job is then completed if the machine is configured to that color during all its processing interval.

We are interested in a game-theoretic variant of the above interval scheduling problem. Assuming players know how the machine solves the beam selection problem, players compete for access to the radio resource. That is, players schedule their requests by selecting a time interval such that their requests can be processed. We assume that each player controls jobs of one color. The strategy of a player is to decide on a processing interval for each job of its color. The player's goal is to assign the jobs such that the machine will complete as many jobs of its color as possible.

We consider three different problems related to the above description. First, we solve the machine scheduling problem that decides which jobs are covered given the processing interval of each job. Second, we study the problem of assigning jobs to processing intervals so that the sum of weights of all covered jobs is maximized. Third, we provide answers to basic problems in the analysis of the corresponding game. Specifically, we study the existence and computation of a pure Nash equilibrium, computation and convergence of best-response dynamics, and the equilibrium inefficiency.

2 Model

An interval scheduling game is given by a tuple $\langle \mathcal{J}, \mathcal{C}, T, (p_j)_{j \in \mathcal{J}}, (w_j)_{j \in \mathcal{J}} \rangle$, containing a set of jobs $\mathcal{J} = \{1, \ldots, n\}$, a set of colors $\mathcal{C}$ with $|\mathcal{C}| = c$ and a time interval $[0, T)$, where every job $j \in \mathcal{J}$ has a color $c_j \in \mathcal{C}$, a length $0 \leq p_j \leq T$ and a weight $w_j \geq 0$.

For $i \in \mathcal{C}$, denote by S_i the jobs having color i. We assume that all the jobs of S_i are controlled by one player. A strategy, σ_i, of player i assigns a processing interval $[s_j, f_j) \subseteq [0, T)$ with $f_j - s_j = p_j$ to each job j with $c_j = i$. A profile $\sigma = (\sigma_i)_{i \in \mathcal{C}}$ assigns a strategy to each player.

Given a strategy profile σ, the machine faces the following scheduling problem. We say that job j is *covered* in a given schedule if the machine is configured to process color c_j during $[s_j, f_j)$. Note that if the machine is configured to a specific color, the machine can service an unlimited number of jobs from that color simultaneously. Let $\mathcal{S} \subseteq \mathcal{J}$ be the set of covered jobs. The goal of the machine is to maximize $\sum_{j \in \mathcal{S}} w_j$. Formally, the output for the machine scheduling problem is a configuration for the machine, i.e., a partition of the interval $[0, T)$ to intervals $\{[0, t_1), \ldots, [t_{m-1}, t_m = T)\}$ and a mapping $\gamma : \{1, \ldots, m\} \to \mathcal{C}$, such that for every $1 \leq k \leq m$, the machine is configured to process jobs of color $\gamma(k)$ during $[t_{k-1}, t_k)$.

Given strategy profile σ, the machine solves its optimization problem. Thus, determining for each job whether it is covered or not. The utility of each player $i \in \mathcal{C}$, denoted by $u_i(\sigma)$, is given by the sum of weights of covered jobs j with $c_j = i$. Given $i \in \mathcal{C}$ and $\sigma_{-i} = (\sigma_j)_{j \neq i}$, we say a strategy σ_i is a best-response for player i if $u_i(\sigma_i, \sigma_{-i}) \geq u_i(\sigma_i', \sigma_{-i})$ for all σ_i'. A strategy profile σ is called a *Nash equilibrium* (NE) if for all $i \in \mathcal{C}$, $u_i(\sigma_i, \sigma_{-i}) \geq u_i(\sigma_i', \sigma_{-i})$ for all σ_i'.

Best-response dynamics (BRD) is a local-search method where in each iteration some player is chosen and plays its best strategy given the strategies of the other players. When applied to our game, every iteration consists of two steps. First, an arbitrary player $i \in \mathcal{C}$ is chosen and may modify the location of the intervals of S_i. Then, as a response, the machine may modify its configuration along $[0, T)$. The dynamics then proceed to the next iteration, until no player has a beneficial deviation. Note that BRD need not always stop.

Example 2.1. Consider the following game with $T = 4$ and $c = 2$. Player 1 controls the set S_1, which includes two jobs (in blue in Fig. 1), where $p_1 = 4$ and $p_2 = 1$, both having weight 2. Player 2 controls the set S_2, which includes a single job (in red in Fig. 1) of length $p_3 = 1$ and weight 3.

If the two unit jobs are placed in disjoint intervals (See Fig. 1(a)) then the machine will process them. The utilities of the players are $(2, 3)$. If the two unit jobs are placed in overlapping intervals (Fig. 1(b)) then the machine will cover only jobs of S_1. The utilities of the players are $(4, 0)$. Therefore, the game has no NE: Player 2 will place its unit job such that it does not overlap with the unit-job of player 1, and player 1 will place its unit-job such that it overlaps with job 3. Since $T = 4$, player 2 always has a valid move (Fig. 1(c)).

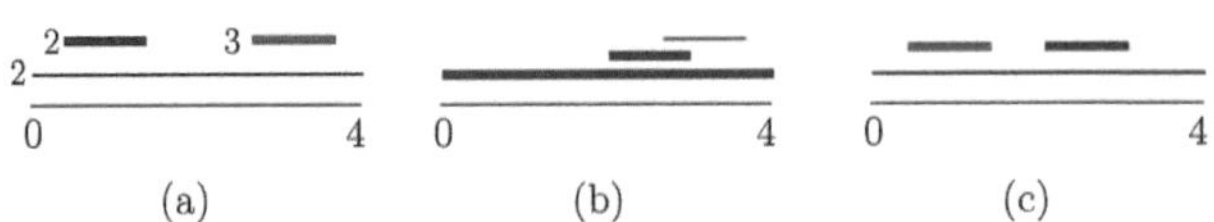

Fig. 1. A game G with $c = 2$ that has no NE. Intervals are labeled by their weights. Bold intervals are covered by the machine.

Denote the set of Nash equilibria of a given game G by $\mathcal{E}$. Define the profit of strategy profile σ by $\text{val}(\sigma) = \sum_{i \in C} u_i(\sigma)$. We identify classes for which a NE is guaranteed to exist, provide algorithms for computing a NE, study the convergence of best-response dynamics, and analyze the inefficiency of Nash equilibria. To this end, the strategy profile σ that maximizes $\text{val}(\sigma)$ is denoted the social optimum solution (OPT) and its profit is denoted by $\text{val}(\text{OPT})$. The *price of anarchy* (PoA) and the *price of stability* (PoS) of a game G are defined as follows.

$$\text{PoA}(G) = \frac{\text{val}(\text{OPT})}{\min_{\sigma \in \mathcal{E}} \text{val}(\sigma)} \quad and \quad \text{PoS}(G) = \frac{\text{val}(\text{OPT})}{\max_{\sigma \in \mathcal{E}} \text{val}(\sigma)}.$$

Some of our results refer to restricted classes of games, specifically

1. $\mathcal{G}_{single}$ - games corresponding to the classic interval scheduling problem – in which there is exactly one job from each color, that is, $n = c$.
2. $\mathcal{G}_{unit}$ - games with unit-length jobs, that is, for every job $j \in \mathcal{J}$ it holds that $p_j = 1$.
3. $\mathcal{G}_{prop}$ - games in which the weight of a job is proportional to its length, that is, for every job $j \in \mathcal{J}$ it holds that $w_j = p_j$.

2.1   Our Results

Our first result, Theorem 3.1, shows that given a strategy profile of the players, the machine scheduling problem can be solved in polynomial time using dynamic programming.

We then proceed to show in Theorem 4.2 that computing the socially optimal solution for the players can be done in polynomial time if the number of colors is constant, but in Theorem 4.3 that it is NP-hard for an arbitrary number of colors.

We next analyze Nash equilibria of the interval scheduling game. We show in Example 2.1 that in general, even with two players, a (pure) Nash equilibrium need not exist. However, for the game-theoretic variant of the classic interval scheduling problem, where every player controls a single job, we prove in Theorem 5.1 that a (pure) Nash equilibrium always exists and the price of stability is 1. For this class of games, we present in Theorem 5.3 an algorithm for computing a NE. Then, Theorem 5.4 provides a complete and tight analysis of the inefficiency of Nash equilibria. For $c \leq 5$, we show that the price of anarchy is at most 2 and for $c \geq 6$, we show that the price of anarchy is at most $(c-1)/2$. Moreover, these bounds are tight. We provide a significantly lower upper bound of 3 in Theorem 5.11 for the restricted setting of the classic interval scheduling problems with processing time equal to the weight.

For general games, we prove in Theorem 6.2 and Theorem 6.3 that even with only two players, computing the best-response of a player, as well as deciding whether an instance has a Nash equilibrium is NP-hard. In Theorem 6.5 we present an upper bound of c for the price of anarchy, and show that even the best NE can have poor quality, by proving that the price of stability is at least $\frac{c}{2} - \epsilon'$ for all $\epsilon' > 0$.

A second class of interval scheduling games with a guaranteed Nash equilibrium are games with unit processing times. For this class, the price of anarchy is significantly lower. To be more precise, in Theorem 6.8 we provide a tight bound of $\min\{3 - 2/c, 3 - 2/\lfloor T \rfloor\}$.

Lastly, we define a natural extension of the game, in which jobs may be associated with different release times and due dates, and show in Theorem 7.1 that even instances with unit processing time might lack equilibria. Due to space constraints some of the proofs are omitted.

2.2 Related Literature

The machine scheduling problem we study is a generalization of the classical interval scheduling/activity selection problem. This problem can be solved greedily for unweighted jobs [8,16], and by dynamic programming [21] or min-cost flow computation [2,6] for weighted jobs. For an overview of different variants of interval scheduling, we refer to [22,25]. Our analysis shows a close connection to the famous knapsack problem—one of Karp's NP-complete problems [20].

There are many game-theoretic models of job scheduling problems. The majority of this literature refer to games in which each job selfishly chooses a machine so as to minimize a certain objective. Different authors make various assumptions about the machines' scheduling policy, the cost function of the players, and the social welfare function to be considered, like the makespan of the schedule or the sum of completion times. This line of research was initiated by [24] and later extended by, for example, [5,11–14,29].

Real-time scheduling, refers to a scheduling environment in which jobs are associated with intervals during which they have to be processed. There is wide literature on real-time scheduling, either on a single or on parallel machines (see surveys in [10,19]). Most of the existing work consider systems controlled by an external authority determining the jobs' assignment. When the server has a limited capacity, and jobs have variable-weights, many problems such as minimizing the number of late jobs, or minimizing the servers' busy time are NP-hard, even with unit-length jobs [1,9]. On the other hand, with unit-weight unit-length jobs, these problems are polynomially solvable [3,10]. Real-time scheduling has been studied as a cost-sharing game, in which jobs that are processed in the same interval, share the machine's activation cost in this interval [17,28]. In the above games, the machine may process multiple jobs simultaneously and the congestion on the machine during its processed interval determines the job's cost. The paper [18] considers a strategic variant of the multistage interval scheduling problem, in which jobs consist of several tasks, and all tasks have to be scheduled in order to obtain the profit associated with the job.

Another related game is *selfish bin packing*. The goal in this line of research is to find a cost-sharing rule so that number of bins used by selfish jobs is as close as possible to the optimal number of bins [4,15,30,31]. A different setting in which players correspond to jobs who need to be processed by a machine with a limited capacity arises in *knapsack auctions*, where each job suggests a payment for being processed [7,27]. We note that in the above packing games, a profile does not specify the location of a packed item in the knapsack, unlike our game, in which the specific interval in which a job is processed within the interval $[0, T)$ plays a crucial role.

3 Optimal Algorithm for the Machine Scheduling Problem

In this section we show that we can compute an optimal configuration for the machine in polynomial time. The input for the problem is a placement of the jobs in $[0, T)$, and the output for the machine scheduling problem is a configuration for the machine. The objective is to maximize the weight of covered jobs.

Observe first that if $c = n$, that is, every player controls a single job, the machine scheduling problem is the classical interval scheduling/activity selection problem [21].

We present an optimal solution for the most general instance of arbitrary length, arbitrary weight jobs, and arbitrary number of colors. The following notations are used in our solution. We assume that the jobs are indexed by finish time, that is, $f_1 \leq \ldots \leq f_n$.

- For a set of jobs $J \subseteq \mathcal{J}$, let $w(J) := \sum_{j \in J} w_j$ be the total weight of jobs in J.
- For every job $j \in \mathcal{J}$, let $prev(j) := \max\{k \in \mathcal{J} \mid f_k < s_j\}$, that is, $prev(j)$ is the index of the last job to end before job j. If there is no such job, then define $prev(j) = 0$.
- For every job $j \in \mathcal{J}$, let $In(j) := \{k \in \mathcal{J} \mid [s_k, f_k) \subseteq [s_j, f_j)$ and $c_k = c_j\}$, that is, $In(j)$ is the set of jobs that have the same color as job j and whose interval is fully included in the interval of job j. In particular, $j \in In(j)$.

Theorem 3.1. *There is a dynamic program that, for each strategy profile σ, solves the machine scheduling problem for σ in polynomial time.*

Proof. Define $A[j]$ to be the maximum profit from a solution in which job j is the last covered job. In other words, $A[j]$ represents the maximum profit from an instance that only includes jobs $1, \ldots, j$ when job j is covered.

The base case is $A[0] = 0$. The recursive formula for $j \geq 1$ is $A[j] = \max\{X, Y\}$, where

$$X = \max_{k \leq prev(j)} A[k] + w(In(j))$$

and

$$Y = \max_{k < j \text{ and } c_k = c_j \text{ and } k \notin In(j)} A[k] + w(In(j) \setminus In(k)).$$

The value of X is the maximum profit in case the last job covered before job j ends before job j starts. The value of Y is the maximum profit in case job j

starts while the machine services earlier jobs of color c_j. In this case, we select the intersecting job from j's color, for which the added profit from extending the interval in which the machine is configured to c_j is maximal. Note that the case in which the machine is configured to c_j and is then idle, is covered in both X and Y.

Once the table A is full, the value of an optimal solution is given by $\max_j A[j]$. The optimal schedule itself can be retrieved by backtracking. We assume that the machine applies the following deterministic tie breaking rule: give priority to jobs with lower index. $\qquad\square$

4   Computing the Social Optimum of a Game

In this section we consider the optimization problem of finding a strategy profile that maximizes the sum of weights of covered jobs. Note that this task should not be confused with the problem of computing an optimal schedule for the machine (discussed in Sect. 3). The problem considered below is the following: Given an instance $\langle \mathcal{J}, \mathcal{C}, T, (p_j)_{j\in\mathcal{J}}, (w_j)_{j\in\mathcal{J}} \rangle$ of the game, place the jobs in $[0, T)$, such that an optimal configuration of the machine produces maximal profit. We first prove the following property.

Claim 4.1. *For all G, there exists a socially optimal solution in which the machine processes jobs of each color $i \in \mathcal{C}$ during at most one interval.* $\qquad\square$

Based on the above claim, we show the following:

Theorem 4.2. *If c is constant, then the socially optimal solution can be computed in polynomial time.* $\qquad\square$

Theorem 4.3. *Computing the socially optimal solution is NP-hard, already for the class $\mathcal{G}_{single}$.*

Proof. The proof is by a simple reduction from the $0-1$ knapsack problem. Note that in our reduction $|S_i| = 1$ for all $1 \leq i \leq c$.

An instance of Knapsack is given by a set of c items each associated with a weight p_i and a value w_i. A subset of these items should be placed in a knapsack with capacity T such that the total value of the packed items is maximal.

Given an instance of knapsack, consider a game played in the interval $[0, T)$. There are c colors, where S_i consists of a single job of length p_i and weight w_i. It is easy to see that there is a packing with total value W if and only if there is a valid schedule with total profit W. $\qquad\square$

5   One Job per Color

In this section we analyze the class $\mathcal{G}_{single}$ where $c = n$. This class corresponds to the classic interval scheduling problem. For every color $1 \leq i \leq c$, denote by p_i, w_i the length and the weight of the single job in S_i.

Every game $G \in \mathcal{G}_{single}$ induces a $0-1$ Knapsack problem, with a knapsack of capacity T, and n items, where item i has size p_i and value w_i. Some of the results in this section leverage the relation between the game and its corresponding packing problem. We note the following crucial differences between the problems. First, in the knapsack problem, the physical location of the items is not part of the solution, whereas in our setting, it plays a pivotal role. Second, in the knapsack problem, items that are not packed are simply rejected, whereas in our game, every job must be placed somewhere in the interval $[0, T)$; the machine selects a set of non-overlapping jobs, corresponding to the packed items.

Theorem 5.1. *Every game $G \in \mathcal{G}_{single}$ has a NE profile, and* $\mathrm{PoS}(\mathcal{G}_{single}) = 1$.

Proof. Observe that an optimal solution of the corresponding knapsack problem induces a NE, by placing the corresponding jobs one after the other along the interval $[0, T)$, and all other jobs in $[0, p_j)$. This placement is a NE since the machine will select the 'packed' jobs (in case of a tie, select jobs in a way that agrees with the machine's tie breaking rule), and no non-covered job can be added without rejecting jobs of at least the same weight. This relation with the knapsack problem also implies that $\mathrm{PoS}(G) = 1$ for all $G \in \mathcal{G}_{single}$.

Proposition 5.2. *For every game $G \in \mathcal{G}_{single}$, best-response dynamics converges to a NE.*

Proof. A deviation is beneficial for a job $j \in \mathcal{J}$ only if j is not covered before the deviation and becomes covered afterward. After job j's deviation, the machine can maintain its configuration over the interval $[0, T)$ and retain its profit. The machine modifies its strategy to cover j, as this increases its profit. Consequently, every beneficial best response of a player is associated with an increase in the machine's profit. Since the maximum profit from covered jobs is bounded, the result follows. $\square$

We turn to consider the problem of computing a NE. It might seem that any approximation algorithm for the knapsack problem could easily be adapted to our game by scheduling, one after the other, the jobs corresponding to the packed items. However, the resulting schedule is not necessarily a NE. While best-response dynamics are guaranteed to converge to a NE with at least the same profit, there does not seem to be a straightforward way to bound the convergence time. However, as we show, a NE can be computed efficiently.

Theorem 5.3. *For every game $G \in \mathcal{G}_{single}$, computing a NE profile can be done in polynomial time.*

Proof. We present an algorithm for computing a NE. Recall that for every job $j \in \mathcal{J}$, it holds that $0 \leq p_j \leq T$. We also assume that for at least one pair of jobs, x, y we have that $p_x + p_y \leq T$, as otherwise, covering just the most profitable job is clearly a NE.

The algorithm distinguishes between two cases. In the first case, the most profitable job, h, is more profitable than any pair of jobs that can fit together in $[0, T)$. This case is handled in lines 3–4. In the second case, let a, b be a most profitable pair that can fit in $[0, T)$ and have total profit higher than h. This case is handled in lines 6–16.

Assume first that the condition in line 3 is valid. Thus, for any job $i \neq h$, $p_h + p_i > T$. Indeed, if for some job $i \neq h$, $p_h + p_i \leq T$, then $w_a + w_b \geq w_h + w_i > w_h$, contradicting the condition in line 3. This implies that the schedule produced in step 4 is a NE: all jobs overlap at $t = 0$, the machine processes job h, and no job a can move to an interval disjoint with h or disjoint with a job b such that $w_a + w_b > w_h$.

Assume next that the condition in line 3 is not valid, that is, $w_a + w_b > w_h$. The algorithm first schedules a and b one after the other in the leftmost position of the schedule, and then considers the remaining jobs in non-increasing order by weight. A job that fits is placed in the leftmost idle position; a job that does not fit, is placed such that it overlaps both a and b. Let σ denote the resulting schedule.

Since $w_a + w_b > w_h$, the machine will cover a and b and the jobs that were placed one after the other during the loop in lines 7–16. The jobs that intersect a and b will not be covered. We show that σ is a NE.

For every non-covered job i, at the time i is considered by the algorithm, the total busy time of the machine is more than $T - p_i$. Assume that i moves to an interval that begins after $p_a + p_b$. By the algorithm, such an interval must intersect at least one job that is more profitable than i, and therefore, covering i is not beneficial for the machine. Assume next that i moves to an interval that intersects $[0, p_a + p_b]$. Note that at most one additional job that intersects $[0, p_a + p_b]$ (possibly a or b) can be covered together with job i. However, if

---

Algorithm 1 - Computing a NE schedule of a game $G \in \mathcal{G}_{single}$

1: Let h be a job with maximal weight.
2: Let $\{a, b\}$ be a pair of jobs for which $w_a + w_b$ is maximal among all pairs x, y
    fulfilling $p_x + p_y \leq T$. Possibly, $a = h$ or $b = h$.
3: **if** $w_a + w_b \leq w_h$ **then**
4:     For every $i \in \mathcal{J}$, schedule job i in $[0, p_i)$ and halt
5: **else**
6:     Schedule job a in $[0, p_a)$ and job b in $[p_a, p_a + p_b)$.
7:     Sort $\mathcal{J} \setminus \{a, b\}$ such that $w_1 \geq w_2 \geq \ldots \geq w_{n-2}$.
8:     Let $C = p_a + p_b$.
9:     **for** $i = 1$ to $n - 2$ **do**
10:       **if** $C + p_i \leq T$ **then**
11:         Schedule job i in $[C, C + p_i)$.
12:         $C = C + p_i$.
13:       **else**
14:         Schedule job i such that it overlaps both a and b.
15:       **end if**
16:     **end for**
17: **end if**

---

covering a different pair that begins in $[0, p_a + p_b)$ is beneficial for the machine, we get a contradiction to the choice of $\{a, b\}$ in step 2 of the algorithm. $\square$

We turn to analyze the equilibrium inefficiency. While the price of stability is 1, we show that the price of anarchy is linear in c, which means that highly inefficient equilibria exist as well.

Theorem 5.4. *Let $G \in \mathcal{G}_{single}$. If $c \leq 5$ then $\mathrm{PoA}(G) \leq 2$. If $c \geq 6$, then $\mathrm{PoA}(G) \leq \frac{c-1}{2}$.*

Proof. Let OPT be an optimal profile. Denote by $c' \leq c$ the number of jobs that are covered in OPT. Sort the jobs covered by OPT such that $w_1 \geq w_2 \geq \dots, \geq w_{c'}$.

Since job 1 can be selected by the machine, for any NE profile σ it holds that $\mathrm{val}(\sigma) \geq w_1$. If $c' = 2$ then $\mathrm{PoA}(G) \leq 2$, since $\mathrm{OPT} = w_1 + w_2$ and $w_1 \geq w_2$.

Consider next the case $c' = 3$. If $w_1 \geq \mathrm{OPT}/2$, then clearly, $\mathrm{PoA}(G) \leq 2$. If $w_1 < \mathrm{OPT}/2$ then any two jobs in $A_3 = \{1, 2, 3\}$ have total profit at least $\mathrm{OPT}/2$. Consider a NE σ. If at least two jobs from A_3 are covered, then $\mathrm{val}(\sigma) \geq \mathrm{OPT}/2$. Otherwise, assume that job 1 is assigned to interval $[t, t + p_1)$. Note that at least one of the intervals $[0, t)$, and $[t + p_1, T)$ have length at least $\frac{T - p_1}{2}$. Since all the jobs in A_3 are covered in OPT, we have that $p_2 + p_3 \leq T - p_1$, thus $\min\{p_2, p_3\} \leq \frac{T - p_1}{2}$. If $\mathrm{val}(\sigma) < \mathrm{OPT}/2$, each of job 2 and 3 intersects job 1. However, in this case, at least one of 2 and 3 fits into $[0, t)$ or $[t + p_1, T)$, implying that at least one of these two jobs has a beneficial migration. Therefore, if $c' = 3$ then $\mathrm{PoA}(G) \leq 2$.

We turn to consider the case $c' \geq 4$. Our proof distinguishes between the case $c' = c$ and the case $c' \leq c - 1$.

Case 1: $c' = c$: Assume that all jobs are covered in OPT. Note that this implies that $\sum_{i=1}^{n} p_i \leq T$. Let σ be a NE profile. Denote by $\mathcal{J}_{in}(\sigma)$ and $\mathcal{J}_{out}(\sigma)$ the sets of jobs that are covered and non-covered, respectively, by the machine in σ. Let $n_{in}(\sigma) = |\mathcal{J}_{in}(\sigma)|$ and $n_{out}(\sigma) = |\mathcal{J}_{out}(\sigma)|$. Note that $n_{out}(\sigma) + n_{in}(\sigma) = c$.

Claim 5.5. $n_{out}(\sigma) \leq n_{in}(\sigma)$.

Proof. Let $B = \sum_{i \in J_{in}(\sigma)} p_i$ be the total busy time of the machine in σ. Since all jobs in the instance can fit into $[0, T)$, the machine is idle at least $\sum_{i \in J_{out}(\sigma)} p_i$ time units. Thus, $\sum_{i \in J_{out}(\sigma)} p_i \leq T - B$. There are $n_{in}(\sigma)$ covered jobs, hence, at most $n_{in}(\sigma) + 1$ idle intervals, where at least one of the idle intervals has length at least $\frac{T - B}{n_{in}(\sigma) + 1}$.

By averaging, the shortest non-covered job has length at most $\frac{\sum_{i \in J_{out}(\sigma)} p_i}{n_{out}(\sigma)} \leq \frac{T - B}{n_{out}(\sigma)}$. Given that σ is a NE, no non-covered job can fit into an idle interval, therefore, $\frac{T - B}{n_{out}(\sigma)} > \frac{T - B}{n_{in}(\sigma) + 1}$, implying $n_{out}(\sigma) < n_{in}(\sigma) + 1$, therefore, $n_{out}(\sigma) \leq n_{in}(\sigma)$. $\square$

Claim 5.6. *For any two jobs $a, b \in J_{out}(\sigma)$, it holds that $w_a + w_b \leq \mathrm{val}(\sigma)$.*

Proof. Let x be the leftmost job in $J_{in}(\sigma)$ such that $f_x \geq p_a$. Let X be the set of jobs in $J_{in}(\sigma)$ that are covered in $[0, f_x)$. For an illustration, see Fig. 2. Since σ is a NE, $w_a \leq \mathrm{val}(X)$. Similarly, let y be the rightmost job in $J_{in}(\sigma)$ such that $s_y \leq T - p_b$. Let Y be the set of jobs in $J_{in}(\sigma)$ that are covered in $[s_y, T)$. Since σ is a NE, $w_b \leq \mathrm{val}(Y)$. Also, $X \cap Y = \emptyset$ since all jobs can fit into $[0, T)$ and in particular $p_a + p_b + p_x + p_y \leq T$. We conclude that $w_a + w_b \leq \mathrm{val}(X \cup Y) \leq \mathrm{val}(\sigma)$.

Fig. 2. The non-covered jobs a, b, and the sets X, Y. The jobs of $J_{in}(\sigma)$ are bold.

Combining the above claims concludes the analysis for $c = 4$ and the first case for $c \geq 5$.

Claim 5.7. *If $c = c' = 4$, then* $\mathrm{PoA}(G) \leq 2$. $\qquad\square$

Claim 5.8. *If $c = c' \geq 5$, then* $\mathrm{PoA}(G) \leq \frac{c-1}{2}$. $\qquad\square$

Case 2: $c' \leq c - 1$: If $w_1 > \frac{2\mathrm{OPT}}{c'}$, then we are done. Otherwise, by averaging, for all $1 \leq i \leq c'$, we have that $\sum_{k=1}^{i} w_i \geq \frac{i \cdot \mathrm{OPT}}{c'}$. It is possible to show (details are omitted) that job 1, together with any of 2 or 3 are sufficient to achieve profit $\frac{2 \cdot \mathrm{OPT}}{c'}$. Formally:

Claim 5.9. *For $i = 2, 3$ it holds that* $w_1 + w_i \geq \frac{2 \cdot \mathrm{OPT}}{c'}$. $\qquad\square$

Consider a NE profile σ. If job 1 is covered, then, similar to the analysis of $c' = 3$, at least one of job $2, 3$ is covered, or has a beneficial migration, implying that either $\mathrm{val}(\sigma) \geq \frac{2 \cdot \mathrm{OPT}}{c'}$ (by Claim 5.9), or contradicting the stability of σ.

Therefore, we are left with the case that job 1 is not covered. If $\mathrm{val}(\sigma) < \frac{2\mathrm{OPT}}{c'}$ it must be that job 1 intersects with both $2, 3$. We first analyze the case $w_2 + w_3 \geq \frac{2\mathrm{OPT}}{c'}$:

- If both 2 and 3 are covered in σ, then $\mathrm{val}(\sigma) \geq \frac{2\mathrm{OPT}}{c'}$.
- If one of 2 and 3 is covered, say J_a, then assume that J_a is assigned in interval $[t, t + p_a)$. Note that at least one of the intervals $[0, t)$, and $[t + p_a, T)$ has length at least $\frac{T - p_a}{2}$. Let $J_b = J_{5-a}$ be the other job in $\{2, 3\}$. Since all the jobs in A_3 are covered in OPT, we have that $p_1 + p_b \leq T - p_1$, thus $\min\{p_1, p_b\} \leq \frac{T - p_1}{2}$, implying that the shortest unassigned job in A_3 has a beneficial migration if $\mathrm{val}(\sigma) < \frac{2\mathrm{OPT}}{c'}$.
- If both 2 and 3 are not covered, then the shortest of these two jobs has a beneficial migration by moving before or after job 1 if $\mathrm{val}(\sigma) < \frac{2\mathrm{OPT}}{c'}$ (see the analysis for $c' = 3$).

We turn to analyze the case $w_2+w_3 < \frac{2\mathrm{OPT}}{c'}$. Consider the 4th most profitable job in OPT. Recall that $\sum_{i=1}^{4} w_i \geq \frac{4\cdot\mathrm{OPT}}{c'}$. Since we analyze the case $w_1 < \frac{2\mathrm{OPT}}{c'}$, and $w_2 + w_3 < \frac{2\mathrm{OPT}}{c'}$, we have that $w_2 + w_3 + w_4 \geq \frac{2\mathrm{OPT}}{c'}$ and $w_1 + w_4 \geq \frac{2\mathrm{OPT}}{c'}$. That is, for all $k \in \{2,3,4\}$ we have that $w_1 + w_k \geq \frac{2\mathrm{OPT}}{c'}$. Consider the three jobs $\{2,3,4\}$.

- If all the three are covered in σ then $\mathrm{val}(\sigma) \geq w_2 + w_3 + w_4 \geq \frac{2\mathrm{OPT}}{c'}$.
- If at most one of the three is covered, then the shortest uncovered job has a beneficial migration by moving before or after job 1 if $\mathrm{val}(\sigma) < \frac{2\mathrm{OPT}}{c'}$ (see the analysis for $c' = 3$).
- If exactly two are covered, then let x and y be covered, while z is not. Assume the covered jobs are placed in $[s_x, f_x)$ and $[s_y, f_y)$, respectively, where w.l.o.g., that $f_x \leq s_y$.
  If $\mathrm{val}(\sigma) < \frac{2\mathrm{OPT}}{c'}$ and σ is a NE, it must be that job 1 cannot be placed before y, thus, $s_y < p_1$. In addition, z cannot be placed after y, thus $T - f_y < p_z$. Given that OPT processes all four jobs, we have that $p_1 + p_x + p_y + p_z \leq T$. However, the above inequalities imply that $p_1 + p_y + p_z > s_y + (f_y - s_y) + T - f_y = T$, contradicting the stability of σ or the assumption that $\mathrm{val}(\sigma) < \frac{2\mathrm{OPT}}{c'}$.

We conclude that if $c' < c$, then $\mathrm{PoA}(G) \leq \frac{c'}{2} \leq \frac{c-1}{2}$. $\qquad\square$
Next, we show that the above analysis is tight up to ϵ.

Theorem 5.10. *For every $c \geq 2$, there exists a game $G_c \in \mathcal{G}_{single}$ with c players such that $\mathrm{PoA}(G_c) = 2$. For every $\epsilon > 0$ and $c > 5$, there exists a game G_c with c players such that $\mathrm{PoA}(G_c) \geq \frac{c-1}{2+\epsilon}$.*

Proof. For $c \geq 2$, the game G_c consists of c unit weight jobs of length 1. Let $T = 2$. In a possible NE profile, all the jobs are placed in $[t, t + 1)$ for some $0 < t < 1$, thus $\mathrm{val}(NE) = 1$, while $\mathrm{OPT} = 2$.

For $c \geq 5$, the game G_c is defined as follows: Let $T = c - 1$. Player 1 has one job with length $p_1 = T$ and $w_1 = 2 + \epsilon$. For $i = 2, \ldots, c$, i has one job with $p_i = w_i = 1$. In the Nash equilibrium, player 1 places its job on $[0, T)$ and all players $i = 2, \ldots, c$ place their jobs on $[0, 1)$. Job 1 will be covered and even if job $i \neq 1$ deviates to a different interval the machine will still process job 1 as $2 + \epsilon > 2$. In the social optimum, jobs $i = 2, \ldots, c$ each choose interval $[i - 2, i - 1)$ and are covered for a weight of $c - 1$. Hence, $\mathrm{PoA}(G_c) \geq (c - 1)/(2 + \epsilon)$ for every $\epsilon > 0$. $\qquad\square$

5.1   Weight Proportional to Length

For the restricted class for games in $\mathcal{G}_{prop} \cap \mathcal{G}_{single}$, we show that the PoA is bounded by a constant. Recall that $G \in \mathcal{G}_{prop}$ if for all $i \in \mathcal{J}$, we have that $w_j = p_j$. Thus, the goal is to cover as much of the interval as possible in $[0, T)$.

Theorem 5.11. *For every $G \in \mathcal{G}_{prop} \cap \mathcal{G}_{single}$, $\mathrm{PoA}(G) \le 3$.*

Proof. Let $G \in \mathcal{G}_{prop}$ and let σ be a NE profile of G. If all the jobs are covered, then clearly, $\mathrm{val}(\sigma) = \mathrm{OPT}$. Thus, we assume below that at least one job is not covered. During the interval $[0, T)$, the machine alternates between being idle and busy in σ. Let $u_1, b_1, u_2, b_2, \ldots, u_k, b_k, u_{k+1}$ denote the lengths of the intervals in which the machine is idle and busy. If two jobs are covered one after the other we consider them as two busy intervals with an idle interval of length 0 between them. We show that the total idle time is strictly less than two times the total busy time.

Consider the first idle interval u_1, and any non-covered job, i. Assume that job i is placed in $[0, p_i)$. If the point p_i is within an idle interval, then σ is not a NE, since it is profitable for the machine to cover p_i instead of the jobs in $[0, p_i)$. Therefore, the point p_i must be within a busy interval, say b_a (See Fig. 3). Since σ is a NE, placing job i in $[0, p_i)$ is not beneficial. Specifically, if the machine covers job i, its added profit will be p_i and its lost profit will be $\sum_{j=1}^{a} b_j$. Therefore, $p_i < \sum_{j=1}^{a} b_j$. The choice of a is such that $p_i > \sum_{j=1}^{a-1}(u_j + b_j) + u_a$. Combining the two inequalities, we get that $b_a > \sum_{j=1}^{a} u_j$.

The same argument can be applied on the suffix of the schedule, starting from u_{a+1}. If $\sum_{j=1}^{a}(u_j + b_j) + p_i \le T$, that is, job i can fit after b_a, then we repeat the above procedure to the suffix of the schedule starting after b_a. If $\sum_{j=1}^{a}(u_j + b_j) + p_i > T$, then we assume that job i is placed in $[T - p_i, T)$. If point $T - p_i$ is within an idle interval, then σ is not a NE. Therefore, the point $T - p_i$ must be in a busy interval, say $b_{a'}$, where $a' \le a$ (because job i does not fit after b_a). Using the same argument as above implies that $b_{a'} > \sum_{j=a'+1}^{k+1} u_j$.

Adding the inequalities on the suffix and the prefix of σ we get that $2\sum_{j=1}^{k} b_j > \sum_{j=1}^{k+1} u_j$.

The interval T is partitioned such that $T = \sum_{j=1}^{k} b_j + \sum_{j=1}^{k+1} u_j$. Hence, $3\mathrm{val}(\sigma) = 3\sum_{j=1}^{k} b_j > \sum_{j=1}^{k} b_j + \sum_{j=1}^{k+1} u_j = T \ge \mathrm{OPT}$, implying $\mathrm{PoA}(G) < 3$. $\square$

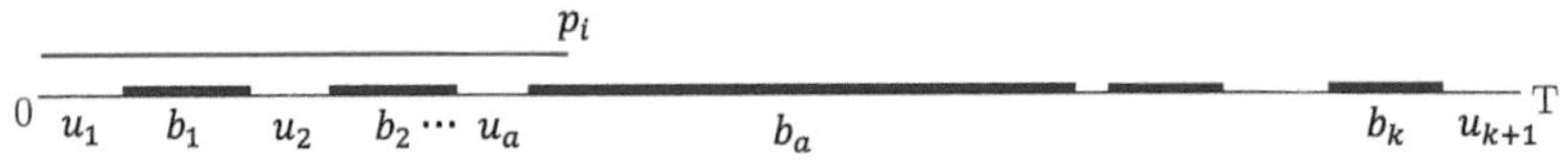

Fig. 3. The stability of σ implies that point p_i is within a busy interval.

6 Arbitrary Number of Jobs per Color

For games in $\mathcal{G}_{single}$, we have shown that a NE always exists, the price of stability is 1 and the price of anarchy is $(c-1)/2$ for $c \ge 5$. In general, when several jobs may have the same color, the game becomes less stable, and the equilibrium inefficiency increases. Since most of the challenges arise already in games with two players, we first analyze this setting.

6.1   Two Players

As shown in the introduction, there exists a game with $c = 2$ that has no NE profile. We strengthen this negative result and show that NE is not guaranteed to exist even in the class $\mathcal{G}_{prop}$ where jobs' weights are proportional to their lengths.

Observation 6.1. *There exists a game $G \in \mathcal{G}_{prop}$ with $c = 2$ and $w_j = p_j$ for all $j \in \mathcal{J}$ that has no NE profile.*

Next, we show that the problem of deciding whether a game has a NE, as well as the simpler problem of best-response computation are both NP-hard.

Theorem 6.2. *For $c = 2$, deciding whether a game has a NE is NP-hard.*   □

Theorem 6.3. *For $c = 2$, computing the best-response of a player is NP-hard.* □

Finally, we provide tight analysis of the equilibrium inefficiency in a 2-player game.

Theorem 6.4. *For $c = 2$, $\mathrm{PoA}(G) \leq 2$. Moreover, there exists a game G with $c = 2$ and $\mathrm{PoA}(G) = 2$, and for every $\epsilon > 0$, there exists a game G' with $c = 2$ and $\mathrm{PoS}(G') = 2 - \epsilon$.*   □

6.2   Equilibrium Inefficiency Arbitrary Number of Players

We show that both the price of anarchy and the price of stability are linear in the number of colors.

Theorem 6.5. *For all G, $\mathrm{PoA}(G) \leq c$ and for every $c > 2$ and $\epsilon' > 0$, there exists a game G with $\mathrm{PoS}(G) \geq \frac{c}{2} - \epsilon'$.*

Proof. Let σ be a NE. Since the machine can always fully cover all jobs of the most profitable color, $\mathrm{val}(\sigma) \geq \frac{1}{c} \sum_{i=1}^{c} w(S_i)$. Since $\mathrm{val}(\mathrm{OPT}) \leq \sum_{i=1}^{c} w(S_i)$, we have that $\mathrm{PoA}(G) \leq c$.

For the lower bound on the price of stability, Given $c > 2$ and $\epsilon' > 0$, let $T = 2c + 1$ and let ϵ be a small number such that $\frac{c + \frac{c+1}{c+3}\epsilon}{2+\epsilon} = \frac{c}{2} - \epsilon'$. The game G is defined as follows. Every player $i = 1, \ldots, c$ has one job with $p_i = w_i = 1$. Player 1 has, in addition, one job with length $p_{1'} = T$ and weight $w_{1'} = 1 + \epsilon$. Player 2 has, in addition, $c + 2$ light jobs of lengths $2, \ldots, c + 3$ and weight $\frac{\epsilon}{c+3}$ each. In a possible NE profile, s_0 (see Fig. 4(a), where $c = 4$), player 1 puts its long job in $[0, T)$ and all players $i = 1, \ldots, c$ put their unit job in $[0, 1)$. Player 2 puts each job of length t in $[0, t)$. The two jobs of player 1 will be covered, for a total profit of $2 + \epsilon$. Player 1 is clearly stable. If player $i > 2$ deviates to a different interval the machine will still process the two jobs of player 1 as $2 + \epsilon \geq 2 + \frac{c+2}{c+3}\epsilon$. Since the total weight of the light jobs of player 2 is less than ϵ, player 2 does not have a beneficial migration as well.

We show that every NE has profit $2 + \epsilon$. Consider a profile σ. If the long job of S_1 is covered, then only jobs of S_1 are covered and the profit is $2 + \epsilon$. If the long job of S_1 is not covered, then we show that σ is not a NE. Since $T = 2c + 1$, all the unit-jobs are covered. Indeed, a player that controls a non-covered unit-job can place it on an idle unit slot or overlap (and be preferred) over light jobs of S_2. Let $x > 0$ be the length of the longest interval in σ that has no unit job of S_j, $j \neq 2$. If all the unit jobs are covered, then $c - 1$ out of the T available slots are busy processing unit jobs not in S_2, implying that $1 \leq x \leq T - (c - 1) = c + 2$.

Let j be a player whose unit-job is covered adjacent to the interval of length x. Player 2 can deviate such that its unit job overlaps j and all the light jobs of length at most $x+1$ are covered (see Fig. 4(c)). Thus, σ is not a NE. The resulting schedule is not a NE as well, since job j is non-covered, and as mentioned above, if the long job of S_1 is not covered, then all unit-jobs are.

In the social optimum, all the jobs except for the long job of S_1 and the longest light job of S_2 are covered. Hence, $\mathrm{PoS}(G) = \frac{c + \frac{c+1}{c+3}\epsilon}{2+\epsilon} = \frac{c}{2} - \epsilon'$. $\square$

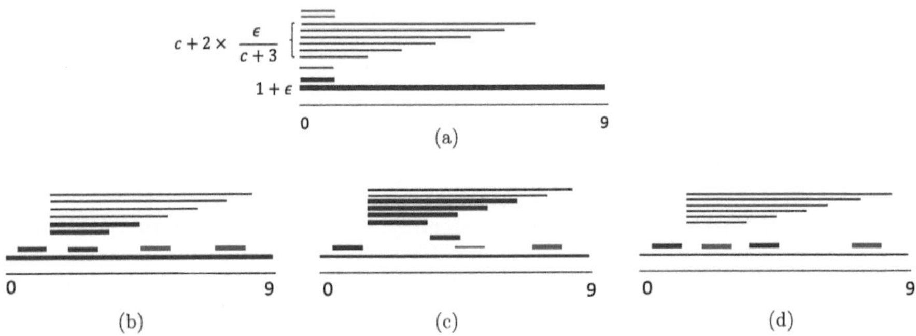

Fig. 4. A game with $c = 4$ and $\mathrm{PoS} = 2 - \epsilon'$. Bold intervals are covered. (a) a NE profile. (b) all unit jobs and some jobs of S_2 are covered. (c) a profile resulting from a beneficial deviation of player 2. (d) a best-response of player 3; once again, all unit jobs are covered.

6.3   Unit-Length Jobs

In this section we analyze games with unit-length jobs. For this class, we provide positive results. Specifically, some optimal solution is a NE, BRD converges to a NE, and the PoA is bounded by a constant less than 3.

Theorem 6.6. *For every game $G \in \mathcal{G}_{unit}$, G has a NE profile and $\mathrm{PoS}(G) = 1$.*

Proposition 6.7. *For every $G \in \mathcal{G}_{unit}$, best-response dynamics converges to a NE.*

Proof. For all $i \in C$, if at least one job $j \in S_i$ is covered, then since all jobs have unit length, by placing non-covered jobs in the unit interval in which job j

is covered, player i can have utility $w(S_i)$. Therefore, the best-response of i will lead to utility 0 or $w(S_i)$. Consider any application of best-response dynamics. After some warm-up, during which all players get a chance to deviate, for all i, player i will have utility 0 or $w(S_i)$. From this point on, the profit of the machine increases with every iteration. The machine selects to cover jobs of S_i since it gives away total profit less than $w(S_i)$, so the total profit of the machine increases. $\square$

Theorem 6.8. *Let $G \in \mathcal{G}_{unit}$ and let $k = \lfloor T \rfloor$. We have $\mathrm{PoA}(G) \leq \min\{3 - \frac{2}{k}, 3 - \frac{2}{c}\}$. In addition, for every even c, there exists a game $G \in \mathcal{G}_{unit}$ with $\mathrm{PoA}(G) = 3 - \frac{2}{k} = 3 - \frac{2}{c}$.*

Proof. Let $G \in \mathcal{G}_{unit}$. We show that $\mathrm{PoA}(G) \leq 3 - \frac{2}{k}$. Consider a NE schedule σ of G. Clearly, if some job of color i is covered in σ, then all jobs of color i are covered, since uncovered jobs can be added to fully overlap a covered one.

Recall that the sets are sorted in non-increasing order of total weight. Let $\ell > 1$ be the lowest index of a non-covered color. For every $0 \leq t \leq T - 2$, jobs of total weight at least W_ℓ start processing in the interval $[t, t+2)$, as otherwise, by assigning all the jobs of S_ℓ in $[t+1, t+2)$, it would be beneficial for the machine to cover the jobs of S_ℓ.

If k is even, consider the partition of $[0, T)$ into $\frac{k}{2}$ intervals $\{[0,2), [2,4), \dots [k-2, T)\}$. The first $\frac{k}{2} - 1$ intervals are of length 2, and the interval $[k-2, T)$ is of length at least 2. We conclude that $\mathrm{val}(\sigma) \geq \frac{k}{2} \cdot W_\ell$, that is, $W_\ell \leq \frac{2 \cdot \mathrm{val}(\sigma)}{k}$. If k is odd, then consider the partition of $[0, T)$ into $\lceil \frac{k}{2} \rceil$ intervals $\{[0,2), [2,4), \dots [k-1, T)\}$. The first $\lfloor \frac{k}{2} \rfloor$ intervals are of length 2 and the interval $[k-1, T)$ is of length at least 1. No job can start its processing after time $T - 1$ and complete on time. Thus, jobs of total weight at least W_ℓ start their processing during $[k-1, T-1)$, as otherwise it would be beneficial for the machine to cover the jobs of S_ℓ in the interval $[T-1, T)$. We conclude that $\mathrm{val}(\sigma) \geq \lceil \frac{k}{2} \rceil \cdot W_\ell \geq \frac{k}{2} \cdot W_\ell$, that is, $W_\ell \leq \frac{2 \cdot \mathrm{val}(\sigma)}{k}$.

By the choice of ℓ, $\mathrm{val}(\sigma) = \sum_{i=1}^{\ell-1} W_i$. In addition $\mathrm{val}(\sigma^*) = \sum_{i=1}^{k} W_i \leq \sum_{i=1}^{\ell-1} W_i + (k - \ell + 1)W_\ell$. Since $\ell > 1$, we have $\mathrm{val}(\sigma^*) \leq \mathrm{val}(\sigma) + \frac{2(k-1)\mathrm{val}(\sigma)}{k} = (3 - \frac{2}{k})\mathrm{val}(\sigma)$. That is, $\mathrm{PoA}(G) \leq 3 - \frac{2}{k}$.

If $k \leq c$, then $\min\{3 - \frac{2}{k}, 3 - \frac{2}{c}\} = 3 - \frac{2}{k}$, and we are done. If $k > c$ then note that $W_\ell \leq \frac{2 \cdot \mathrm{val}(\sigma)}{c}$. Also, $\mathrm{val}(\sigma^*) = \sum_{i=1}^{c} W_i \leq \sum_{i=1}^{\ell-1} W_i + (c - \ell + 1)W_\ell$. Since $\ell > 1$, we have $\mathrm{val}(\sigma^*) \leq \mathrm{val}(\sigma) + \frac{2(c-1)\mathrm{val}(\sigma)}{c} = (3 - \frac{2}{c})\mathrm{val}(\sigma)$. That is, $\mathrm{PoA}(G) \leq 3 - \frac{2}{c}$.

For the lower bound, given an even number c, consider a game G in which $c = T = k$. The set S_1 consists of $\frac{k}{2}$ unit-weight jobs, and for all $2 \leq i \leq k$, the set S_i consists of a single unit-weight job. For $1 \leq j \leq \frac{k}{2}$, let $a_j = j(2 - \epsilon)$. Consider a schedule in which for all $1 \leq j \leq \frac{k}{2}$ there is one job of S_1 in the slot $[a_j - 1, a_j)$, and all other jobs are in $[1 - \epsilon, 2 - \epsilon)$. Note that the idle intervals between the jobs have length $1 - \epsilon$, and the last idle interval $[a_{k/2}, T)$ has length $k\epsilon/2$. Therefore, a schedule in which only the jobs of S_1 are covered is a NE (we assume that the tie-breaking of the machine in $[1 - \epsilon, 2 - \epsilon)$ is in favor of 1. This assumption can be removed by increasing to $(1 + \epsilon)$ the weight of the job of S_1 placed in this slot). The players' utility vector is $(\frac{k}{2}, 0, \ldots, 0)$. The total revenue is $\frac{k}{2}$. The social optimum for this instance has profit $\sum_{i=1}^{k} W_i = \frac{k}{2} + k - 1 = \frac{3k}{2} - 1$. We conclude that $\mathrm{PoA}(G) = 3 - \frac{2}{k}$. $\qquad \square$

7 Extension: Non-symmetric Games

A natural extension to our game considers a setting in which every job $j \in \mathcal{J}$ is associated also with a release time, r_j, and a due-date, d_j. The player controlling S_i should place every job colored i in an interval $[t, t + p_j) \subseteq I_j = [r_j, d_j)$. Note that from the machine's point of view, the problem remains the same. However, for the players, this setting is computationally harder, and even a 2-player game with unit-length unit-weight jobs, may not have a NE.

Theorem 7.1. *There exists a game $G \in \mathcal{G}_{unit}$ with $c = 2$ that has no NE.*

Proof. Let G be the following game with $T = 3$, $|S_1| = 7$, and $|S_2| = 5$. The set S_1 consists of seven unit-length unit-weight jobs. The first two are restricted to go to $[0, 1)$, the next two are restricted to go to $[2, 3)$, and the remaining three can be placed anywhere in $[0, 3)$. The set S_2 consists of five unit-length unit-weight jobs. The first is restricted to go to $[0, 1)$, the second is restricted to go to $[2, 3)$, and the remaining three can be placed anywhere in $[0, 3)$. Consider a profile σ. For $i = 1, 2$, denote by x_i and y_i the number of jobs of S_i that intersects with $[0, 1)$ and $[2, 3)$, respectively. Note that a unit-job cannot intersect with both $[0, 1)$ and $[2, 3)$, thus $x_1 + y_1 \leq 7$ and $x_2 + y_2 \leq 5$. In addition, the restricted jobs imply that $x_1 \geq 2, y_1 \geq 2, x_2 \geq 1$ and $y_2 \geq 1$.

Assume that the utility of player 2 in σ is less than 4. Since $\min\{x_1, y_1\} \leq 3$, player 1 has at most 3 jobs intersecting at least one of $[0, 1)$ or $[2, 3)$. Player 2 has a beneficial migration - by placing all its flexible jobs in the corresponding interval, it increases its utility to 4. Thus, σ is not a NE.

Assume now that the utility of player 2 in σ is at least 4. Since only three jobs of S_2 can be covered in $[1, 2)$, the machine must processes S_2 also in an interval I that contains $[0, 1)$ or $[2, 3)$. Now, either 2 has a beneficial migration - by moving all its flexible jobs to I, or, if all the flexible jobs of S_2 are already in I, player 1 can increase its utility to 7 by placing all its flexible jobs in I. Thus, σ is not a NE. $\qquad \square$

Theorem 7.2. *Computing the best-response of a player is NP-hard even for $G \in \mathcal{G}_{unit}$ with $c = 2$.* $\qquad \square$

References

1. Albers, S.: Energy-efficient algorithms. Commun. ACM **53**(5), 86–96 (2010)
2. Arkin, E.M., Silverberg, E.B.: Scheduling jobs with fixed start and end times. Discret. Appl. Math. **18**(1), 1–8 (1987)

3. Baptiste, P.: Batching identical jobs. Math. Meth. Oper. Res. **52**(3), 355–367 (2000)
4. Bilò, V.: On the packing of selfish items. In: Proceedings 20th IEEE International Parallel & Distributed Processing Symposium (2006)
5. Bilò, V., Vinci, C.: Congestion games with priority-based scheduling. In: International Symposium on Algorithmic Game-Theory, pp. 67–82. Springer (2020)
6. Bouzina, K.I., Emmons, H.: Interval scheduling on identical machines. J. Global Optim. **9**, 379–393 (1996)
7. Briest, P., Krysta, P., Vöcking, B.: Approximation techniques for utilitarian mechanism design. SIAM J. Comput. **40**(6), 1587–1622 (2011)
8. Carlisle, M.C., Lloyd, E.L.: On the k-coloring of intervals. Discret. Appl. Math. **59**(3), 225–235 (1995)
9. Chang, J., Erlebach, T., Gailis, R., Khuller, S.: Broadcast scheduling: algorithms and complexity. ACM Trans. Algorithms **7**(4), 47:1–47:14 (2011)
10. Chang, J., Gabow, H.N., Khuller, S.: A model for minimizing active processor time. Algorithmica **70**(3), 368–405 (2014)
11. Cole, R., Correa, J., Gkatzelis, V., Mirrokni, V., Olver, N.: Decentralized utilitarian mechanisms for scheduling games. Games Econom. Behav. **92**, 306–326 (2015)
12. Correa, J., Queyranne, M.: Efficiency of equilibria in restricted uniform machine scheduling with total weighted completion time as social cost. Nav. Res. Logist. **59**(5), 384–395 (2012)
13. Czumaj, A., Vöcking, B.: Tight bounds for worst-case equilibria. ACM Trans. Algorithms **3**(1), 4 (2007)
14. Dürr, C., Nguyen, K.T.: Non-clairvoyant scheduling games. In: International Symposium on Algorithmic Game-Theory, pp. 135–146. Springer (2009)
15. Epstein, L., Kleiman, E.: Selfish bin packing. Algorithmica **60**, 368–394 (2011)
16. Faigle, U., Nawijn, W.M.: Note on scheduling intervals on-line. Discret. Appl. Math. **58**(1), 13–17 (1995)
17. Georgoulaki, E., Kollias, K., Tamir, T.: Equilibrium inefficiency and computation in cost-sharing games in real-time scheduling systems. Algorithms **14**(4) (2021)
18. Herzel, A., Hopf, M., Thielen, C.: Multistage interval scheduling games. J. Sched. **22**, 359–377 (2019)
19. Irani, S., Pruhs, K.R.: Algorithmic problems in power management. SIGACT News **36**(2), 63–76 (2005)
20. Karp, R.: Reducibility among combinatorial problems. In: Miller, R., Thatcher, J. (eds.) Complexity of Computer Computations, pp. 85–103. Plenum Press (1972)
21. Kleinberg, J., Tardos, E.: Algorithm Design. Pearson Education India (2006)
22. Kolen, A.W.J., Lenstra, J.K., Papadimitriou, C.H., Spieksma, F.: Interval scheduling: a survey. Naval Res. Logistics (NRL) **54**(5), 530–543 (2007)
23. Kose, A., Foh, C., Lee, H., Moessner, K.: Profiling vehicles for improved small cell beam-vehicle pairing using multi-armed bandit. In: 2021 International Conference on Information and Communication Technology Convergence (ICTC), pp. 221–226 (2021)
24. Koutsoupias, E., Papadimitriou, C.: Worst-case equilibria. In: Annual Symposium on Theoretical Aspects of Computer Science, pp. 404–413. Springer (1999)
25. Kovalyov, M.Y., Ng, C.T., Cheng, T.C.E.: Fixed interval scheduling: models, applications, computational complexity and algorithms. Eur. J. Oper. Res. **178**(2), 331–342 (2007)
26. Li, D., Wang, S., Zhao, H., Wang, X.: Context-and-social-aware online beam selection for mmWave vehicular communications. IEEE Internet Things J. **8**(10), 8603–8615 (2020)

27. Mu'alem, A., Nisan, N.: Truthful approximation mechanisms for restricted combinatorial auctions. Games Econ. Behav. **64**(2), 612–631 (2008). Special Issue in Honor of Michael B. Maschler
28. Tamir, T.: Cost-sharing games in real-time scheduling systems. Int. J. Game Theor. **52**(1), 273–301 (2022)
29. Vijayalakshmi, V.R., Schröder, M., Tamir, T.: Scheduling games with machine-dependent priority lists. Theoret. Comput. Sci. **855**, 90–103 (2021)
30. Wang, C., Zhang, G.: A best cost-sharing rule for selfish bin packing. arXiv preprint arXiv:2204.09202 (2022)
31. Yu, G., Zhang, G.: Bin packing of selfish items. In: Papadimitriou, C., Zhang, S. (eds.) WINE 2008. LNCS, vol. 5385, pp. 446–453. Springer, Heidelberg (2008). https://doi.org/10.1007/978-3-540-92185-1_50

Coordination Mechanisms with Rank-Based Utilities

Gilad Lavie and Tami Tamir[(✉)]

School of Computer Science, Reichman University, Herzliya, Israel
`giladlavie@gmail.com, tami@runi.ac.il`

Abstract. In classical job-scheduling games, each job behaves as a selfish player, choosing a machine to minimize its own completion time. To reduce the equilibria inefficiency, coordination mechanisms [8] are employed, allowing each machine to follow its own scheduling policy. In this paper we study the effects of incorporating *rank-based utilities* within coordination mechanisms across environments with either identical or unrelated machines.

With rank-based utilities, players aim to perform well *relative to their competitors*, rather than solely minimizing their completion time. We first demonstrate that even in basic setups, such as two identical machines with unit-length jobs, a pure Nash equilibrium (NE) assignment may not exist. This observation motivates our inquiry into the complexity of determining whether a given game instance admits a NE. We prove that this problem is NP-complete, even in highly restricted cases. In contrast, we identify specific classes of games where a NE is guaranteed to exist, or where the decision problem can be resolved in polynomial time. Additionally, we examine how competition impacts the efficiency of Nash equilibria, or sink equilibria if a NE does not exist. We derive tight bounds on the price of anarchy, and show that competition may either enhance or degrade overall performance.

Keywords: Coordination mechanisms · Rank-based utilities · Equilibrium existence and inefficiency

1 Introduction

Scheduling problems have traditionally been studied from a centralized point of view in which the goal is to find an assignment of jobs to machines so as to minimize some global objective function. In practice, many resource allocation services lack a central authority, and are often managed by multiple strategic users, whose individual payoff is affected by the assignment of other users. As a result, game theory has become an essential tool in the analysis of scheduling environments. This stems from the understanding that customers (the jobs) as well as resource owners (the machines) act independently so as to maximize their own benefit.

© ICST Institute for Computer Sciences, Social Informatics and Telecommunications Engineering 2026
Published by Springer Nature Switzerland AG 2026. All Rights Reserved
V. Aggarwal et al. (Eds.): GameNets 2025, LNICST 657, pp. 143–162, 2026.
https://doi.org/10.1007/978-3-032-12915-4_9

Job-scheduling games are singleton congestion games that represent situations which commonly occur in roads, and communication networks. In these well-studied models, each job acts as a selfish player, choosing a machine to minimize its own completion time. An algorithmic tool that is commonly utilized by the designer of such a system is a *coordination mechanism* [8]. The coordination mechanism uses a scheduling policy within each machine that aims to mitigate the impact of selfishness to performance. The scheduling policy defines the order according to which jobs are scheduled within a machine. For example, the jobs assigned to a machine that applies a *ShortestFirst* policy, are processed from shortest to longest. The assignment is non-preemptive and each job is processed uninterruptedly.

A coordination mechanism induces a game in which the strategy space of each player is the set of machines. An *assignment* is a strategy profile, defined by the jobs' selections. Every machine processes the jobs assigned to it according to its scheduling policy. The profile induces a completion time for each job - the time when its processing is done.

Traditionally, in such scheduling games, the goal of a player is to select a machine such that its completion time is minimized (Christodoulou et al. [8], Immorlica et al. [18]). In this work, inspired by Rosner and Tamir [25], we study *coordination mechanisms with rank-based utilities*. Formally, all players are competitors. A player's main goal is to do well relative to its competitors, i.e., to minimize the *rank* of its completion time among all players, while minimizing the completion time itself is a secondary objective. This natural objective arises in several computational environments. For example, (i) in high-frequency trading, the absolute time to execute a trade is irrelevant as long as it is faster than competitors, since only the first trade secures a profit. The focus is entirely on being ahead of others. The competitive nature of this environment ensures that speed is the sole priority, as market conditions can shift so rapidly that even minor delays result in missed opportunities. (ii) In cloud computing, users compete for access to shared servers, where the allocation of computational resources is often determined by relative performance metrics. For instance, during high-demand events like Black Friday, where e-commerce platforms experience surges in traffic, users with higher priority - such as premium subscribers or those leveraging performance-optimized instances - receive faster task processing. In these scenarios, the focus is not on minimizing absolute completion time but on being processed ahead of others to gain a competitive edge. This prioritization is especially critical in time-sensitive operations, such as real-time analytics or transaction processing, where delays can significantly impact business outcomes. (iii) On e-commerce platforms like Amazon, sellers optimize metrics such as response and delivery times to achieve higher rankings in search results. These rankings are based on relative performance, where sellers with faster responses and better fulfillment times gain increased visibility. Higher visibility directly translates into increased sales, creating a competitive environment where outperforming others matters more than achieving an absolute delivery speed.

An assignment is a *pure Nash equilibrium* (NE) if no player can benefit from unilaterally deviating from its strategy, that is, no player has an incentive to deviate from the machine on which its job is assigned. In games with rank-based utilities, a NE is a profile in which no job can reduce the rank of its completion time, nor to keep its rank and reduce its completion time.

We study several aspects of coordination mechanisms with rank-based utilities: the existence and computation of a NE, its quality, and the effect of competition on the equilibrium inefficiency, compared to games without competition.

1.1 Notation and Problem Statements

An instance of a *coordination mechanism with rank-based utilities* is given by a tuple $G = \langle J, M, (p_j)_{j \in J}, (r_i)_{M_i \in M}, (\pi_i)_{M_i \in M} \rangle$, where J is a finite set of $n \geq 1$ jobs (also denoted *players*), M is a finite set of $m \geq 1$ machines, $p_j \in \mathbb{R}^+$ is the processing time of job $j \in J$, $r_i \in \mathbb{R}^+$ denotes the rate or speed of machine $M_i \in M$, and $\pi_i : J \to \{1, \ldots, n\}$ is the *priority list* of machine $M_i \in M$. We assume that jobs have no release times. We denote by $j_1 \prec_i j_2$ the fact that job j_1 is prioritized over job j_2 in the priority list of machine M_i, that is $\pi_i(j_1) < \pi_i(j_2)$. For every job $j \in J$, the other jobs in J are referred to as the competitors of j.

A strategy profile $s = (s_j)_{j \in J} \in M^{|J|}$ assigns a machine $s_j \subset M$ to every job $j \in J$. A strategy profile s induces a *schedule* in which the jobs are processed according to their order in the machines' priority lists. We use s to denote both the strategy profile and its induced schedule. The set of jobs that delay $j \in J$ in s is denoted by $E_j(s) = \{j' \in J | s_{j'} = s_j \wedge \pi_{s_j}(j') \leq \pi_{s_j}(j)\}$. Note that job j itself also belongs to $E_j(s)$. Let $P_j(s) = \sum_{j' \in E_j(s)} p_{j'}$. The completion time of job $j \in J$ is given by $C_j(s) = P_j(s)/r_{s_j}$. For machine $M_i \in M$ let $L_i(s) = \sum_{j|s_j=i} p_j$ be the load on M_i in s, i.e., the total length of the jobs assigned to it.

Unlike classical job-scheduling games, in which the goal of a player is to minimize its completion time, in games with rank-based utilities, the goal of a player is to do well relative to its competitors. That is, every profile induces a ranking of the players according to their completion time, and the goal of each player is to have the lowest possible rank among all players. Formally, for a profile s, let $C^s = \langle C_1^s, \ldots, C_n^s \rangle$ be a sorted vector of the completion times of the players in J. That is, $C_1^s \leq \ldots \leq C_n^s$, where C_1^s is the minimal completion time of a player in s, etc. The *rank* of player $j \in J$ in profile s, denoted by $rank_j(s)$, is the rank of its completion time in C^s. If several players have the same completion time, then they all have the same rank, which is the corresponding average value. For example, if $n = 4$ and $C^s = \langle 7, 8, 8, 13 \rangle$, then the players' ranks are $\langle 1, 2.5, 2.5, 4 \rangle$, and if all players have the same completion time, then they all have rank $(n + 1)/2$.

The primary objective of every player is to minimize its rank. The secondary objective is to minimize its completion time. Formally, player j prefers profile s' over profile s if $rank_j(s') < rank_j(s)$ or $rank_j(s') = rank_j(s)$ and $C_j(s') < C_j(s)$. In this case, a deviation from profile s to profile s' is called beneficial for player j. A strategy profile s is a *pure Nash equilibrium (NE)* if for all $j \in J$, job j does not have a beneficial deviation.

For a strategy profile s, let $SC(s)$ denote the social cost of s. The social cost is defined with respect to some objective, e.g., the makespan, i.e., $C_{max}(s) = \max_{j \in J} C_j(s)$, or the sum of completion times, i.e., $\sum_{j \in J} C_j(s)$. It is well known that decentralized decision-making may lead to sub-optimal solutions from the point of view of the society as a whole. For a game G, let $P(G)$ be the set of feasible profiles of G. We denote by $OPT(G)$ the social cost of a social optimal solution, i.e., $OPT(G) = \min_{s \in P(G)} SC(s)$. We quantify the inefficiency incurred due to self-interested behavior according to the *price of anarchy* (PoA) [21], and *price of stability* (PoS) [1]. The PoA is the worst-case inefficiency of a pure Nash equilibrium, while the PoS measures the best-case inefficiency of a pure Nash equilibrium.

Definition 1.1. *Let $\mathcal{G}$ be a family of games, and let G be a game in $\mathcal{G}$. Let $\mathcal{E}(G)$ be the set of pure Nash equilibria of the game G. Assume that $\mathcal{E}(G) \neq \emptyset$.*

- *The* price of anarchy *of G is the ratio between the* maximum *cost of a NE and the social optimum of G, i.e., $PoA(G) = \max\limits_{s \in \mathcal{E}(G)} SC(s)/OPT(G)$. The* price of anarchy *of $\mathcal{G}$ is $PoA(\mathcal{G}) = sup_{G \in \mathcal{G}} PoA(G)$.*
- *The* price of stability *of G is the ratio between the* minimum *cost of a NE and the social optimum of G, i.e., $PoS(G) = \min\limits_{s \in \mathcal{E}(G)} SC(s)/OPT(G)$. The* price of stability *of $\mathcal{G}$ is $PoS(\mathcal{G}) = sup_{G \in \mathcal{G}} PoS(G)$.*

The strategy profile of all players except player j is denoted by s_{-j}, and it is convenient to denote a strategy profile s as $s = (s_j, s_{-j})$.

Best-Response Dynamics (BRD) is a natural method by which players proceed toward a NE via the following local search method: Given a strategy profile s, the best response of player j is $BR_j(s) = \arg\min_{s'_j \in M} \langle rank_j(s'_j, s_{-j}), C_j(s'_j, s_{-j}) \rangle$; i.e., the set of strategies that maximize job j's utility, fixing the strategies of all other players. Player j is said to be *suboptimal* in s if it has a beneficial deviation (reduce its rank, or maintain its rank and reduce its completion time), i.e., if $s_j \notin BR_j(s)$. If no player is suboptimal in s, then s is a NE.

Given an initial strategy profile s^0, a best response sequence from s^0 is a sequence $\langle s^0, s^1, \ldots \rangle$ in which for every $T = 0, 1, \ldots$ there exists a player $j \in J$ such that $s^{T+1} = (s'_j, s^T_{-j})$, where $s'_j \in BR_j(s^T_{-j})$.

Given a game G, the strategy profile graph of G is a directed graph whose vertex set consists of all possible strategy profiles of G, and there is a directed edge (s_1, s_2), if the profile s_2 can be obtained from profile s_1 by a best-response deviation of a single player.

A *deviator rule* is a function that, given a profile s, chooses a deviator among all suboptimal players in s. The chosen player then performs a best response move (breaking ties arbitrarily). Given an initial strategy profile s^0 and a deviator rule D we denote by $NE_D(s^0)$ the set of NE that can be obtained as the final profile of a BR sequence $\langle s^0, s^1, \ldots \rangle$, where for every $T \geq 0$, s^{T+1} is a profile resulting from a deviation of $D(s^T)$. Note that every BR-sequence corresponds to some path in the strategy profile graph. Therefore, the analysis of this graph is a major tool in understanding BRD convergence and the quality of possible BRD outcomes.

As we are going to show, a game with rank-based utilities may not have a NE. In order to analyze the quality of the profiles to which natural dynamics may converge, we use the concept of a *Sink Equilibrium*, introduced in [16]. A sink equilibrium is a strongly connected component with no outgoing edges in the strategy profile graph. A sink equilibrium always exists. Thus, even in games that do not admit a NE, we can still analyze the expected quality of a steady state of the game.

The definition of a sink equilibrium in [16] refers to a random walk in the strategy profile graph. When BRD is applied with a specific deviator rule, the choice of the deviating player is deterministic, however, we can still have several different BR-sequences, depending on the initial profile and the tie breaking applied by a player in case it has more than one best-response move. For a game G and a deviator rule, D, a sink equilibrium of (G, D) is a strongly connected component with no outgoing edges in the strategy profile graph, to which G may converge when D is applied.

The following definitions extend the definitions from [16] to sink equilibria reached via a specific deviator rule.

Definition 1.2. *Let $\mathcal{Q}(G, D)$ be the set of sink equilibria of G reached by applying BRD with deviator rule D. For a sink $Q \in \mathcal{Q}(G, D)$, let $f_Q : Q \to \mathbb{R}^+$ be the steady state distribution of a BR-sequence over states in Q.*

- *The (expected) social cost of a sink equilibrium $Q \in \mathcal{Q}(G, D)$, denoted by $SC(Q)$, is the expected social cost of the states in a BR-sequence that reaches Q, i.e., $SC(Q) = \Sigma_{s \in Q} f(s) \cdot SC(s)$.*
- *The price of sinking of G, D is the ratio between the maximum cost of a sink equilibrium and the social optimum of G, i.e., $PoSINK(G, D) =$*

$\max_{Q \in \mathcal{Q}(G,D)} SC(Q)/OPT(G)$. *The* price of sinking *of* $\mathcal{G}, D$ *is* $PoSINK(\mathcal{G}, D) = sup_{G \in \mathcal{G}} PoSINK(G, D)$.

1.2   Rank-Based vs. Cost-Based Utilities

The crucial difference between rank-based utilities and cost-based utilities is demonstrated already in the following simple game with two identical machines $\{M_1, M_2\}$ and two unit-length jobs $J = \{a, b\}$ (see Fig. 1). Assume that in both machines $a \prec b$. It is easy to see that with rank-based utilities, the game has no NE profile. Specifically, let s be a profile in which both jobs are assigned to the same machine. We have that $rank_a(s) = 1, rank_b(s) = 2$, thus job b would benefit from deviating to the other machine. In the resulting profile, s', we have that $rank_a(s') = rank_b(s') = 1.5$. Any profile in which the jobs are on different machines, and in particular s', is not stable as well, since both jobs have the same completion time and rank, therefore, job a would benefit from joining the machine of job b. Such a deviation will not affect a's completion time, and will delay job b. Note that in the traditional model, in which jobs only care about their completion time, any balanced schedule is a NE.

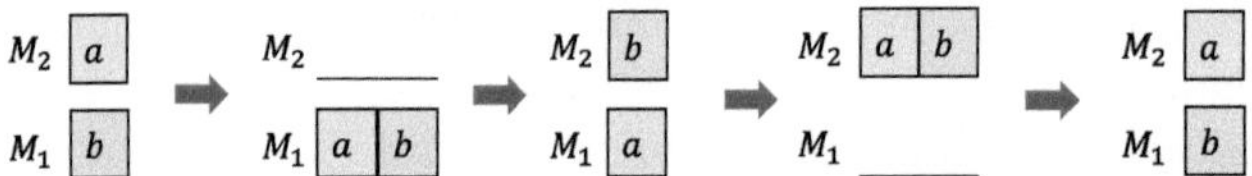

Fig. 1. A BR-sequence in a game with two unit-length players and no NE.

On the other hand, if the two machines have different priority lists, for example if $a \prec_1 b$ (that is, M_1 prioritize a over b), and $b \prec_2 a$ then the assignment in which job a is on M_1, and job b is on M_2 is a NE. Both jobs have rank 1.5 and will have rank 2 if they deviate.

The above example highlights the fact that games with rank-based utilities are significantly different from classical job-scheduling games; the competition creates interesting problems already with unit-length jobs, a class whose analysis in the competition-free setting is straightforward.

The next example demonstrates that in a game with rank-based utilities, jobs may perform non-intuitive beneficial migrations. Specifically, a job may reduce its rank even though it increases its cost (completion time). Consider an instance with two identical machines $\{M_1, M_2\}$ and three jobs $J = \{a, b, c\}$, where $p_b > p_a + p_c$. Assume that in both machines $a \prec b \prec c$. Consider a schedule, s, in which jobs a, c are on one machine and job b is on the other machine (see left schedule in Fig. 2). We have that $rank_a(s) = 1, rank_b(s) = 3, rank_c(s) = 2$. Job b can reduce its rank from 3 to 2 by deviating to M_1. This deviation increases its completion time from p_b to $p_a + p_b$, but is beneficial in our model. It is not difficult to see that this game has no NE.

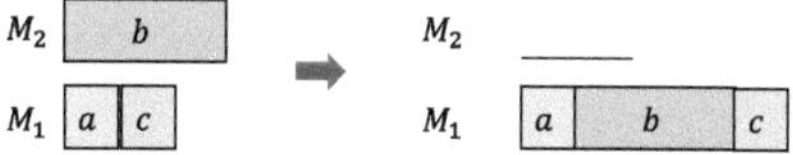

Fig. 2. A cost-increasing rank-reducing deviation.

1.3   Related Work

Scheduling games were initially studied in the setting in which each machine processes its jobs in parallel so that the completion time of each job depends on the total load on the machine [3,11,15]. The high equilibrium inefficiency of these games motivated the study of coordination mechanisms, i.e., games with local scheduling policies.

Christodoulou et al. [8] introduced coordination mechanisms and studied the price of anarchy with priority lists based on longest processing time (LPT) first. These initial results were generalized in [4,7,9,18,20,23] were additional scheduling policies as well as their inefficiency and convergence time were studied. Vijayalakshmi et al. [24] considered a more general setting in which machines have arbitrary individual priority lists. The paper characterizes four classes of instances in which a pure Nash equilibrium is guaranteed to exist, and analyzes the equilibrium inefficiency for these classes. Our paper consider this setting with competition-based utilities.

Best Response Dynamics (BRD) has been a significant area of study in the analysis of congestion games. Research in this domain often examines the existence of NE, the convergence of BRD to these equilibria, and the inefficiencies introduced by selfish behavior. The papers [12–14,19] analyze various deviator rules, and compared their effects on the convergence time and the solution quality in several classes of congestion games.

Research has also delved into scenarios where BRD does not converge to a pure Nash Equilibrium. Goemans et al. [16] introduced the concept of sink equilibria, and defined the *Price of Sinking* that quantifies the inefficiency of sink equilibria. Berger et al. [5] introduced the notion of dynamic inefficiency, examining the average social cost across an infinite sequence of best responses.

Rank-based scheduling games where studied so far only on parallel machines (without priority lists). Ashlagi et al. [2] presented a social context game with rank competition. The competition structure in their model is arbitrary and defined by a network. Immorlica et al. [18] consider a model with arbitrary competition structure, in which players' utility combine their payoff and ranking.

General ranking games are studied in Brandt et al. [6], where it is shown that computing a NE is NP-complete in most cases. In Goldberg et al. [17] a player's utilization combines its rank with the effort expended to achieve it. Rosner and Tamir introduced in [25] a scheduling game with rank-based utilities. These works show that the analysis of games with rank-based utilities tends to be very different from the analysis of classical games.

Our model combines the study of coordination mechanism with rank-based utilities. This combination was not considered in the past.

1.4 Our Results

As demonstrated in Sect. 1.2, even in simple games with just two jobs and two machines, a pure Nash equilibrium may not exist. The natural problem of deciding whether a given game has a pure NE is central in our study. In Sect. 2, we establish that this problem is NP-complete, even when job lengths are restricted to $\{1,2\}$. On the positive side, we identify several classes of instances where a Nash equilibrium is guaranteed to exist or where the decision problem can be solved efficiently.

The following classes of games are analyzed in our work:

- $\mathcal{G}^P$ - games played on identical (unit-rate) machines.
- $\mathcal{G}^Q$ - games played on related machines.
- $\mathcal{G}^{global}$ - games with a global priority list, π. That is, for every machine $M_i \in M$, it holds that $\pi_i = \pi$.
- $\mathcal{G}_{unit}$ - games with unit-length jobs.

Some of our results refer to games in the intersection of some classes. For example, a game $G \in \mathcal{G}_{unit}^{Q2,global}$ is played on two related machines with a global priority list and unit-length jobs.

In Sect. 2 we propose two simple greedy algorithms for computing a schedule: one for identical machines and one for related machines. Next, we provide necessary and sufficient conditions for the stability of the resulting schedule. A run of the algorithm may require $O(n)$ tie-breaking steps. We show that the question of deciding whether a game has a NE is reduced to the problem of deciding whether there exists a run of the algorithm whose output fulfills the stability conditions. Some of our results below are based on showing that even though the number of potential outputs is exponential, it is possible to trace them efficiently.

In Sect. 3 we study equilibrium existence and computation in games played on identical machines. We first introduce a coordination mechanism denoted *Inversed-Policies*, that ensures the existence of a NE on any game with two machines. Next, we characterize games in $\mathcal{G}_{unit}^{P,global}$ that admit a NE, and provide a linear time algorithm for games in $\mathcal{G}_{unit}^{P2}$.

In Sect. 4 we study equilibrium existence and computation in games played on two related machines. We provide an exact characterization of games in $\mathcal{G}_{unit}^{Q2}$ that admit a NE, distinguishing between global and machine-dependent priority lists, and between games where the ratio of the machines' rates is a rational or irrational number.

Focusing on games that admit a Nash equilibrium (NE), we turn in Sect. 5 to examine how competition impacts the efficiency of these equilibria. Our efficiency metric is the makespan, defined as the maximum completion time across all jobs. We first verify that the tight bounds established in prior work for traditional scheduling games without competition remain valid when rank-based utilities are introduced. Specifically, we find that the PoA and PoS of $\mathcal{G}^P$ are both $2 - \frac{1}{m}$, a result which also extends to games in $\mathcal{G}^{P2}$ with *Inversed-Policies* mechanism. For related machines, we show that the PoA and PoS of a game in $\mathcal{G}^{Q2}$ depend on the machine's speed ratio r: they are equal to $r + 1$ when $r \leq \frac{\sqrt{5}-1}{2}$ and $\frac{r+2}{r+1}$ when $r > \frac{\sqrt{5}-1}{2}$. Notably, when $r = \frac{\sqrt{5}-1}{2}$, the system reaches its highest inefficiency, with both PoA and PoS equal $\frac{\sqrt{5}+1}{2}$.

While the bounds are similar to those in traditional scheduling games, our analysis reveals instances where competition either mitigates or worsens the equilibrium inefficiency. Specifically, we present cases where a game without competition attains the worst possible price of stability (PoS) in its class, but with the introduction of competition, the price of anarchy (PoA) improves to 1. Conversely, we present games where introducing competition degrades the equilibrium quality.

For games in $\mathcal{G}_{unit}^{P,global}$ that do not admit a NE, we propose a deviator rule and show that when it is applied, the price of sinking (PoSINK) is as low as $1 + \frac{1}{2 \cdot \lceil \frac{n}{m} \rceil}$. On the other hand, for games in $\mathcal{G}^{Q2}$ that do not admit a NE, we show that the price of sinking is not bounded by a constant.

Due to space constraints, some proofs and examples are omitted from this extended abstract. A full version is available in [22].

2   Computational Complexity, Greedy Algorithms and Stability Conditions

We first show that the problem of deciding whether a game has a NE is NP-complete already in the case that job lengths are in $\{1, 2\}$. Formally,

Theorem 2.1. *Given a coordination mechanism with rank-based utilities, the problem of deciding whether the game has a NE is NP-complete, even when the machines are identical and for all jobs $p_j \in \{1, 2\}$.* $\square$

Next, we present greedy scheduling algorithms and provide sufficient and necessary conditions for the stability of their output. These algorithms will be analyzed further in our work.

2.1 Identical Machines

The first algorithm is for identical machines. It assigns the jobs greedily one after the other in non-decreasing order of starting time.

Algorithm 1 - Computing a schedule s, identical machines

1: For $1 \leq i \leq m$, set $L_i(s) = 0$.
2: **repeat**
3:     Let $i^{\star} = \arg\min_i \; (L_i(s))$, breaking ties arbitrarily.
4:     Assign on machine $i^{\star}$ the first unassigned job in $\pi_{i^{\star}}$, j.
5:     $L_{i^{\star}}(s) = L_{i^{\star}}(s) + p_j$.
6: **until** all jobs are scheduled

An important property of Algorithm 1 is that, as shown in [10], it generates a schedule in which no job can decrease its completion time, that is, a schedule stable against cost-reducing deviations. However, as demonstrated in Sect. 1.2, such a profile may not be a NE in the presence of competition.

Algorithm 1 will be analyzed for various classes of games in this paper. The following discussion refers to the class $\mathcal{G}_{unit}$ of games with unit-length jobs. We begin by presenting a sufficient and necessary condition for having a beneficial deviation of a single job in a schedule of a game $G \in \mathcal{G}_{unit}$. Recall that a deviation is *cost-reducing* if it reduces the completion time of the deviating job.

Claim 2.2. *Let s be a schedule of $G \in \mathcal{G}_{unit}$, such that s is stable against cost-reducing deviations. A job j on machine M_i has a rank-decreasing deviation iff*

1. *Job j is processed last on its machine, and*
2. *There exists a job j' on M_z, for which $C_{j'}(s) = C_j(s)$ and $j \prec_z j'$.*   □

Based on the above claim, we now describe the conditions under which a schedule produced by Algorithm 1 is a NE for a game $G \in \mathcal{G}_{unit}$. Let $n = \ell \cdot m + c$ for $0 \leq c < m$. Note that when the algorithm is executed on an instance with unit-length jobs, then in the resulting schedule, $m - c$ machines have load $\ell = \lfloor n/m \rfloor$, and c machines have load $\ell + 1 = \lceil n/m \rceil$.

Theorem 2.3. *Let s be a schedule produced by Algorithm 1 for a game $G \in \mathcal{G}_{unit}$. Schedule s is a NE iff the two following conditions hold:*

1. *Let P be the set of c jobs with completion time $\ell + 1$. If $j \in P$ is processed on machine i, then j has the highest priority in π_i among the jobs in P.*

2. *Let P_1 be the set of $m - c$ jobs with completion time ℓ that are processed last on their machines, and P_2 be the set of c jobs with completion time ℓ that are not processed last on their machines. If $j \in P_1$ is processed on machine i, then j has the highest priority in π_i among the jobs in P_1. If $j \in P_2$ is processed on machine i, then j has higher priority in π_i than any $j' \in P_1$.*

Proof. Let s be a NE schedule produced by Algorithm 1. Since all jobs in P share the same completion time, and similarly, all jobs in P_1 and P_2 share their respective completion times, conditions 1 and 2 follow directly from Claim 2.2 (see example in Fig. 3). Specifically, in P, each job is assigned to the machine where it has the highest priority among the jobs with the same completion time, and similarly, the prioritization within P_1 and P_2 ensures no beneficial deviations.

For the other direction, let s be a schedule in which both conditions are satisfied. Since no job can decrease its completion time, it follows from Claim 2.2 that only jobs that are processed last on their machines, i.e., jobs in P or P_1, might potentially benefit from migrating. By condition 1 and Claim 2.2, no job in P has a beneficial migration. Similarly, by condition 2 and Claim 2.2, no job in P_1 has a beneficial migration.

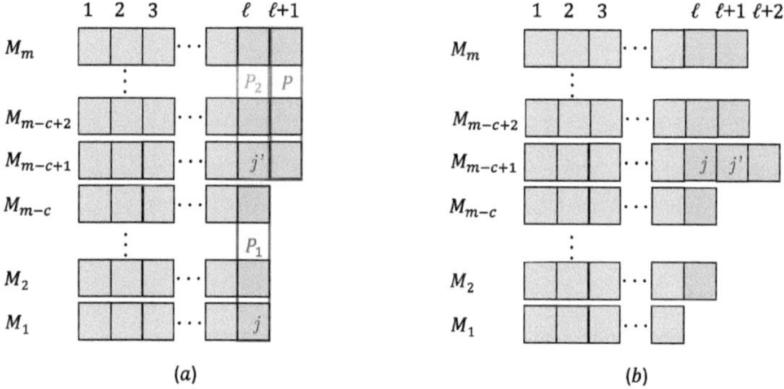

Fig. 3. (a) The sets P, P_1 and P_2 in s. (b) A beneficial migration of job $j \in P_1$ from M_1 to $M_{m-\,c+1}$, assuming condition 2 is not satisfied and $j \prec_{m-c+1} j'$.

2.2   Related Machines

The second algorithm is for related machines. It assigns the jobs greedily one after the other according to their expected *completion time*.

Algorithm 2 - Computing a schedule s, related machines and unit-jobs

---

1: For $1 \leq i \leq m$, set $L_i(s) = 0$.
2: **repeat**
3:     Let $i^\star = \arg\min_i \ (L_i(s) + 1)/r_i$, breaking ties arbitrarily.
4:     Assign on machine $i^\star$ the first unassigned job in $\pi_{i^\star}$.
5:     $L_{i^\star}(s) = L_{i^\star}(s) + 1$.
6: **until** all jobs are scheduled

Clearly, with identical machines, this algorithm is equivalent to Algorithm 1. We refer to Algorithm 1 when analyzing identical machines, since its greedy choice is more intuitive.

Section 4 considers the class $\mathcal{G}_{unit}^{Q2}$ of games with unit-jobs and two related machines, M_1 and M_2, with rates $r_1 = 1$ and $r_2 = r \leq 1$. We now establish a condition regarding the stability of a profile produced by Algorithm 2 for this class. As shown in [24], Algorithm 2 produces a schedule in which no job can decrease its completion time. However, with rank-based utilities, such a schedule is not necessarily stable.

Given a schedule s, for $i \in \{1, 2\}$, let j_i be the last job on M_i in s.

Theorem 2.4. *Let s be a schedule of a game $G \in \mathcal{G}_{unit}^{Q2}$ produced by Algorithm 2. Schedule s is a NE iff one of the three following conditions holds:*

1. *$L_1(s) < L_2(s)/r$.*
2. *$L_1(s) = L_2(s)/r$, and each of the two last jobs is prioritized on its machine over the other last job. Formally, $j_1 \prec_1 j_2$ and $j_2 \prec_2 j_1$.*
3. *$L_1(s) > L_2(s)/r$, and either no job on M_1 has completion time $C_{j_2}(s)$, or for the job j such that $C_j(s) = C_{j_2}(s)$ it holds that $j \prec_1 j_2$.* $\square$

3 Identical Machines Equilibrium Existence and Computation

In this section we analyze games with identical machines, i.e., $\forall M_i \in M, r_i = 1$.

Machine-Dependent Priority Lists and Arbitrary Job Lengths: For the case of $m = 2$ identical machines, (M_1, M_2), with machine-dependent priority list and arbitrary job lengths, Christodoulou et al. [8] introduced the mechanism *Increasing-Decreasing* with tiebreak based on the lexicographic order of the jobs. We generalize their result and introduce the *Inversed-Policies* coordination mechanism, in which the priority lists of M_1 and M_2 are inversed. That is, $\forall j = 1, \ldots, n \quad \pi_1(j) = n - \pi_2(j) + 1$. Note that the order is independent of the job lengths.

We show that a game with *Inversed-Policies* has a NE, and that Algorithm 1 produces a NE profile.

Theorem 3.1. *With Inversed-Policies, Algorithm 1 produces a Nash equilibrium.*   □

Global Priority List and Unit-Length Jobs: For games with unit-length jobs and a global priority list we show that no NE exists if the game is played on more than two machines, and we give a simple characterization of instances on two machines that have a NE. Moreover, if a NE exists, then it can be computed efficiently.

Theorem 3.2. *A game $G \in \mathcal{G}_{unit}^{P,global}$ has a NE iff $m = 2$ and n is odd.*   □

Machine-Dependent Priority Lists and Unit-Length Jobs: For $m = 2$ machines with arbitrary priority lists and unit-size jobs, we present a linear time algorithm for deciding whether a given game has a NE, and producing a NE if one exists.

Theorem 3.3. *Given a coordination mechanism with rank-based utilities and arbitrary priority list, with $m = 2$ machines and unit-size jobs, it is possible to decide in linear time whether the game has a NE, and to produce a NE if one exists.*

Proof. Recall Algorithm 1, which ensures that no job can decrease its completion time in the generated schedule. We utilize this property to prove that if n is odd, the game G has a NE.

Claim 3.4. *If n is odd, any game $G \in \mathcal{G}_{unit}^{P2}$ has a NE, and a NE can be computed in time $O(n)$.*   □

On the other hand, if n is even, the existence of a NE is not guaranteed. We begin by showing that if a NE does exist, then Algorithm 1 has the capability to generate it, or at least a schedule closely resembling it with identical *layers*, which we define as follows: Let s be an assignment of J. Denote the jobs assigned to machine M_i by $j_{i1}, \ldots, j_{ix}$ according to their order in π_i, with x representing the total number of jobs assigned to M_i. For any $k \geq 1$, the kth layer of s is denoted by $L_k^{(s)}$ and consists of the two jobs $\{j_{1k}, j_{2k}\}$.

Claim 3.5. *Any stable assignment s has a run of Algorithm 1 that produces a schedule with the same layers as in s, and in which the jobs in the last layer are processed on the same machines as in s.*   □

We now establish the condition for a schedule produced by Algorithm 1 to be stable.

Claim 3.6. *Let $n = 2\ell$, and let s be an assignment produced by Algorithm 1. Let $j_{1\ell}$ and $j_{2\ell}$ be the last jobs on M_1 and M_2 in s, respectively. Schedule s is a NE iff $j_{1\ell} \prec_1 j_{2\ell}$ and $j_{2\ell} \prec_2 j_{1\ell}$.*   □

From Claims 3.5 and 3.6, we infer that by examining the last layers of all the potential schedules generated by Algorithm 1, we can determine the existence of a NE and even produce one if it exists. We show that at most two potential last layers exist, and we can identify them efficiently in linear time.

Recall that $n = 2\ell$. For $1 \leq k \leq \ell$, let Γ_k be the set of sets of jobs such that $S_k \in \Gamma_k$ if and only if $|S_k| = 2k$ and there exists a run of Algorithm 1 in which the jobs of S_k are assigned on the first k layers.

We show that for $1 \leq k \leq \ell$, $|\Gamma_k| \leq 2$. Moreover, if $|\Gamma_k| = 2$ then the two sets are identical up to a single job. For $1 \leq k \leq \ell$, denote by $\hat{\pi}_i^{(k)}$ the unassigned jobs in π_i, at the beginning of the $(2k-1)^{th}$ iteration of Algorithm 1, i.e., after assigning jobs in the first $k-1$ layers, and before assigning jobs in the kth layer. Note that $\hat{\pi}_i^{(1)} = \pi_i$, and that $|\hat{\pi}_i^{(k)}| = n - 2 \cdot (k-1)$. Denote by $\hat{\pi}_i^{(k)}(x)$ the job in the xth place in $\hat{\pi}_i^{(k)}$.

Claim 3.7. *For all $1 \leq k \leq \ell$, $|\Gamma_k| \leq 2$. If $S_k^1, S_k^2 \in \Gamma_k$, then*

1. *$|S_k^1 \cap S_k^2| = 2k - 1$, and*
2. *$\hat{\pi}_1^{(k)}(1) = \hat{\pi}_2^{(k)}(1)$, $\hat{\pi}_1^{(k)}(2) \neq \hat{\pi}_2^{(k)}(2)$, and*
3. *denote $\hat{\pi}_1^{(k)}(2) = a_k$ and $\hat{\pi}_2^{(k)}(2) = b_k$, then $S_k^1 \setminus S_k^2 = \{a_k\}$, $S_k^2 \setminus S_k^1 = \{b_k\}$, w.l.o.g.* □

If $n = 2\ell$, then every schedule s produced by Algorithm 1 has exactly ℓ layers. Notice that for any $k = 1, \ldots, \ell$, the kth layer is $L_k^{(s)} = S_k \setminus S_{k-1}$. Specifically, the last layer is $L_\ell^{(s)} = S_\ell \setminus S_{\ell-1}$. By Claim 3.7, there are at most 2 options for $S_{\ell-1}$, and since $S_\ell = J$, there are at most 2 options for the last layer $L_\ell^{(s)}$.

Based on the above observations, we present Algorithm 3. The following claim establishes the statement of Theorem 3.3.

Algorithm 3 - Determines existence of a NE in $G \in \mathcal{G}_{unit}^{P2}$ and produces one if it exists

---

1: **if** n is odd **then**
2:    Use Algorithm 1 to produce a schedule s and assign the first $n-1$ jobs.
3:    Assign the last job in s according to Claim 3.4.
4:    Return s
5: **end if**
6: Determine all different options for $S_\ell, S_{\ell-1}$, where $n = 2\ell$.
7: **for** each option of $S_{\ell-1}$ **do**
8:    Compute $L_\ell^{(s)} = S_\ell \setminus S_{\ell-1}$, where s is a schedule corresponding to $S_{\ell-1}$.
9:    **if** $L_\ell^{(s)}$ satisfies the condition in Claim 3.6 **then**
10:       Return s
11:    **end if**
12: **end for**
13: Return "no NE exists"

Claim 3.8. *Algorithm 3 has a runtime of $O(n)$, and returns a NE schedule s iff a NE exists.*   □

4 Related Machines Equilibrium Existence and Computation

In this section, we consider the class $\mathcal{G}^{Q2}_{unit}$, in which unit-jobs are assigned to two related machines. W.l.o.g., the two machines, M_1 and M_2, have rates $r_1 = 1$ and $r_2 = r \leq 1$. Thus, M_1 is denoted *the fast machine*, while M_2 is denoted *the slow machine*.

In the following analysis, we distinguish between rational r, that is, $r = \frac{a}{b}$ for some integers $a \leq b$, and irrational r. Our analysis is based on analyzing the possible outputs of Algorithm 2, presented in Sect. 2.2. Recall that the algorithm assigns the jobs greedily according to their completion time. The following observations are valid for both global and machine-dependent priority lists.

Theorem 4.1. *If r is an irrational number, then G has a NE, and it can be calculated in linear time.*

We turn to consider the case that r is a rational number, that is, $r = \frac{a}{b}$ for some integers $a \leq b$. Let s be a schedule produced by Algorithm 2. Let $n = \ell \cdot (a + b) + c$ for $0 \leq c < a + b$. The algorithm assigns the jobs in blocks of $a + b$ jobs. In every block, there are b jobs on the fast machine and a jobs on the slow machine (see Fig. 4). Specifically, for $k \geq 1$, the kth block is $B_k(s) = \{j \mid (k - 1) \cdot b < C_j(s) \leq k \cdot b\}$. When s is clear from the context, we omit it. We denote the jobs in B_k by non-decreasing order of their completion time $j_1^{(k)}, j_2^{(k)}, \ldots, j_{a+b}^{(k)}$.

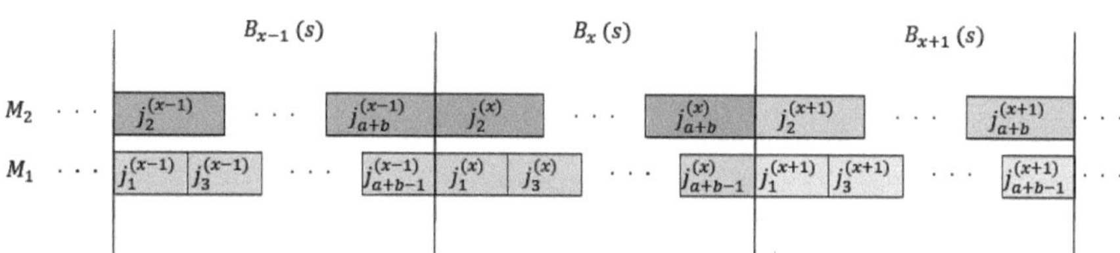

Fig. 4. Blocks in schedule s on two related machines having rates 1 and $r = a/b$.

Note that the last two jobs in a block, $(j_{a+b-1}^{(k)}, j_{a+b}^{(k)})$, have the same completion time, and that these are the only pairs that share a completion time.

In the sequel we show that for games with a global priority list, having $c \neq 0$ is a necessary and sufficient condition for having a NE, while for games with machine-dependent priority lists, games for which $c = 0$ may also have a NE assignment, and their analysis is more involved.

We start by showing that, without any assumptions regarding the priority lists, having $c \neq 0$ is a sufficient condition to ensure that a NE exists and can be produced efficiently. Recall that Algorithm 2 produces a schedule stable against cost-reducing deviations. We utilize this property to prove the following claim.

Claim 4.2. *For every $G \in \mathcal{G}_{unit}^{Q2}$, if $c \neq 0$, then G has a NE, and a NE can be computed in time $O(n)$.*

Proof. Let $n = \ell \cdot (a + b) + c$, with $c \neq 0$. If $c \geq \lceil \frac{b}{a} \rceil$, then let s be a schedule produced by Algorithm 2, and let j_1 and j_2 be the last jobs processed on M_1 and M_2, respectively. Because $c \geq \lceil \frac{b}{a} \rceil$, both j_1 and j_2 are in $B_{\ell+1}$, and neither of them has a job on the opposite machine with the same completion time. Thus, by Theorem 2.4, s is a NE.

If $0 < c < \lceil \frac{b}{a} \rceil$, assume that Algorithm 2 is executed. After the first $\ell \cdot (a+b) - 2$ jobs are assigned, we enter the $(\ell \cdot (a + b) - 1)^{th}$ iteration. Let j_1 be the first unassigned job in π_1. In Step 3 of the algorithm, machine i^* might be either M_1 or M_2. Suppose the tiebreaker resolves in favor of assigning j_1 to M_1. Let s be the produced schedule, and let j_2 be the last job processed on M_2. Since $0 < c < \lceil \frac{b}{a} \rceil$, it follows that $L_1(s) > L_2(s)/r$. Note that $C_{j_1}(s) = C_{j_2}(s)$ and $j_1 \prec_1 j_2$. Therefore, by Theorem 2.4 s is a NE. $\qquad\square$

Global Priority List: Assume that both machines have the same priority list $\pi = \langle 1, 2, \ldots, n \rangle$.

Theorem 4.3. *Let G be a game with $m = 2$ related machines, $r_1 = 1$, $r_2 = r = \frac{a}{b}$ for two integers $a \leq b$, a global priority list π and $n = \ell \cdot (a + b) + c$ unit-jobs for $0 \leq c < a + b$. G has a NE iff $c \neq 0$.*

Machine-Dependent Priority Lists: We turn to discuss instances in which $\pi_1 \neq \pi_2$. We present a linear time algorithm for deciding whether a given game has a NE, and producing a NE if one exists.

As a warm-up, we demonstrate that a tie-breaking decision during a run of Algorithm 2 may by crucial for the stability of the resulting schedule. This example highlights the need to trace multiple possible outcomes of the algorithm.

Example 4.1. Consider the game G with $m = 2$ related machines, where $r = \frac{2}{3}$ and $J = \{1, 2, \ldots, 10\}$. The priority lists are: $\pi_1 = \langle 1, 2, 3, 4, 5, 6, 7, 8, 9, 10 \rangle$ and $\pi_2 = \langle 1, 2, 3, 4, 10, 9, 6, 7, 8, 5 \rangle$. Now, consider the scheduling process of Algorithm 2. After assigning the first three jobs, a tie-break occurs as job 4 is the first unassigned job in both π_1 and π_2, with its possible completion time on both machines being equal. At this point, the algorithm's outcome may diverge, as job 4 can either be assigned to M_1 or M_2. If the algorithm assigns job 4 to M_2, *then the resulting schedule is a NE (see Fig. 5(a)), as the last jobs to complete, jobs 8 and 9, are each prioritized on their respective machines over the other. However, if job 4 is assigned to M_1, the last jobs to complete are jobs 7 and 8 (see Fig. 5 (b_1) and (b_2)). Since job 7 is prioritized over job 8 on both priority lists, an endless sequence of best response moves arises between them, preventing convergence to a NE.*

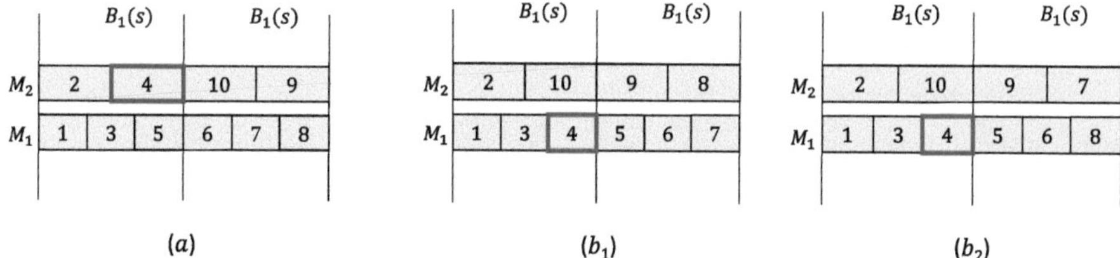

(a)   (b_1)   (b_2)

Fig. 5. (a) A NE schedule produced by Algorithm 2 in case that job 4 is assigned on M_2. (b_1, b_2) The unstable schedules Algorithm 2 produces when job 4 is assigned on M_1. In both schedules, job 7 can reduce its rank from 9.5 to 9 by deviating to the other machine and precede job 8.

By manipulating the priority lists, we can build an instance in which an assignment of job 4 on the fast machine yields a NE, while its assignment on the slow machine leads to an unstable schedule. Thus, no tie-breaking rule can be used to promote stability. However, we show that even if the algorithm faces multiple tie-breaking decisions, there are only two possible sets of jobs that may be processed last in any schedule produced by the algorithm.

Theorem 4.4. *Given a coordination mechanism with rank-based utilities and $m = 2$ related machines, $r_1 = 1$, $r_2 = r = \frac{a}{b}$ for some $a \leq b$, and unit-size jobs, it is possible to decide in linear time whether the game has a NE, and to produce a NE if one exists.* □

5   The Effect of Competition on the Equilibrium Inefficiency

In this section, we analyze the equilibrium inefficiency with respect to the objective of minimizing the makespan, focusing on whether competition improves or worsens it. We show that the PoA bounds from [24] for games without competition also hold for games with competition that have a NE. Additionally, we show that competition can be either beneficial or harmful. For games without a NE, we analyze the price of sinking.

5.1 Identical Machines

Recall that Algorithm 1 produces a Nash equilibrium for any game on two identical machines with *Inversed-Policies*. We first bound the PoA of the resulting NE. Our bound is higher than the bound (of $\frac{4}{3}$) presented in [8] for *Increasing-Decreasing* policies without competition.

Theorem 5.1. *A coordination mechanism with* Inversed-Policies *has a price of anarchy of* $\frac{3}{2}$. $\qquad\square$

Next, we analyze the class $\mathcal{G}^P$ of games played on m identical machines, and n arbitrary jobs.

Theorem 5.2. $PoA(\mathcal{G}^P) = PoS(\mathcal{G}^P) = 2 - \frac{1}{m}$. $\qquad\square$

In the full version [22] we show that competition may be both helpful and harmful for the social cost. We first present an instance G_1 for which the corresponding game without competition has $PoS(G_1) = 2 - \frac{1}{m}$, while the same game with competition has $PoA(G_1) = 1$. We then present an instance G_2 for which without competition $PoA(G_2) = 1$, and with competition we get a game for which $PoS(G_2) = 2 - \frac{1}{m}$.

Sink Equilibria Analysis: Let $G \in \mathcal{G}_{unit}^{P,global}$ be a game played by $n = \ell \cdot m + c$, for $0 \leq c < m$, unit-length jobs, on m identical machines, with a global priority list π. Assume that G has no NE. By Theorem 3.2, either $m \geq 3$ or $m = 2$ and n is even. We analyze the sink equilibria of G. As we show, natural dynamics lead to sink equilibria with good social cost.

Assume w.l.o.g., that $J = \{1, \ldots, n\}$ and that $\pi = \langle 1, \ldots, n \rangle$. Given a profile s, let $Sub(s)$ be the set of suboptimal players in s, and let $Lag(s)$ denote the set of jobs such that $j \in Lag(s)$ iff $rank_j(s) > m \cdot \lceil j/m \rceil - \frac{m-1}{2}$. Note that $Lag(s) \subseteq Sub(s)$.

Recall that BRD is a natural dynamics, in which, as long as the system is not in a stable state, a suboptimal player is chosen by applying some deviator rule, and performs a best response move. We suggest the following deviator rule for selecting the next player to deviate in an (infinite) sequence of best response moves, and bound the expected cost of a profile in the resulting sink equilibrium.

Priority-Based Deviator Rule: If $Lag(s) \neq \emptyset$, then choose the player with the highest priority in $Lag(s)$. Else, if $Sub(s) \setminus Lag(s) \neq \emptyset$ then choose the player with the lowest priority in $Sub(s)$.

Theorem 5.3. *Let* $G \in \mathcal{G}_{unit}^{P,global}$ *be a game with* $n = \ell \cdot m + c$ *jobs. If* $c \neq 1$, *then* $PoSINK(G, \pi-based) = 1 + \frac{1}{2 \cdot \lceil \frac{n}{m} \rceil}$, *and if* $c = 1$, *then* $PoSINK(G, \pi-based) = 1$. $\qquad\square$

5.2   Related Machines

Consider the class $\mathcal{G}^{Q2}$. Recall that the two machines are denoted by M_1 and M_2, such that $r_1 = 1$ and $r_2 = r \leq 1$. The proof of the following theorem builds on the corresponding proof in [24] for games without competition.

Theorem 5.4. *If* $r \leq \frac{\sqrt{5}-1}{2}$ *then* $PoA(\mathcal{G}^{Q2}) = PoS(\mathcal{G}^{Q2}) = r + 1$, *and if* $r > \frac{\sqrt{5}-1}{2}$ *then* $PoA(\mathcal{G}^{Q2}) = PoS(\mathcal{G}^{Q2}) = \frac{r+2}{r+1}$. $\qquad\square$

As with identical machines, in the full version [22] we show that competition may be both helpful and harmful for the social cost.

Finally, we analyze the price of sinking for games in $\mathcal{G}^{Q2}$ with arbitrary job lengths. As we show, the price of sinking - regardless of the deviator rule applied - cannot be bounded by any constant, since it depends on $1/r$.

Example 5.1. Consider the game G' with two jobs a and b, where $p_a = 1$, $p_b = r$, and $\pi_1 = \pi_2 = \langle a, b \rangle$. G' has no pure NE. Profile s_1 is the social optimum. The sink consists of 4 profiles (see Fig. 6), and has price of sinking of $\frac{r+3}{4} + \frac{1}{2r}$. The high cost of the sink is due to the fact that the long job is on the slow machine in two out of the four profiles.

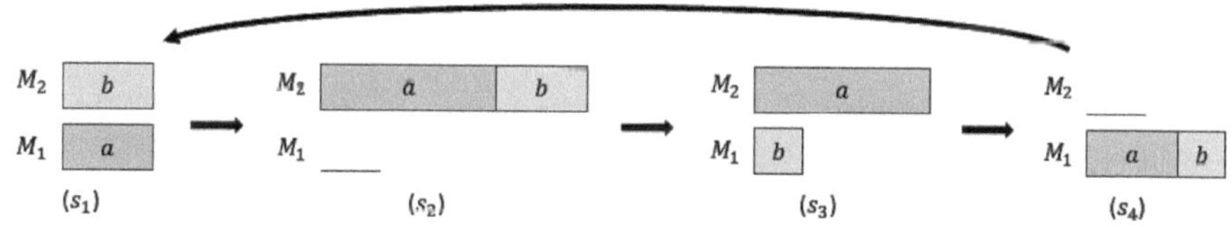

Fig. 6. The sink equilibrium of G'. Job a benefits from a migration in s_1 and s_3, job b benefits from a migration in s_2 and s_4.

References

1. Anshelevich, E., Dasgupta, A., Kleinberg, J., Tardos, E., Wexler, T., Roughgarden, T.: The price of stability for network design with fair cost allocation. SIAM J. Comput. **38**(4), 1602–1623 (2008)
2. Ashlagi, I., Krysta, P., Tennenholtz, M.: Social context games. In: International Workshop on Internet and Network Economics, pp. 675–683. Springer, Heidelberg (2008)
3. Awerbuch, B., Azar, Y., Richter, Y., Tsur, D.: Tradeoffs in worst-case equilibria. Theoret. Comput. Sci. **361**(2), 200–209 (2006)
4. Azar, Y., Jain, K., Mirrokni, V.: (Almost) optimal coordination mechanisms for unrelated machine scheduling. In: Proceedings of the 19th Annual ACM-SIAM Symposium on Discrete Algorithms, SODA '08, pp. 323–332 (2008)

5. Berger, N., Feldman, M., Neiman, O., Rosenthal, M.: Dynamic inefficiency: anarchy without stability. In: Proceedings of the 4th SAGT, pp. 57–68 (2011)

6. Brandt, F., Fischer, F., Harrenstein, P., Shoham, Y.: Ranking games. Artif. Intell. **173**(2), 221–239 (2009)

7. Caragiannis, I., Fanelli, A.: An almost ideal coordination mechanism for unrelated machine scheduling. Theor. Comput. Syst. **63**(1), 114–127 (2019)

8. Christodoulou, G., Koutsoupias, E., Nanavati, A.: Coordination mechanisms. In: Proceedings of the 31st ICALP, pp. 345–357 (2004)

9. Cohen, J., Dürr, C., Kim, T.N.: Non-clairvoyant scheduling games. Theor. Comput. Syst. **49**(1), 3–23 (2011)

10. Correa, J.R., Queyranne, M.: Efficiency of equilibria in restricted uniform machine scheduling with total weighted completion time as social cost. Naval Res. Logist. (NRL) **59**(5), 384–395 (2012)

11. Czumaj, A., Vöcking, B.: Tight bounds for worst-case equilibria. ACM Trans. Algorithms **3**(1), 4:1–4:17 (2007)

12. Even-Dar, E., Kesselman, A., Mansour, Y.: Convergence time to Nash equilibria. In: Proceedings of the 30th ICALP, pp. 502–513 (2003)

13. Feldman, M., Snappir, Y., Tamir, T.: The efficiency of best-response dynamics. In: The 10th International Symposium on Algorithmic Game Theory (SAGT) (2017)

14. Feldman, M., Tamir, T.: Convergence of best-response dynamics in games with conflicting congestion effects. Inf. Process. Lett. **115**(2), 112–118 (2015)

15. Gairing, M., Lücking, T., Mavronicolas, M., et al.: Computing Nash equilibria for scheduling on restricted parallel links. Theor. Comput. Syst. **47**(2), 405–432 (2010)

16. Goemans, M.X., Mirrokni, V.S., Vetta, A.: Sink equilibria and convergence. In: 46th Annual IEEE Symposium on Foundations of Computer Science (FOCS), pp. 142–154 (2005)

17. Goldberg, L.A., Goldberg, P.W., Krysta, P., Ventre, C.: Ranking games that have competitiveness-based strategies. Theoret. Comput. Sci. **476**, 24–37 (2013)

18. Immorlica, N., Li, L.E., Mirrokni, V.S., Schulz, A.S.: Coordination mechanisms for selfish scheduling. Theor. Comput. Sci. **410**(17), 1589–1598 (2009)

19. Kawald, B., Lenzner, P.: On dynamics in selfish network creation. In: Proceedings of the 25th ACM Symposium on Parallelism in Algorithms and Architectures (SPAA), pp. 83–92 (2013)

20. Kollias, K.: Nonpreemptive coordination mechanisms for identical machines. Theor. Comput. Syst. **53**(3), 424–440 (2013)

21. Koutsoupias, E., Papadimitriou, C.: Worst-case equilibria. Comput. Sci. Rev. **3**(2), 65–69 (2009)

22. Lavie, G., Tamir, T.: Coordination Mechanisms with Rank-Based Utilities. arXiv arXiv:2502.03113 (2025)

23. Lu, P., Yu, C.: Worst-case Nash equilibria in restricted routing. J. Comput. Sci. Technol. **27**(4), 710–717 (2012)

24. Ravindran Vijayalakshmi, V., Schröder, M., Tamir, T.: Scheduling games with machine-dependent priority lists. Theoret. Comput. Sci. **855**, 90–103 (2021)

25. Rosner, S., Tamir, T.: Scheduling games with rank-based utilities. Games Econom. Behav. **140**, 229–252 (2023)

Applications of Game Theory

Diffusion Control of Wildland Fire
via a Cooperative Game-Theoretic Model

Patrizia Bagnerini[1] , Mauro Gaggero[2] , Giorgio Gnecco[3] ,
and Marcello Sanguineti[1,2](✉)

[1] University of Genoa, Genoa, Italy
`{patrizia.bagnerini,marcello.sanguineti}@unige.it`
[2] National Research Council of Italy, Genoa, Italy
`mauro.gaggero@cnr.it`
[3] IMT Alti Studi Lucca, Lucca, Italy
`giorgio.gnecco@imtlucca.it`

Abstract. Various modeling approaches have been proposed in the literature to forecast the evolution of wildland fires over time and space and to control them. Here, a methodology based on cooperative game theory is proposed to optimize the use of limited resources to control a fire, such as firefighters, Canadair, drones, etc. In particular, the Shapley value, i.e., a solution concept of cooperative games, is exploited. It provides a measure of the value of each player in a so-called transferable-utility game, and recently it has been used to evaluate the importance of edges or nodes in a network. In the proposed approach, the wildland area is modeled as a network, in which nodes represent areas of particular interest. Some of them may become fire outbreaks, from which the fire can reach other nodes. The edges represent possible directions of fire evolution and can be weighted by taking into account several features, including elevation of the terrain, kind of vegetation, and estimated rate of spread. A temperature diffusion process is considered, where the global rate of diffusion is given by the second smallest eigenvalue of the weighted Laplacian matrix of the network. Then, a transferable-utility game is defined, where players form a subset of the edge set, and the utility function is related to the decrease of the global rate of diffusion of the fire when one or more edges are removed. This corresponds to control diffusion paths from a fire outbreak. The Shapley values are exploited to decide the order in which the edges should be removed, that is, how one should act with fire-extinguishing resources, in such a way as to effectively reduce the global fire diffusion rate.

Keywords: Wildland Fires · Transferable-Utility Games · Shapley Value

1   Introduction

In recent decades, fighting forest fires has become increasingly important due to their growth in frequency, incidence, and magnitude. According to San-Miguel-Ayanz et al. (2020), an average of 47,000 fires per year in Mediterranean European countries have

V. Aggarwal et al. (Eds.): GameNets 2025, LNICST 657, pp. 165–177, 2026.
https://doi.org/10.1007/978-3-032-12915-4_10

affected about 44,200 ha of vegetated areas since 1980. Forest fires are fought through a series of air/ground interventions and through the coordination of various actors, such as firefighters, civil defense, police, and volunteers.

From a logistic point of view, it is important to determine where to intervene with firefighting operations to minimize the fire spread, based on a suitable model of fire evolution and on a proper measure of the "importance" of each area of possible intervention. The former calls for the application of a suitable fire simulation model, whose importance has been recognized for several decades (see, e.g., Hanson et al. 2000), whereas the latter suggests the application of solution concepts from cooperative game theory (Maschler et al. 2020). In this context, the Shapley value (Shapley 1953) is a well-established solution concept, which serves as a metric for assessing the importance of each player in a so-called transferable utility game. Recently, it has found application in evaluating the relevance of individual nodes or edges within a network (Hadas et al. 2017; Michalak et al. 2013; Passacantando et al. 2021), representing an alternative to classical measures of centrality in a network. Analyzing the importance of nodes/edges can assist decision-makers in identifying weak components in a network, detecting and preventing failures, and improving its connectivity (for instance, in the case of a transportation network, in terms of travel time, costs, reliability, access, and flow).

The Shapley value has diverse applications across various fields. In economics, it has traditionally been used in areas such as taxation, redistribution, public goods production, and fixed-price economies (see, e.g., Aumann 1994). More recently, Yeung et al. (2021) applied it to trade analysis. The concept has also gained traction in machine learning, particularly in feature importance evaluation for tasks like binary classification (Strumbelj and Kononenko 2014). Indeed, the Shapley value has become a key tool in the emerging field of interpretable machine learning, offering a versatile method for understanding model behavior (Molnar 2022). This expansion into machine learning is especially significant given the growing influence of these techniques in economics, as highlighted by Athey and Imbens (2019). Moreover, Michalak et al. (2014) have contributed to the implementation and computation of suitable extensions of the Shapley value in generalized utility function games, broadening its applicability. Its utility extends to critical areas such as cybersecurity, with Bataineh et al. (2024) demonstrating its use in detecting poisoning attacks in collaborative intrusion detection systems for vehicular networks.

In this work, which develops preliminary results presented in Bagnerini et al. (2024), we apply the Shapley value to a transferable-utility game on a network modeling cooperation of firefighters in controlling wildland fire diffusion, with the aim of identifying important edges in the network. The proposed approach consists of the following steps. First, we model the wildland area as a network. The nodes represent areas of particular interest and some of them may become fire outbreaks, from which the fire can reach other nodes. Possible directions of fire evolution are modeled by the edges, which can be weighted by taking into account, for instance, elevation of the terrain, kind of vegetation, estimated rate of spread, and other features. Then, we consider a temperature diffusion process, where the global rate of diffusion is given by the second smallest eigenvalue of the weighted Laplacian matrix of the network. As a further step, we introduce a transferable-utility game, where the players form a subset of the edge set and the utility function is defined in terms of the decrease of the global rate of diffusion of the fire when one or more edges are removed, i.e., the corresponding diffusion paths from a fire outbreak are controlled. Finally, we exploit the Shapley values to decide the order in which the edges should be removed, that is, how one should act with fire-extinguishing resources, in such a way to effectively reduce the global fire diffusion rate.

Wildfire suppression efforts have significant economic implications, extending beyond the immediate costs of firefighting. For instance, Baylis and Boomhower (2023) found that public expenditures on wildfire protection can act as substantial implicit subsidies for development in high-risk areas, potentially encouraging construction in fire-prone zones. Meier et al. (2023) quantified the regional economic impact of wildfires in Southern Europe, revealing significant negative effects on the growth of gross domestic product and heterogeneous impacts on employment across sectors. Their study estimated yearly production losses of 13–21 billion euros for the region. Hand et al. (2014) developed models for understanding suppression expenditures, emphasizing the need for a comprehensive approach to wildfire management.

The paper is organized as follows. In Sect. 2, the model of wildland fire diffusion is presented. In Sect. 3, a wildland fire game based on that model is introduced. In Sect. 4, the game is analyzed and examples are provided. In Sect. 5, extensions of this research are discussed.

2 Model of Wildland Fire Diffusion

Let $G = (V, E, W)$ be a *weighted undirected graph* with *non-negative weights*, where V is the *set of vertices*, E is the *set of edges*, and W is a *weighted adjacency matrix*, which models the local fire diffusion rate of each edge. For each vertex i, let φ_i denote its "temperature". We assume that each φ_i evolves with respect to the time t according to the following *diffusion* process:

$$\frac{d\varphi_i}{dt} = \sum_{j \in V} W_{i,j}(\varphi_j - \varphi_i). \tag{1}$$

By introducing the temperature column vector $\boldsymbol{\varphi}$ and the *weighted Laplacian matrix* $\boldsymbol{L} = \boldsymbol{D} - \boldsymbol{W}$ (where $\boldsymbol{D}$ is the *weighted degree matrix*), the system of ordinary differential Eqs. (1) can be also written as

$$\frac{d\boldsymbol{\varphi}}{dt} + \boldsymbol{L}\boldsymbol{\varphi} = 0,$$

whose solution, in terms of the matrix exponential, is

$$\boldsymbol{\varphi}(t) = e^{-\boldsymbol{L}t}\boldsymbol{\varphi}(0).$$

It is well-known (see, e.g., Chung 1997) that the eigenvalues of the weighted Laplacian matrix $\boldsymbol{L}$ satisfy the chain of inequalities

$$0 = \lambda_1 \leq \lambda_2 \leq \cdots \leq \lambda_{|V|},$$

and that for a connected graph (the case considered in the following) one has $\lambda_2 > 0$ (Chung 1997).

The *global rate of the fire diffusion process* is defined as λ_2. The first smallest eigenvalue λ_1 is not associated with diffusion, but with the steady state, which is constant over the set of vertices of the graph in the case of a connected graph, as it follows from Eq. (1). The smaller λ_2, the smaller the rate. The other eigenvalues $\lambda_3 \leq \cdots \leq \lambda_{|V|}$ refer to faster dynamics, and are also related to diffusion. The focus is given here to λ_2, which refers to the slowest dynamic, which basically determines the duration of the transient behavior.

Example 1. Figure 1 *reports the evolution of the diffusion process for a given initial condition at $t = 0$ (all the weights $W_{i,j}$ being equal to 0.5, from which one gets $\lambda_2 = 0.5$). Each node temperature is proportional to the radius of the associated circle. In Fig. 2, the evolution of the diffusion process for the same initial condition is reported (all the weights $W_{i,j}$ being equal to a smaller value, namely 0.1, from which one gets $\lambda_2 = 0.1$). A comparison of Figs. 1 and 2 clarifies the role of λ_2 as global rate of the diffusion process: the diffusion is faster in the first example, with $\lambda_2 = 0.5$, than in the second one, for which $\lambda_2 = 0.1$.*

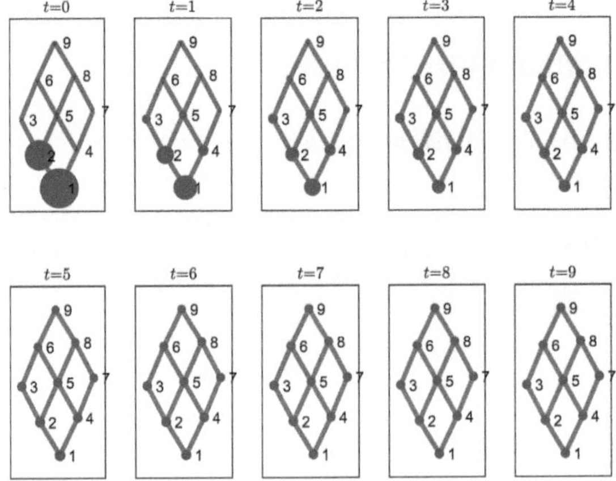

Fig. 1. Evolution of the diffusion process for a given initial condition, for a weighted undirected graph with global diffusion rate $\lambda_2 = 0.5$.

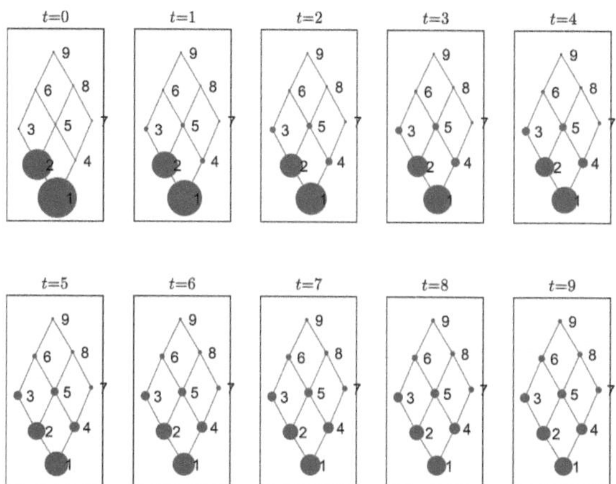

Fig. 2. Evolution of the diffusion process for the same initial condition as in Fig. 1, for a weighted undirected graph with global diffusion rate $\lambda_2 = 0.1$.

3   The Wildland Fire Game

Recall that a *Transferable-Utility cooperative game* (*TU game*; see, e.g., Maschler et al. 2020) is a pair (N, v), defined as follows: $N = \{1, \ldots, n\}$ is a set of *players*, which is also called the *grand coalition*. $S \subseteq N$ denotes a generic *coalition*. The function $v: 2^N \to \mathbb{R}$ is called *utility function* (or *characteristic function*). For each $S \in 2^N$, $v(S)$ represents the *utility* that can be achieved jointly by all the players in S. For the empty coalition, one has $v(\varnothing) = 0$ by definition. TU games are called in this way since, in this class of cooperative games, there is the possibility of transferring utility from one player to another one without incurring any loss.

A measure of importance of players in a TU game is the *Shapley value,* defined as

$$\sum_{S \subseteq N} \left[(v(S) - v(S \setminus \{i\})) \frac{(|S| - 1)!(n - |S|)!}{n!} \right], \forall i \in N. \tag{2}$$

Equation (2) can be interpreted as the average marginal utility of player i, when it joins the coalition formed by all the players that precede it in a random permutation of the grand coalition (assuming that all the permutations are equally likely). To reduce the computational burden needed for its exact evaluation, the Shapley value is often approximated via the Monte Carlo method (see, e.g., Castro et al. 2009; Gnecco et al. 2021).

Several properties satisfied by the Shapley value (such as *symmetry* and the so-called *null-player property*, which show, together, that the Shapley value represents a fair measure of importance of the players) are well-known (see, e.g., Maschler et al. 2020). In particular, it follows from the definition (2) that the Shapley value is non-negative when the utility function $v(S)$ is *monotonic*, i.e., when

$$v(S) - v(S \setminus \{i\}) \geq 0 \ \forall S \subseteq N, \forall i \in N.$$

This means that, in this case, every player has non-negative importance. In some TU games the Shapley value of some players may be negative (hence, by removing those players from a randomly-formed coalition has a beneficial average effect).

In the TU game that we are going to associate with wildland fire diffusion and control, the players form a subset E of edges. A coalition S of players acts as follows: the edges in S are removed from the graph G, for instance, as a consequence of firefighters intervention on those edges (in other words, the edges can be modeled as locations of possible firefighters intervention). The resulting graph is denoted by G_S. For simplicity we assume that the remaining edges (which are not players of the game) make the graph connected (so, removing a subset of players from the graph G never makes it disconnected, and $\lambda_2 > 0$ holds for every G_S). For graphs G_S with $\lambda_2(G_S) = 0$ this assumption can be relaxed by replacing $\lambda_2(G_S)$ with the eigenvalue $\lambda_h(G_S)$ having the smallest index h for which $\lambda_h(G_S) > 0$. However, relaxing such an assumption may invalidate the conclusions reported in the next Remark 1.

We consider the following choice for the utility function, which models the reduction in the global fire diffusion rate when all the edges in S are removed from the graph:

$$v(S) =: \lambda_2(G) - \lambda_2(G_S). \tag{3}$$

We refer to the TU game defined above as *Wildland Fire game (WF game)*. Its properties can be investigated by exploiting a characterization of the global fire diffusion rate λ_2 provided by the Courant-Fischer theorem.

Remark 1. *The utility function* (3) *of the WF game is monotonic and so the Shapley values are non-negative. Indeed, since the weighted Laplacian matrix L is symmetric, we can apply the Courant-Fischer theorem (see, e.g., Parlett 1998), which expresses λ_2 as the optimal objective value of the following optimization problem:*

$$\lambda_2 = \min_{\varphi \in \mathbb{R}^{|V|}} \varphi^T L \varphi = \tfrac{1}{2} \sum_{i,j \in V} W_{i,j}(\varphi_j - \varphi_i)^2,$$
$$\text{s.t. } \|\varphi\|_2 = 1, \tag{4}$$
$$\sum_{i \in V} \varphi_i = 0.$$

Removing the edges in S corresponds to removing some non-negative terms from the summation in the objective function of the optimization problem (4)*, without changing its constraints (since the resulting graph remains connected). Thus, we get*

$$\lambda_2(G_S) \leq \lambda_2(G), \text{ or } \lambda_2(G) - \lambda_2(G_S) \geq 0.$$

Through the same argument we conclude that, if $S_1 \subseteq S_2$, then $\lambda_2(G_{S_2}) \leq \lambda_2(G_{S_1})$, i.e., $\lambda_2(G_{S_1}) - \lambda_2(G_{S_2}) \geq 0$.

We remark that a similar result holds if one modifies the definition of the utility function (3) *in such a way that each edge in a coalition has a reduced weight with respect to its original weight in G.*

Remark 1 implies that the edge removal cannot increase the global fire diffusion rate (since the second eigenvalue of the new network is either the same of the one of the original network or smaller) and decreases the rate when the second eigenvalue of the new network is strictly smaller. The Shapley value of each edge is the average reduction in the global fire diffusion rate due to the removal of the corresponding edge.

Example 2. *As a simple example of Shapley value computation in the WF game, we consider a weighted undirected graph for which all the weights $W_{i,j}$ are equal to 1. Edge players are highlighted in red in* Fig. 3.

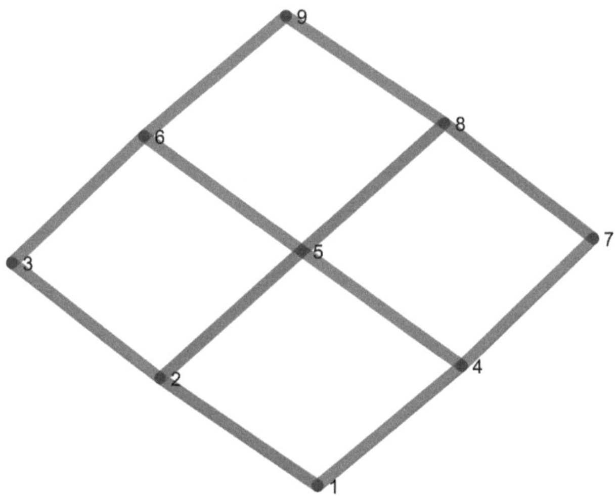

Fig. 3. Example of a set of edge players (in red).

In this example there are 4 players and $2^4 = 16$ possible coalitions (including the empty one). The definition (2) of the Shapley value provides the following values:

$$Sh(e_{1,2}) = Sh(e_{7,8}) = 0.2574,$$

$$Sh(e_{2,5}) = Sh(e_{5,8}) = 0.1450.$$

These values agree with a symmetry argument (i.e., $e_{1,2}$ and $e_{7,8}$ are so-called symmetric players, hence their Shapley values are equal; the same occurs for $e_{2,5}$ and $e_{5,8}$).

4 Edge Removal Strategy and Model Matching

We consider the following goal: removing a given number $k \leq |N|$ of edges that reduce the global fire diffusion rate the most. This is a combinatorial optimization problem, whose optimal solution can be approximated by computing recursively the (approximate) Shapley values of the players. The following strategy can be adopted:

i) Compute the Shapley values of the edges (average reductions of the global fire diffusion rate due to their removal) in the WF game and order them non-increasingly.

ii) Remove the first edge $e_1 \in N$ in the ranking.

iii) Compute the Shapley values of the remaining edges for a new instance of the game, whose set of players is $N \setminus \{e_1\}$.

iv) Remove the first edge $e_2 \in N \setminus \{e_1\}$ in the new ranking and so on, until k edges have been removed.

Similar strategies were already adopted in the literature, both for the Shapley value (e.g., by selecting k players with the k largest Shapley values, see Narayanam and Narahari 2011) and for the generalized Shapley value (Metulini and Gnecco 2023).

Example 3. *The following toy example illustrates the situation in which no wind is present during the wildfire diffusion, so an undirected graph model can be used (see Sect. 5 for an extension to the case of a directed graph model). Five kinds of terrain are considered, modeled as vertical strips with constant weights (equal to 1, 2, 3, 4, 5, respectively) for the edges either inside each strip or between two consecutive strips (see Fig. 4).*

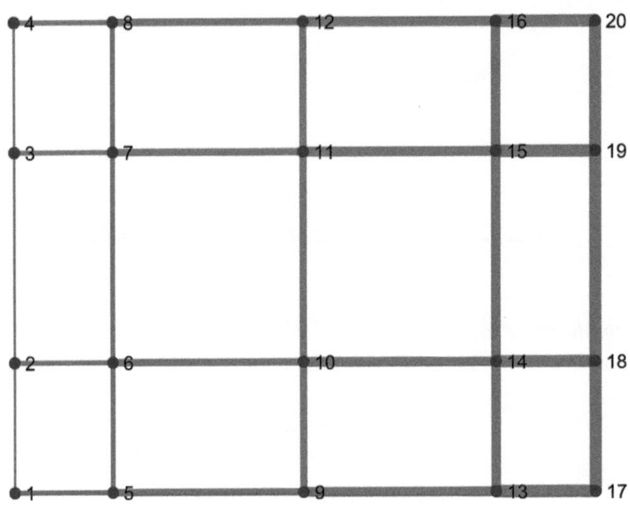

Fig. 4. Toy example.

In the figure, the edge widths are proportional to their weights. We consider an instance of the WF game with 8 players, depicted in red in the figure: two edges for each strip, apart from the middle strip. Each edge touches an end of the corresponding strip and the graph obtained by removing any subset of edges is connected. In this example there are $2^8 = 256$ possible coalitions (including the empty one). Based on the definition (2) of the Shapley value and the one (3) of the utility function of the WF game, we get the following results:

$$Sh(e_{1,2}) = Sh(e_{3,4}) = 0.1221,$$

$$Sh(e_{5,6}) = Sh(e_{7,8}) = 0.1124,$$

$$Sh(e_{13,14}) = Sh(e_{15,16}) = 0.0935,$$

$$Sh\big(e_{17,18}\big) = Sh\big(e_{19,20}\big) = 0.0957.$$

Again, these values agree with a symmetry argument.

The model parameters (e.g., the local diffusion rates) could be learned by matching as closely as possible the output of the graph-theoretical model with the one of a more detailed physical model of fire evolution (e.g., a *fire-front propagation model* based on *level set methods*, such as the model by Alessandri et al. 2021), able to take into account issues such the type of terrain, its elevation, and wind velocity.

As an illustrative example, we report the following hill case study from Alessandri et al. (2021). In Fig. 5, part (a) represents the 3D elevation map, while part (b) represents the initial condition. The initial fire front is represented in red, the wind direction is in blue, the elevation level curves are in black, fuel A (modeling the first terrain) is in light-yellow, and fuel B (modeling the second terrain) is in light-green.

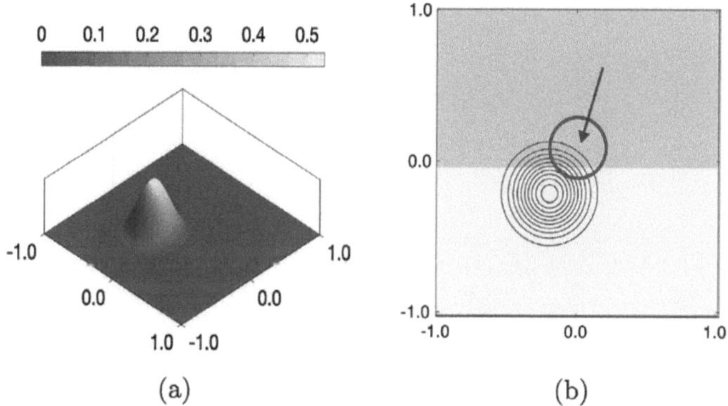

(a)   (b)

Fig. 5. Hill case study (from Alessandri et al. 2021). 3D elevation map (a); initial condition (b).

The matching of the two models could be stated as an optimization problem, similar to the training problem of a feedforward neural network, in which the supervision is provided by the more detailed physical model. Alternatively, one could work directly on a graph-based discretization of the more detailed physical model.

However, it is worth noting that the model considered in the present work is a fire diffusion model, not a fire propagation model, that is, a different mechanism of fire evolution is considered. Moreover, although it allows one to identify a fire front, the level set function does not represent a temperature. This is an issue to be faced when searching for a matching of the two models. Moreover, an application of Courant-Fischer theorem similar to the one considered above may not be possible in a graph-based discretization of the physical model by Alessandri et al. (2021). Hence, given a suitable TU game based on this discretized model, it may be more difficult to prove non-negativeness of the Shapley values of its players.

5 Extensions and Discussion

The inclusion of wind velocity in the more detailed physical model would motivate using a weighted directed graph instead of a weighted undirected one also in the model considered in the present work. The graph-theoretical model considered in this work can be easily extended to the case of a weighted directed graph, using a special form of the weighted Laplacian matrix for that kind of graph, which is called *weighted in-degree Laplacian matrix* (Mesbahi and Egerstedt 2010). In this case, a condition analogous to $0 = \lambda_1 < \lambda_2 \leq \cdots \leq \lambda_{|V|}$ holds for the real parts of the eigenvalues, and is obtained by imposing that the graph contains a so-called *arborescence*, i.e., a directed rooted tree (indicated in green in Fig. 6, with node 1 as the root).

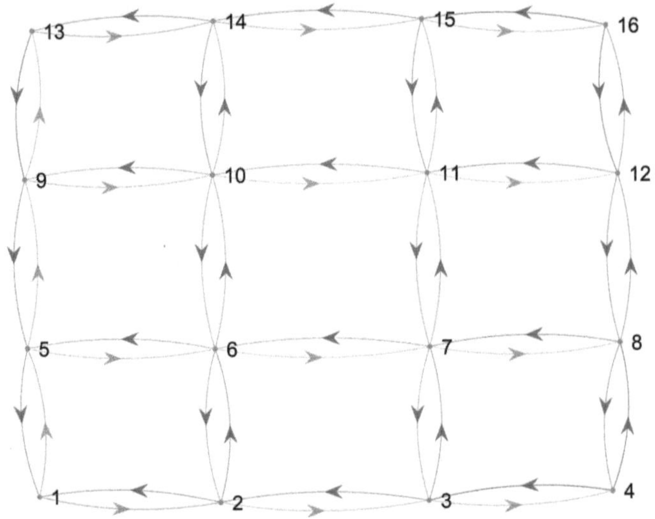

Fig. 6. Weighted directed graph with an arborescence (in green).

However, an important difference is that the in-degree Laplacian matrix is typically not symmetric, hence the Courant-Fischer theorem cannot be applied to prove the monotonicity of the utility function of the resulting TU game.

In the graph-theoretic model presented in this work, focus has been given only to the second-smallest eigenvalue λ_2 of the weighted Laplacian matrix. However, also the other eigenvalues $\lambda_3 \leq \cdots \leq \lambda_{|V|}$ may be important when studying the diffusion process. As a possible extension of the analysis, one could investigate conditions under which the property $\lambda_2(G_S) \leq \lambda_2(G)$ extends to some of these eigenvalues. In this case, removing one edge would also slow down the faster dynamics.

We have analyzed edge removal with the aim of slowing down the fire diffusion process, by increasing the duration of the transient behavior. Still, when $t \to +\infty$, a possible non-desirable steady state could be reached, i.e., a constant temperature steady state is obtained in the graph, which could correspond either to fire extinction or to fire diffusion to the whole graph.

Enforcing fire extinction could require a more complex model of firefighters intervention, not limited to edge removal. For instance, one could include control variables (e.g., negative self-loops or heat sinks) in selected vertices. These would be inserted in the set of players of the resulting game model, with the aim of obtaining a "lower-temperature" steady state. Moreover, the model would become more realistic by including heat sources, integrating other mechanisms of fire evolution different from diffusion.

The model could be extended to a dynamic context (possibly depending on various parameters), based on concepts from *dynamic cooperative game theory*, such as the dynamic Shapley value (Petrosyan et al. 2021; Yeung et al. 2021) and the dynamic Owen value (Petrosyan and Pankratova 2022). The latter is based on the hierarchical application of the Shapley value at two different levels. In the outer level the player set is a pre-defined set of coalitions, while in the inner level the Shapley value is evaluated for various cooperative games (for each of them, the grand coalition is assumed to be a pre-defined coalition arising at the outer level). In both cases, the utility of each coalition is evaluated by solving an optimal control problem for a dynamical system, in which the components of the coalition act as a single decision maker. Computational issues that may arise in the case of parameterized utility functions (especially in the case of a large number of players) could be handled based on machine-learning approaches recently proposed for cooperative games on networks (Gnecco et al. 2025, forthcoming).

Finally, another possible extension concerns moving from a cooperative game-theoretical framework to a non-cooperative one, by investigating a related network formation problem, in which the players would control the weights of the edges or of the arcs, and the payoff of each player could represent, e.g., a trade-off between the global diffusion rate and an individual activation cost. In this context, a possible way to ensure a fair use of resources could be to consider a symmetrized modified version of the resulting non-cooperative game (obtained, e.g., by randomly assigning each player to an edge or arc), then looking for a symmetric mixed strategy Nash equilibrium (i.e., a Nash equilibrium in which all the players play the same mixed strategy).

Acknowledgements. This work was partially supported by the European Union – Next Generation EU program (PNRR 2022 project "MOTUS", code CUP: D53D23017470001), by the Italian Ministry of Enterprises and Made in Italy (project F/310027/02/X56 "Distributed and coordinated drone swarm for fire detection and suppression activities"), by the Italian Ministry of Research (PRIN 2022S8XSMY "Optimal robust shape control for distributed parameter systems"), by the GNAMPA-INdAM 2023 project "Sviluppo di metodi di machine learning per la stima del valore Shapley e di sue generalizzazioni" (code CUP: E53C22001930001), and by the GNAMPA-INdAM 2024 project "Variational inequality approach to network games", and by the Tuscany Region (project ROBOFARM, code CUP: D63C23000520009). P. Bagnerini, M. Gaggero, and M. Sanguineti were partially supported by the FISA-2022-00827 project "UAV-FIRE" ("UAV platform for monitoring forest fire outbreaks and detecting post-fire recovery hotspots"). P. Bagnerini was partially supported by the PNRR project "RETURN" ("Multi risk science for resilient communities under a changing climate"). M. Sanguineti was partially supported by the project of the PDGP DIT.AD021.104 "Optimization and Control Techniques" of the Institute of Marine Engineering, National Research Council of Italy. M. Gaggero, G. Gnecco, and M. Sanguineti are members of GNAMPA-INdAM.

References

Alessandri, A., Bagnerini, P., Gaggero, M., Mantelli, L.: Parameter estimation of fire propagation models using level set methods. Appl. Math. Model. **92**, 731–747 (2021)

Athey, S., Imbens, G.: Machine learning methods that economists should know about. Ann. Rev. Econ. **11**, 685–725 (2019)

Aumann, R.J.J.: Economic applications of the Shapley value. In: Mertens, J.F., Sorin, S. (eds.) Game-Theoretic Methods in General Equilibrium Analysis, pp. 121–133 (1994)

Bagnerini, P., Gaggero, M., Gnecco, G., Sanguineti, M.: Wildland fire diffusion and control: a cooperative game-theoretic model. In: Book of Abstract of the International Conference on Optimization and Decision Science (ODS 2024), p. 87 (2024)

Bataineh, A.S., Zulkernine, M., Abusitta, A., Halabi, T.: Detecting poisoning attacks in collaborative IDSs of vehicular networks using XAI and Shapley value. J. Auton. Transp. Syst. **2**(3), Article no. 9 (2024)

Baylis, P., Boomhower, J.: The economic incidence of wildfire suppression in the United States. Am. Econ. J. Appl. Econ. **15**, 442–473 (2023)

Castro, J., Gómez, D., Tejada, J.: Polynomial calculation of the Shapley value based on sampling. Comput. Oper. Res. **36**, 1726–1730 (2009)

Chung, F.: Spectral Graph Theory. American Mathematical Society (1997)

Gnecco, G., Hadas, Y., Passacantando, M., Sanguineti, M.: On the approximation of the Shapley value via machine learning in transportation network cooperative games. In: Di Francesco, M., Gorgone, E., Manca, B., Zanda, S. (eds.) Operations Research: Closing the Gap Between Research and Practice. AIRO Springer Series, vol. 15 pp. 27–36. Springer, Cham (2025). https://doi.org/10.1007/978-3-031-90095-2_3

Gnecco, G., Hadas, Y., Sanguineti, M.: Public transport transfers assessment via transferable utility games and Shapley value approximation. Transportmetrica A Transp. Sci. **17**, 540–565 (2021)

Hadas, Y., Gnecco, G., Sanguineti, M.: An approach to transportation network analysis via transferable utility games. Transp. Res. Part B Methodol. **105**, 120–143 (2017)

Hand, M.S., Gebert, K.M., Liang, J., Calkin, D., Thompson, M.P., Zhou, M.: Economics of Wildfire Management: The Development and Application of Suppression Expenditure Models. Springer Briefs in Fire. Springer, New York (2014). https://doi.org/10.1007/978-1-4939-0578-2

Hanson, M., Bradley, M., Bossert, J.E., Linn, R.R., Younker, L.W.: The potential and promise of physics-based wildfire simulation. Environ Sci Policy **3**(4), 161–172 (2000)

Maschler, M., Solan, E., Zamir, S.: Game Theory. Cambridge University Press, Cambridge (2020)

Meier, S., Elliott, R.J.R., Strobl, E.: The regional economic impact of wildfires: evidence from Southern Europe. J. Environ. Econ. Manag. **118**, Article no. 102787 (2023)

Mesbahi, M., Egerstedt, M.: Graph Theoretic Methods in Multiagent Networks. Princeton University Press (2010)

Metulini, R., Gnecco, G.: Measuring players' importance in basketball using the generalized Shapley value. Ann. Oper. Res. **325**, 441–465 (2023)

Michalak, T.P., Aadithya, K.V., Szczepański, P.L., Ravindran, B., Jennings, N.R.: Efficient computation of the Shapley value for game-theoretic network centrality. J. Artif. Intell. Res. **46**, 607–650 (2013)

Michalak, T.P., et al.: Implementation and computation of a value for generalized characteristic function games. ACM Trans. Econ. Comput. **2**, 1–35, Article no. 16 (2014)

Molnar, C.: Interpretable Machine Learning: A Guide for Making Black Box Models Explainable. Independently Published (2022)

Narayanam, R., Narahari, Y.: A Shapley value approach to discover influential nodes in social networks. IEEE Trans. Autom. Sci. Eng. **8**(1), 130–147 (2011)

Parlett, B.N.: The symmetric eigenvalue problem. Soc. Appl. Math. (1998)

Passacantando, M., Gnecco, G., Hadas, Y., Sanguineti, M.: Braess' paradox: a cooperative game-theoretic point of view. Networks **78**, 264–283 (2021)

Petrosyan, L., Pankratova, Y.B.: Owen value for dynamic games on networks. Contrib. Game Theory Manag. **15**, 218–225 (2022)

Petrosyan, L., Yeung, D.W.K., Pankratova, Y.B.: Dynamic cooperative games on networks. In: Strekalovsky, A., Kochetov, Y., Gruzdeva, T., Orlov, A. (eds.) Proceedings of the 20th International Conference on Mathematical Optimization Theory and Operations Research (MOTOR 2021), pp. 403–416 (2021)

San-Miguel-Ayanz, J., et al.: Forest Fires in Europe, Middle East and North Africa 2019. Publications Office of the European Union, JRC:122115 (2020). https://doi.org/10.2760/468688

Shapley, L.S.: A value for N-person games. In: Kuhn, H.W., Tucker, A.W. (eds.) Contributions to the Theory of Games (1953). Annals of Mathematical Studies, 28: 307-317

Strumbelj, E., Kononenko, I.: Explaining prediction models and individual predictions with feature contributions. Knowl. Inf. Syst. **41**, 647–665 (2014)

Yeung, D.W.K., Petrosyan, L.A., Zhang, Y.: Trade with technology spillover: a dynamic network game analysis. Int. Game Theory Rev. **23**(1), Article no. 2050011 (2021)

Retaliation Game for Mitigating Selfish Mining Attacks in Blockchain Networks

Fatemeh Erfan[1], Martine Bellaiche[1], and Talal Halabi[2(✉)]

[1] Polytechnique Montréal, Montréal, QC, Canada
fatemeh.erfan@polymtl.ca
[2] Université Laval, Québec, QC, Canada
talal.halabi@ift.ulaval.ca

Abstract. Blockchain networks are exposed to several security attacks, including selfish mining attacks, which occur when a miner or a group of miners withhold their newly mined blocks and keep them in their private chain rather than immediately broadcasting them to the rest of the network. This strategy forces honest miners to waste their resources and degrades the efficiency of the network. This paper introduces a novel game-theoretic approach leveraging a war of attrition framework to mitigate selfish mining in PoW blockchains. We design reward and punishment mechanisms to incentivize miners to opt for honest strategies and discourage them from choosing selfish tactics. Additionally, a reputation function is utilized to ensure that miners are not indifferent to the presence of selfish miners in the network. Moreover, we examine whether the honest strategy remains stable within the system using the evolutionary game theory. Our findings indicate that the honest strategy is indeed stable under the proposed model. Our solution will help mitigate the threat of selfish mining in blockchain systems.

Keywords: Selfish mining attack · Evolutionary game theory ·
Retaliation game · Threat mitigation · Blockchain systems

1 Introduction

Blockchain is a decentralized peer-to-peer (P2P) network that enables transactions to be verified by a group of untrusted participants. All participant transactions are recorded in a transparent public ledger known as the blockchain. Blockchain users adhere to a set of rules called the consensus protocol to add a new record known as a block to the chain, facilitating the agreement among most users on a unified record. Blockchain offers participants significant features such as integrity, availability, decentralization, immutability, fault tolerance, and transparency [9]. These characteristics have gained substantial attention from academia and industry in recent years.

The pioneering decentralized cryptocurrency, bitcoin, was introduced as a revolutionary concept that leverages proof of work (PoW) as a consensus protocol

© ICST Institute for Computer Sciences, Social Informatics and Telecommunications Engineering 2026
Published by Springer Nature Switzerland AG 2026. All Rights Reserved
V. Aggarwal et al. (Eds.): GameNets 2025, LNICST 657, pp. 178–193, 2026.
https://doi.org/10.1007/978-3-032-12915-4_11

[16]. In a Bitcoin network utilizing a PoW-based consensus algorithm, users do not need to authenticate to enter the network. This feature enhances the scalability of the Bitcoin consensus model, allowing it to support thousands of network nodes [2]. Among the myriad security threats blockchain technology faces are denial of service (DoS) and distributed denial of service (DDoS) attacks. Notably, selfish mining attacks [7] represent a form of DDoS threat designed to force honest miners to squander their resources, disrupting their ability to effectively access blockchain network services.

Selfish mining is an adversarial strategy in PoW blockchain systems where malicious miners or mining pools deliberately withhold newly mined blocks instead of broadcasting them immediately. By strategically releasing these blocks later, they initiate a race for block validation between honest and selfish miners. This tactic causes the blocks mined by honest participants to become orphaned, leading to the rejection of all associated transactions [7].

Multiple works focus on analyzing the behavior of participants in blockchain networks. Many techniques are leveraged to mitigate and detect selfish mining attacks, including game theory, machine learning, and analyzing network indicators such as fork rate and the number of orphan blocks. Game theory has found extensive application in modeling interactions and conflicts among participants. Many works have utilized various types of game theory to mitigate such security attacks. In this paper, we propose a game-theoretic approach to mitigate selfish mining attacks within a Bitcoin network by leveraging a type of retaliation game called a war of attrition.

Our contributions are as follows.

- We leverage a type of retaliation game named a war of attrition to mitigate selfish mining attacks. To the best of our knowledge, this is the first time this game has been used to mitigate selfish mining attacks.
- We introduce the punishment, the reward, and the reputation systems in order to penalize malicious actions and encourage honest actions within the blockchain network.
- We simulate and analyze our model by utilizing an evolutionary game to study the impact of whether the honest strategy is in a stable state.

The rest of the paper is as follows. Section 2 explains background concepts regarding blockchain security and game theory approaches. Section 3 describes existing work proposed to mitigate selfish mining attacks in blockchain systems. Section 4 presents the proposed game framework. In Sect. 5, the proposed game will be analyzed. Section 6 demonstrates the results of the proposed game, and finally, Sect. 7 concludes the paper.

2   Background Concepts

This section presents background information related to some blockchain preliminary concepts and game theoretic approaches.

2.1 Blockchain

Block. Blockchain transactions are recorded in blocks, which miners sequentially link to form the blockchain starting with the genesis block. Each block has a header and a body: the body contains transaction data in a Merkle tree, where hashes combine to form the Merkle Root [8]. The header includes the block's identifier, previous block reference, timestamp, nonce, and Merkle root.

Miner. A miner generates new blocks in the blockchain. Miners solve cryptographic challenges to create new blocks using a consensus mechanism, typically PoW in Bitcoin. These blocks are then verified by the network, utilizing the Merkle tree structure for efficient validation. Upon successful validation, miners are rewarded, and the transactions are permanently recorded on the blockchain.

Consensus Algorithm. The mining process validates the blockchain by verifying transactions in each new block, which is central to the consensus algorithm. In Bitcoin's PoW, participants solve a cryptographic challenge (nonce discovery) using computational power. Ethereum switched to Proof-of-Stake (PoS) in 2022 to reduce energy use and support scaling [12]. Both PoW and PoS are vulnerable to selfish mining attacks, though this study focuses on the Bitcoin network.

Fork. A fork occurs when two miners create and broadcast separate blocks simultaneously. Miners then select the first block they received as the primary one, resulting in only one validated block. Forks can also be exploited for double-spending and selfish mining attacks [11].

2.2 Game Theory

Game theory has proven an effective tool for dealing with strategic challenges in blockchain networks, such as resource competition and decentralized decision-making like the Internet of Things (IoT) [18]. Researchers have used game-theoretic frameworks to analyze security problems in blockchain-enabled networks and create strategic defenses against attackers [4]. Here, some essential concepts, game types, and their application in blockchain will be explained.

Nash Equilibrium (NE). Solution concepts provide a framework of rules for forecasting the outcome of a game by identifying the strategies players are likely to adopt [4]. Nash Equilibrium is one such concept, where a game reaches equilibrium if each player's chosen strategy is optimal, given the strategies of other players. In this state, no player is incentivized to change their strategy to increase their expected payoff while others stick to theirs. When NE is reached, every player adopts a strategy that maximizes their potential reward.

Retaliation Game. The goal of this game is to punish the selfish player. Here, the player replies to the opponent's strategy to punish them if they have an undesirable action and make them pay a cost. The responses can be mirroring their opponent's actions, setting some penalties, paying some cost to the opponent, or even taking a counterattack to neutralize their action. If we consider decreasing value over time, we normally use a war of attrition.

Tit-for-Tat. Tit-for-tat (TFT) is a retaliation strategy where a player mirrors the opponent's previous action. Initially, the player cooperates; if the opponent cooperates, they continue to do so. If the opponent behaves selfishly, the player mirrors it in the next move. This strategy is ineffective against selfish mining because honest miners lack the computational power to match an attacker's selfish behavior. In equilibrium, both players cooperate continuously if they both start by cooperating [10].

War of Attrition. The theory of war of Attrition introduced by Maynard Smith [17] analyzed a scenario where two animals are in competitive encounters over a single resource valued v. As the conflict endures, both parties experience increasing costs. In particular, if players choose to continue fighting, they accumulate costs until one of them concedes. Each player's costs escalate the longer they remain engaged in the encounter, adding pressure to resolve the conflict. Notably, the distinctive symmetric equilibrium manifests as a mixed strategy equilibrium, where participants exhibit decreasing probabilities of getting involved in each encounter. This equilibrium demonstrates dual characteristics, serving as an evolutionarily stable strategy (ESS) and a subgame perfect equilibrium (SPE) - a NE enhancement. If there is an imbalance between players - if one starts with a resource advantage, choosing not to fight can be an ESS [15].

Evolutionary Game. The study of evolutionary games examines how players with limited rationality can augment their outcomes over time through repeated interactions [20]. In this model, players who gain more revenues are more likely to continue participating in successive rounds, whereas those with lower payoffs tend to drop out. Through this iterative process, the system naturally favors strategies that yield better payoffs, leading to an equilibrium where dominant strategies stabilize across the population. Using evolutionary and retaliation game concepts, we propose a solid model that captures both the strategic, long-term dynamics of conflict escalation and the tactical, situational decision-making processes within individual encounters known as the War of Attrition.

3   Related Work

Some existing work focuses on mitigating selfish mining attacks in blockchain-based networks. A few papers study the application of game theory in blockchain-based networks to prevent, mitigate, and detect security attacks, including selfish mining attacks [4,13]. Eyal [6] models a non-cooperative game to examine relationships between mining pools. In this scenario, a selfish pool can increase its utility by exploiting honest nodes and infiltrating miners who perform block withholding (BWH) attacks within the targeted pool. However, this strategy is effective only when one pool controls a substantial share of computational power; otherwise, mutual attacks reduce profitability.

Luu et al. [14] use the Computational Power Splitting (CPS) game to model pool block Withholding attacks. In this attack, miners or pools can boost their rewards by either redirecting computational power for BWH attacks or following the pool's protocol. When attacking, they allocate a portion of their computational power to maximize the attack's effectiveness. Zhen et al. [21] model mining between two miners as an iterative game and introduce a Zero Determinant (ZD) strategy to alleviate the miners' dilemma. This pinning strategy enables an altruistic miner to influence the selfish miner's payoff, encouraging cooperation and increasing overall social welfare.

Eyal et al. [7] indicated that an attacker must possess a computational power of at least $\frac{1-\gamma}{3-2\gamma}$ for selfish mining to yield a profit, where γ represents the fraction of blocks created by honest miners that the attacker successfully adopts or observes. Consequently, the attacker would require a minimum computing power of 0.09, even under optimal network conditions. Based on [3], in the case of Nash equilibrium on multiple, non-uniform bitcoin block withholding, the smallest pools might maximize their profits by not retaliating at all. In other words, retaliation is not considered a rational move for the smallest pools. In some existing works, the authors utilize the TFT strategy to mitigate any deviation from honest mining through the blockchain network. The TFT strategy is a mutual strategy [19] in which the player chooses his strategy based on his opponent's strategy. The goal is to maximize your payoff. First, the player selects a cooperation strategy and watches the opponent. If the opponent decides to cooperate with player A, player A will choose to continue cooperation for the next move. If player B selects selfishly, player A mirrors the opponent's strategy.

After analyzing existing works on mitigating selfish mining attacks, we find that game-theoretic models like non-cooperative games, CPS, and ZD strategies provide insights into miner behavior and interactions. However, these approaches have limitations: they often rely on specific network conditions and computational power distribution, which can favor larger pools. Our research extends these findings by developing a more adaptive model that considers diverse network conditions, miner types, and resource allocation challenges.

4   The Proposed Game Framework

Prior to delving deeply into the dynamics of retaliatory strategies, we explain the model, players, objectives, actions, and potential states of selfish mining attacks. We consider a repeated game involving two players (malicious and honest) within a discrete time horizon. The individual game within this repeated game is (S_i, u_i), where $i \in \{1, 2\}$. Here, S_i denotes the set of all possible actions for player i, $s_i \in S_i$, $S \equiv S_1 \times S_2$, $s \equiv (s_1, s_2) \in S$, $u_i : S \to \mathbb{R}$, and $u_i(s)$ represents the payoff for player i resulting from action profile $s \in S$. The notations are shown in Table 1.

Players. Our game assumes two types of miners: selfish and honest miners. The selfish miner is incentivized to maximize their payoff by deviating from the consensus protocol. The honest miner aims to maximize their payoff and protect the integrity of the blockchain.

Strategies. Players have two options to choose from and build their strategy: mining honestly or maliciously. The attacker intends to conceal his newly mined block, whereas the honest miner reveals his block (avoids concealing it).

Actions. The players have the following options:

Table 1. Notations used in our model

Notation	Definition
P_0	The initial punishment value
$P(t)$	Punishment system
$\phi(t)$	Decreasing function for the reward system
$\psi(t)$	Increasing function for the punishment system
$R(t)$	Reward function: $R(t) = \phi(t) \cdot r$
C_m	The net cost of mining for the miner m
r	The value of a successfully mined block
rep	The reputation score representing miner contribution

- **Concealing:** the miner opts to keep their newly mined block and avoid broadcasting it.
- **Revealing:** The miner tends to publish their block and propagate it through the network.
- **Retaliating:** the player intends to respond to their opponent's actions in the previous round. The miner (assumed honest) aims to rent sufficient hash power from other honest miners to counter the attacker. In this scenario, the interaction between the attacker and the victim resembles a War of Attrition, where both players compete for a fixed prize by taking turns attacking each other. However, each attack incurs an additional cost for the attacker. Our findings indicate that, over time, the profit from each new attack diminishes for at least one player. Eventually, it becomes unwise for a player to continue counterattacking, leading to the end of the game, as it becomes more detrimental for a player to keep fighting than to stop. This action will be part of a concealing strategy, where the defender aims to retaliate by concealing their block in the next round. Therefore, we focus on concealing and revealing as the main actions in this game.

There are cases where a player might choose to retaliate against his opponent:

- *State transitions:* We can model the behavior of miners across the network using state transitions, where each state represents a particular configuration of actions and outcomes. The progression between states can be captured through the Markov process [7,19]. Choosing the retaliation strategy becomes an option when one party's actions prompt a shift to a new state, requiring a strategic response. For instance, if the selfish miner conceals a block in State S_0, the honest miners might retaliate by enforcing a fork when informed of the concealed block.
- *Revealing blocks:* If the Selfish Miner conceals blocks to gain an advantage, the honest miners might retaliate by revealing their own blocks or enforcing forks to maintain the integrity of the blockchain and reduce the selfish miner's potential rewards.

- *Fork Competition:* When both parties compete to secure the next block, retaliation strategies can be employed as each side strives to gain dominance. These dynamics, which might occur in states such as S_0', motivate each miner to escalate their efforts to outperform the other.
- *Lead in blocks:* When the Selfish Miner maintains a lead in blocks (e.g., in State S_2 or S_n), the honest miners might retaliate by strategically revealing blocks or attempting to catch up in mining efforts to reduce the lead and disrupt the Selfish Miner's dominance.

Reward Function. It is designed to decrease over time to encourage the miners to promptly broadcast their newly mined blocks. We define it as:

$$R(t) = \phi(t) \cdot r \tag{1}$$

where $\phi(t)$ is a decreasing function and r is the base reward for successfully mining a block. By making $\phi(t)$ decreasing over time, miners who delay their broadcasts receive a reduced reward, while those who broadcast immediately maximize their gains. This time-sensitive reward structure aligns miner incentives with the network's goal of maintaining timely and transparent block updates. In our model, t represents the combined delay defined as follows:

$$t = t_m + \delta \tag{2}$$

Where t_m is the mining time and δ is the block propagation delay caused by network latency. This delay influences the reward and punishment mechanisms. Longer propagation delays increase the punishment and decrease the reward, discouraging miners from withholding blocks.

Punishment Function. Prior research often assumes a fixed value for punishment. In contrast, this paper introduces a dynamic punishment model that increases over time. The punishment function should reflect the delay in broadcasting a newly mined block, thereby incentivizing timely behavior among miners. We define the punishment at time t as an increasing function, denoted by $\psi(t)$, which scales the initial punishment P_0 based on the time elapsed since the block was mined but not broadcast.

$$P(t) = \psi(t) \cdot P_0 \tag{3}$$

Here, P_0 represents the initial punishment imposed at the moment a miner fails to broadcast their block (i.e., at $t = 0$), and $\psi(t)$ is a function that grows with time t, representing an increase in punishment the longer the delay persists. To mirror the effect of reward attenuation, we propose that the punishment function $\psi(t)$ could take an inverse form of the component of the reward function $\phi(t)$. This approach implies a more significant penalty for prolonged concealment. Consequently, we define:

$$P(t) = \phi(t)^{-2} \cdot P_0 \tag{4}$$

where $\phi(t)$ is the component of the reward function $R(t)$. Using $\phi(t)^{-2}$ in this manner ensures that as $\phi(t)$ decreases, the punishment $P(t)$ correspondingly increases, thus creating a disincentive for prolonged concealment.

Reputation Score. If a player conceals, they receive a negative reputation score $(-rep)$, while if they reveal the block, they gain a positive reputation score $(+rep)$. This scoring system can enhance miners' incentives to choose revealing actions over concealing. Therefore, we assume that each node possesses its reputation matrix, updated after each block is published on the ledger. Upon request from other nodes, this matrix will be shared with them. This system is utilized to verify the blocks broadcast through the network. Hence, the reputation score of the publisher influences whether their block is accepted or rejected.

Given the above definitions, the following inequality holds:

$$|\psi(t)| > |\phi(t) \cdot r - C| > |rep| \tag{5}$$

to discourage selfish strategies among miners - the dynamic punishment grows large enough over time to outweigh the rewards for concealing, while reputation penalties remain impactful but secondary to the immediate financial incentives.

Assumptions. We consider some assumptions to render the payoff matrix dynamic and responsive to player strategies.

Assumption 1: Free entry logic derived from [1] states that in a blockchain network, anyone can freely join and contribute his computational power to the network; the equilibrium level of computational power allocated to blockchain mining denoted as n is determined by $n = R/C_m$, where C_m and R are considered the cost of mining and the reward of mining a block, respectively. If there are a few miners in the network $(n < R/C_m)$, the reward of mining a block is higher than the cost of each miner. So, mining in this network (pool) is profitable. If there are too many miners in this pool, it means that the reward is less than the cost that a miner should tolerate.

Assumption 2: If the net payoff turns negative for any player, this signals the end of the game.

Assumption 3: The net cost of the selfish mining attack, c, remains constant (or changes at a slower rate than $\phi(t)$).

Assumption 4: Both miners should pay a cost of C for the mining process. These costs are C_a and C_d for the attacker and the defender, respectively.

Assumption 5: If the attacker reveals his block, he gets $\phi(t) \cdot r$ as a reward, where in time 0 this reward is r.

Assumption 6: If the defender retaliates (chooses to conceal his block), he should pay a cost of P as punishment as well as a C_d for their mining efforts.

Assumption 7: If one conceals while another reveals, the player who reveals the block is not rewarded. This is because honest miners should cooperate to have a healthy network. If both reveal their blocks, the one who broadcasts first receives the reward, while the other does not, and their block becomes orphaned.

5   Equilibrium Analysis

$C_a, C_d > 0$ are considered the cost of a mining process for the attacker and the defender, respectively, and $r > 0$ is the reward for mining a block through the blockchain network. The malicious miner (M) chooses to reveal or conceal. We consider a function of time $\phi(t)$ to prove that the net cost of the attack falls over time, with $\phi(t) = 1$ when $t = 0$. We consider t as the period to mine a block.

5.1   Time to Stop

The strategic aspects of this model involve optimizing the timing of stopping the retaliation for the miner, considering the costs of attack or mining C, the decreasing value of the reward $\phi(t) \cdot r$, and the potential reputation loss for the defender rep if they lose a round.

We consider that the player (honest miner) has two options: revealing (immediately broadcasting their mined blocks) and concealing (retaliating by withholding their blocks). The honest miner aims to determine the point, denoted as T_{stop}, at which it becomes unprofitable to continue retaliating against the selfish miner. We consider the cumulative revenue from the revealing and concealing actions to calculate T_{stop}.

If the revenue from choosing to reveal up to time t is represented by the cumulative sum:

$$R_{total}(t) = \sum_{k=0}^{t} \left(\phi(k) \cdot r - C_a + rep\right), \tag{6}$$

and the cumulative loss from concealing up to time t is given by the value:

$$L_{total}(t) = \left| \sum_{k=0}^{t} \left(-C_a - P - rep\right) \right|, \tag{7}$$

then, the stopping condition arises when the total revenue from retaliating equals the absolute cumulative cost of concealing. Thus, we find T_{stop} by solving:

$$R_{total}(T_{stop}) = L_{total}(T_{stop}), \tag{8}$$

or equivalently,

$$\sum_{k=0}^{T_{stop}} \left(\phi(k) \cdot r - C_a + rep\right) = \left| \sum_{k=0}^{T_{stop}} \left(-C_a - P - rep\right) \right|. \tag{9}$$

This condition indicates that retaliation should stop when the total accumulated revenue from revealing no longer exceeds the absolute cumulative losses incurred by concealing.

If a player chooses to conceal a block, his payoff is $R = -C_a - P - rep$ as P is the punishment function that is explained in 4. If he chooses to reveal the block, his payoff is $\phi(t) \cdot r - C_a + rep$ as rep is the reputation score explained in 4. It is worth mentioning that C_d and C_a depend on the cost of mining, the cost of renting computation resources, and the fee of joining any pool (if they are mining in a group).

Table 2. Payoff Matrix for the Selfish Mining Attack

Attacker\Defender	Reveal	Conceal
Reveal	$(\phi(t) \cdot r - C_a + rep, \phi(t) \cdot r - C_d + rep)$	$(-C_a + rep, -C_d - P - rep)$
Conceal	$(-C_a - P - rep, -C_d + rep)$	$(-C_a - P - rep, -C_d - P - rep)$

5.2   Strategies

As shown in Table 2, this game has two primary players: the attacker and the defender. Each player can reveal or conceal the newly mined block. When a player conceals, they face a penalty, represented by P, and their reputation score will decrease, which refers to a financial deduction affecting their reputation.

If the attacker chooses to reveal the block, they stand to gain $\phi(t) \cdot r - C_a + rep$, where $\phi(t)$ represents a function of decreasing value over time t. This function reflects that the longer it takes to complete an action, the less the reward r becomes. C_a represents the cost of mining for the attacker. rep is the reputation score indicating the miner effectively contributes to the pool (or network). Similarly, if the defender chooses to reveal a block, they can gain $\phi(t) \cdot r - C_d + rep$, where C_d is the cost of mining for the defender.

The strategies can be divided into two groups:

- Revealing: If the attacker reveals the block, they gain $\phi(t) \cdot r - C_a + rep$. Likewise, if the defender reveals the block, they gain $\phi(t) \cdot r - C_d + rep$.
- Concealing: If the attacker conceals the block, they gain $-C_a - P - rep$, where P represents the punishment. Similarly, if the defender conceals the block, they gain $-C_d - P - rep$.

It is worth mentioning that if both players choose to reveal their blocks, a competition will happen. The details of the actions are as follows:

- **Reveal (R) vs. Reveal (R):** Neither the attacker nor the defender has the incentive to change their strategy if both choose to reveal as the following inequation holds:

$$\phi(t) \cdot r - C_a + rep \geq -C_a - P - rep \qquad (10)$$

- **Reveal (R) vs. Conceal (C):** If the attacker reveals while the defender conceals, the attacker could also benefit by concealing, given that the punishment for concealment decreases as time passes. The defender has no incentive to deviate. Thus, there is no Nash equilibrium in this cell.
- **Conceal (C) vs. Reveal (R):** If the attacker conceals while the defender reveals, the attacker could benefit by revealing, as the punishment for concealment increases over time. The defender has no incentive to deviate. Thus, no Nash equilibrium in this cell.

- **Conceal (C) vs. Conceal (C):** If both players choose to conceal the block, then the payoff is less than the revealing option. This scenario would not lead to a Nash equilibrium because both players would be incentivized to deviate from choosing to conceal.

Our model assumes perfect information, but practical detection of concealed blocks is achievable using network monitoring and anomaly detection techniques. Methods like analyzing fork rates, orphan block patterns, and machine learning can help miners detect selfish mining [5].

5.3   Using Evolutionary Game

The game between miners is assumed to be dynamic to make it more realistic. As the players' strategies evolve over time, leveraging *evolutionary game* becomes a suitable approach based on their received payoff. This game illustrates how strategies that perform better will become more prevalent in the population of attackers and honest miners. Evolutionary game theory helps identify stable strategy profiles, known as ESS. This game demonstrates whether a particular mix of revealing and concealing strategies will persist in the long run or if the system will evolve toward a different equilibrium.

Let x be the proportion of attackers using the Reveal strategy and y the proportion of defenders using the Conceal strategy. The expected payoffs for the attacker and defender using the Reveal and Conceal strategies are as follows. Attacker revealing:

$$\pi_A^R = y \cdot (\phi(t) \cdot r - C_a + rep) + (1 - y) \cdot (-C_a + rep) \tag{11}$$

Attacker concealing:

$$\pi_A^C = y \cdot (-C_a - P_a - rep) + (1 - y) \cdot (-C_a - P_a - rep) \tag{12}$$

Defender revealing:

$$\pi_D^R = x \cdot (\phi(t) \cdot r - C_d + rep) + (1 - x) \cdot (-C_d + rep) \tag{13}$$

Defender concealing:

$$\pi_D^C = x \cdot (-C_d - P_d - rep) + (1 - x) \cdot (-C_d - P_d - rep) \tag{14}$$

The replicator dynamics show how the proportions of each strategy evolve based on the payoff differences. For the attacker:

$$\frac{dx}{dt} = x \cdot (\pi_A^R - \overline{\pi_A}) \tag{15}$$

where the average payoff for the attacker, $\overline{\pi_A}$, is given by:

$$\overline{\pi_A} = x \cdot \pi_A^R + (1 - x) \cdot \pi_A^C \tag{16}$$

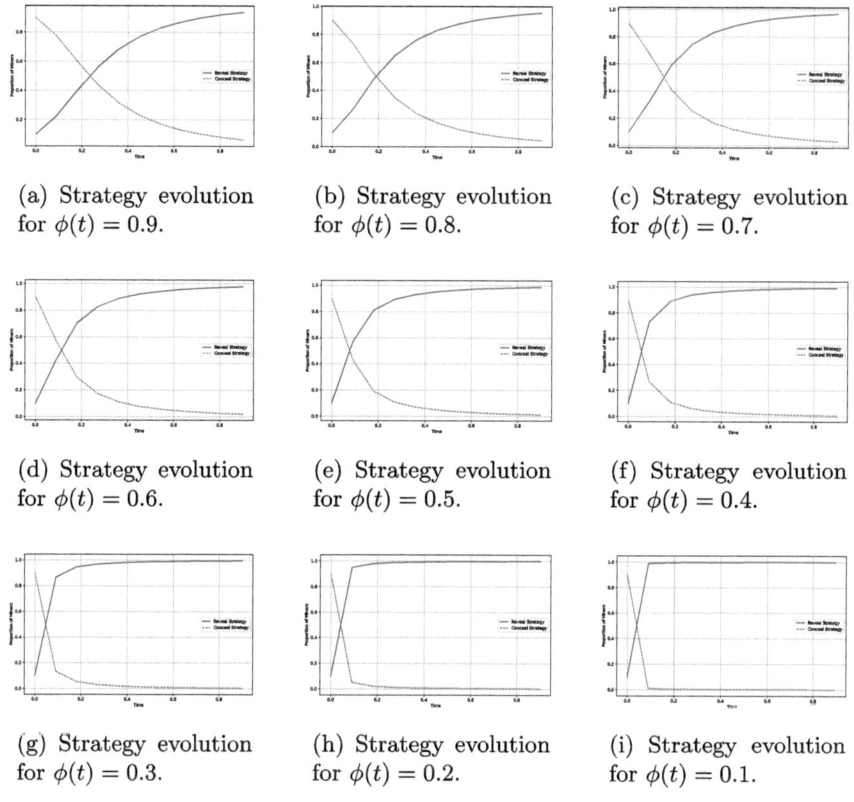

(a) Strategy evolution for $\phi(t) = 0.9$.

(b) Strategy evolution for $\phi(t) = 0.8$.

(c) Strategy evolution for $\phi(t) = 0.7$.

(d) Strategy evolution for $\phi(t) = 0.6$.

(e) Strategy evolution for $\phi(t) = 0.5$.

(f) Strategy evolution for $\phi(t) = 0.4$.

(g) Strategy evolution for $\phi(t) = 0.3$.

(h) Strategy evolution for $\phi(t) = 0.2$.

(i) Strategy evolution for $\phi(t) = 0.1$.

Fig. 1. Strategy evolution for different values of $\phi(t)$.

For the defender:

$$\frac{dy}{dt} = y \cdot (\pi_D^R - \overline{\pi_D}) \tag{17}$$

where the average payoff for the miner, $\overline{\pi_D}$, is given by:

$$\overline{\pi_D} = y \cdot \pi_D^R + (1 - y) \cdot \pi_D^C \tag{18}$$

This analysis demonstrates how miners strategically choose to reveal or conceal blocks based on rewards, costs, and reputation. Honest miners can minimize cumulative losses by identifying the optimal stopping time T_{stop}. Evolutionary game dynamics further reveal the stability of these strategies in a competitive mining environment.

6   Numerical Results

Here, we explain our results to highlight the strategic behavior of miners under different conditions. The analysis focuses on how the parameter $\phi(t)$, which serves as both a reward scaling factor and a vital component of the punishment system, influences the convergence of miners' strategies over time.

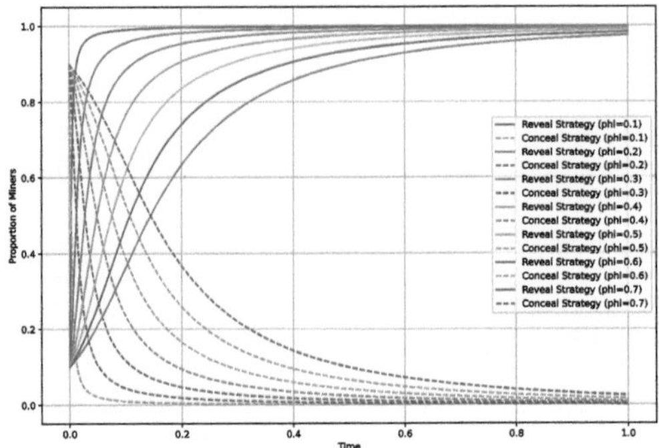

Fig. 2. Evolution of proportion of reveal and conceal strategies for different $\phi(t)$ values over time.

In analyzing the evolution of strategies among miners to counteract selfish mining, fixed points are identified where the strategy proportions stabilize $\frac{dx}{dt} = 0$. These fixed points represent stable equilibria in which miners' choices between concealing and revealing do not vary over time, signifying convergence to either strategy. The parameter $\phi(t)$ plays a significant role in influencing this convergence, modulating the reward-punishment mechanism and thereby shaping miners' strategic preferences across various scenarios. Figure 1 demonstrates this across values of $\phi(t)$ ranging from 0.1 to 0.9, with each scenario exhibiting distinct behaviors. Figure 2 indicates the evolution of the proportion of reveal and conceal strategies for different values of $\phi(t)$ over time.

High Values of $0.9 \geq \phi(t) \geq 0.6$**:** As $\phi(t)$ continues to decrease, convergence occurs gradually, and the incentives for revealing increase. At $\phi(t) = 0.9$, only 35% of miners opt to reveal, showing a strong preference for concealment as severe punishment discourages transparency. As $\phi(t)$ decreases to 0.8, the proportion of revealing miners rises slightly to 42%, suggesting that even under elevated punishment, revealing can be favored under specific conditions. At $\phi(t) = 0.7$, the proportion increases further to 63%, where punishment levels still influence the decision, but miners are more inclined to reveal. By $\phi(t) = 0.6$, about 47% of miners reveal, indicating a near-equal preference for both strategies as transparency becomes more appealing. The decrease in the proportion of miners revealing from 63% at $\phi(t) = 0.7$ to 47% at $\phi(t) = 0.6$ may seem counterintuitive, as we might expect that lower $\phi(t)$ values would increase the incentive to reveal. However, this reduction can occur because, at this boundary, the incentives are balanced between revealing and concealing, creating an equilibrium where concealment becomes more appealing even with decreased punishment.

Moderate Values of $0.6 > \phi(t) > 0.3$**:** there is a noticeable shift towards increased adoption of the reveal strategy as $\phi(t)$ decreases. At $\phi(t) = 0.5$, around 61% of miners choose to reveal, indicating a preference for transparency despite moderate punishment. As $\phi(t)$ decreases to 0.4, the proportion of revealing miners rises to 76%, and by $\phi(t) = 0.3$, it reaches 88%. This trend suggests that lower values of $\phi(t)$ strengthen the incentives for honest behavior, revealing the dominant strategy.

Low Values of $0.3 \geq \phi(t) \geq 0.1$**:** Convergence occurs almost immediately as miners quickly commit to their chosen strategies. At $\phi(t) = 0.3$, approximately 80% of miners favor the *reveal* strategy, indicating a strong preference for transparency under moderate punishment conditions. As $\phi(t)$ decreases to 0.2, the proportion of revealing miners rises slightly to around 87%, and reaches approximately 95% by $\phi(t) = 0.1$. This trend suggests that lower values of $\phi(t)$ further encourage revealing, establishing transparency as the dominant strategy.

These findings underscore that $\phi(t)$ used in the reward and punishment mechanisms is critical in guiding miners' strategic preferences. Notably, moderate values of $0.6 > \phi(t) > 0.3$ emerge as a pivotal region where the game dynamics favor the *Reveal* strategy, with a significant number of miners opting for honest conduct. This suggests that these values of $\phi(t)$ effectively discourage selfish mining behaviors while promoting transparency. The existence of Evolutionarily Stable Strategies (ESS) within this range implies that the system achieves stable equilibria, where revealing is a more attractive strategy than concealing.

7 Conclusion

Selfish mining attacks represent a significant security threat to blockchain networks that allow miners to gain an advantage by holding and not broadcasting newly mined blocks, wasting honest miners' resources. First, this study determines the profitable time for the honest miner to stop the retaliation strategy. Then, we reduce the miners' indifference by utilizing a reputation system. Pursuing the mining process in pools with malicious miners should not continue to protect the resources of honest miners. Moreover, this research considered a reward-punishment system for miners who do not announce their block to the network immediately after being mined will be punished, preventing them from adopting a subversive strategy. In other words, combining these two systems can prevent miners from executing a selfish mining attack as their revenue will decrease over time, and opting for a concealing strategy will not be profitable. In addition, this work leveraged a retaliation game, a war of attrition, to retaliate against selfish miners and discourage them from behaving selfishly. An evolutionary game approach is also employed to analyze how different reward and punishment structures influence the strategies taken by miners.

The results show that the reward scaling factor is crucial in directing the miners' tactics and balancing rewards and punishments effectively, which reduces incentives for selfish mining and enhances blockchain security. When more miners opt to reveal their blocks rather than keep them in their private chains, the game dynamics converge to stable equilibria where the reveal approach is favored. While promoting an honest strategy, the selected reward-punishment balance successfully reduces selfish mining behavior. In the future, we will explore adapting the retaliation game framework to PoS-based networks like Ethereum 2.0 to mitigate such threats.

References

1. Budish, E.: The economic limits of bitcoin and the blockchain. Technical report, National Bureau of Economic Research (2018)
2. Conti, M., Kumar, E.S., Lal, C., Ruj, S.: A survey on security and privacy issues of bitcoin. IEEE Commun. Surv. Tut. **20**(4), 3416–3452 (2018)
3. Elliott, S.: Nash equilibrium of multiple, non-uniform bitcoin block withholding attackers. In: 2019 2nd International Conference on Data Intelligence and Security (ICDIS), pp. 144–151. IEEE (2019)
4. Erfan, F., Bellaiche, M., Halabi, T.: Game-theoretic designs for blockchain-based IoT: taxonomy and research directions. In: 2022 IEEE International Conference on Decentralized Applications and Infrastructures (DAPPS), pp. 27–37. IEEE (2022)
5. Erfan, F., Bellaiche, M., Halabi, T.: Efficient detection of selfish mining attacks on large-scale blockchain networks. In: 2024 IEEE 24th International Conference on Software Quality, Reliability, and Security Companion (QRS-C), pp. 196–205 (2024). https://doi.org/10.1109/QRS-C63300.2024.00035
6. Eyal, I.: The miner's dilemma. In: 2015 IEEE Symposium on Security and Privacy, pp. 89–103. IEEE (2015)
7. Eyal, I., Sirer, E.G.: Majority is not enough: bitcoin mining is vulnerable. Commun. ACM **61**(7), 95–102 (2018)
8. Ferrag, M.A., Shu, L.: The performance evaluation of blockchain-based security and privacy systems for the internet of things: a tutorial. IEEE IoT J. (2021)
9. Guo, H., Yu, X.: A survey on blockchain technology and its security. Blockchain Res. Appl. **3**(2), 100067 (2022)
10. Kayaba, Y., Matsushima, H., Toyama, T.: Accuracy and retaliation in repeated games with imperfect private monitoring: experiments. Games Econom. Behav. **120**, 193–208 (2020)
11. Kwon, Y., Kim, H., Yi, Y., Kim, Y.: An eye for an eye: economics of retaliation in mining pools. In: Proceedings of the 1st ACM Conference on Advances in Financial Technologies, pp. 169–182 (2019)
12. Li, Z., et al.: Demystifying DeFi MEV activities in Flashbots bundle. In: Proceedings of the 2023 ACM SIGSAC Conference on Computer and Communications Security, pp. 165–179 (2023)
13. Liu, Z., et al.: A survey on applications of game theory in blockchain. arXiv preprint arXiv:1902.10865 (2019)
14. Luu, L., Saha, R., Parameshwaran, I., Saxena, P., Hobor, A.: On power splitting games in distributed computation: the case of bitcoin pooled mining. In: 2015 IEEE 28th Computer Security Foundations Symposium, pp. 397–411. IEEE (2015)
15. Moroz, D.J., Aronoff, D.J., Narula, N., Parkes, D.C.: Double-spend counterattacks: threat of retaliation in proof-of-work systems. arXiv preprint arXiv:2002.10736 (2020)
16. Nakamoto, S.: Bitcoin: a peer-to-peer electronic cash system (2008)

17. Smith, J.M.: The theory of games and the evolution of animal conflicts. J. Theor. Biol. **47**(1), 209–221 (1974)
18. Sohail, M.N., Anjum, A., Saeed, I.A., Syed, M.H., Jantsch, A., Rehman, S.: Optimizing industrial IoT data security through blockchain-enabled incentive-driven game theoretic approach for data sharing. IEEE Access (2024)
19. Sun, W., Xu, Z., Chen, L.: Fairness matters: a tit-for-tat strategy against selfish mining. Proc. VLDB Endow. **15**(13), 4048–4061 (2022)
20. Zhang, J., Wu, M.: Cooperation mechanism in blockchain by evolutionary game theory. Complexity **2021**(1), 1258730 (2021)
21. Zhen, Y., Yue, M., Zhong-yu, C., Chang-bing, T., Xin, C.: Zero-determinant strategy for the algorithm optimize of blockchain pow consensus. In: 2017 36th Chinese Control Conference (CCC), pp. 1441–1446. IEEE (2017)

Author Index

© ICST Institute for Computer Sciences, Social Informatics and Telecommunications Engineering 2026
Published by Springer Nature Switzerland AG 2026. All Rights Reserved
V. Aggarwal et al. (Eds.): GameNets 2025, LNICST 657, p. 195, 2026.
https://doi.org/10.1007/978-3-032-12915-4

MIX
Papier aus verantwortungsvollen Quellen
Paper from responsible sources
FSC® C105338

If you have any concerns about our products,
you can contact us on
ProductSafety@springernature.com

In case Publisher is established outside the EU,
the EU authorized representative is:
Springer Nature Customer Service Center GmbH
Europaplatz 3, 69115 Heidelberg, Germany

Printed by Libri Plureos GmbH
in Hamburg, Germany